RUSKIN AND THE
DAWN OF THE MODERN

Ruskin and the Dawn of the Modern

EDITED BY

DINAH BIRCH

OXFORD

UNIVERSITY PRESS

OXFORD
UNIVERSITY PRESS

Great Clarendon Street, Oxford OX2 6DP

Oxford University Press is a department of the University of Oxford
and furthers the University's aim of excellence in research, scholarship,
and education by publishing worldwide in

Oxford New York

Athens Auckland Bangkok Bogotá Buenos Aires Calcutta
Cape Town Chennai Dar es Salaam Delhi Florence Hong Kong Istanbul
Karachi Kuala Lumpur Madrid Melbourne Mexico City Mumbai
Nairobi Paris São Paulo Singapore Taipei Tokyo Toronto Warsaw

with associated companies in Berlin Ibadan

Oxford is a trade mark of Oxford University Press
in the UK and in certain other countries

Published in the United States
by Oxford University Press Inc., New York

British Library Cataloguing in Publication Data

Data available

Library of Congress Cataloging in Publication Data

Ruskin and the dawn of the modern / edited by Dinah Birch.
Includes bibliographical references and index.
1. Ruskin, John, 1819–1900—Knowledge and learning.
2. Civilization, Modern—19th century. 3. Civilization,
Modern—20th century. 4. Ruskin, John, 1819–1900—Influence.
5. Modernism (Aesthetics) I. Birch, Dinah.
PR5264.R7 1999 828'.809—dc21 98–47181
ISBN 0–19–818454–9

1 3 5 7 9 10 8 6 4 2

Typeset in Sabon
by Alliance Phototypesetters, Pondicherry, India
Printed in Great Britain
on acid-free paper by
Biddles Ltd., Guildford and Kings Lynn.

Contents

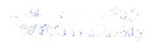

Notes on the Contributors

DINAH BIRCH is a Fellow and Tutor of English Literature at Trinity College, Oxford. Her publications on Victorian literature include two books on Ruskin: *Ruskin's Myths* (1988), and *Ruskin on Turner* (1990). She is currently working on a selected edition of *Fors Clavigera*.

JOSE HARRIS holds a Leverhulme Research Professorship in the Faculty of Modern History at Oxford, and is a Fellow of St Catherine's College. The second edition of her biography of William Beveridge appeared in 1997. Her other books include *Private Lives: Public Spirit 1870–1914* (repr. 1994).

FRANCIS O'GORMAN read English at Lady Margaret Hall, Oxford, and wrote a D.Phil. thesis on Ruskin there. He was lecturer in English at Pembroke College, Oxford, 1993–6, and is now Research Fellow in English at Cheltenham and Gloucester College of Higher Education. He has published articles on Ruskin in British and American journals, and his book *Late Ruskin* is forthcoming from Scolar Press. He has also published articles on Tyndall, Browning, and Charles Kingsley, and co-edited a collection of essays on Margaret Oliphant.

LAWRENCE GOLDMAN is Fellow and Tutor in Modern History at St Peter's College, Oxford, where he teaches British and American History.

DELIA DA SOUSA CORREA is completing a book on music in Victorian literary culture. She has published on George Eliot and German Romanticism (in *George Eliot and Europe*, 1997), and on music and memory in Eliot's novels (*Nineteenth-Century Contexts*); she is a contributor to the forthcoming *Oxford Companion to George Eliot*. She is a Lecturer in Literature at the Open University.

DONATA LEVI is a graduate in Art History from the University of Pisa. Her subsequent doctoral thesis was published as a book, *Cavalcaselle: Il Pioniere della Conservazione dell'arte Italiana* (1988). She is Associate Professor of Museology and the History of Collecting at the University of Udine, and is working on a study of the relations between the art-market and museums in England and Germany in the first half of the nineteenth century.

PAUL TUCKER graduated in English from the University of Cambridge in 1977. In 1983 he completed a thesis on Walter Pater at the University of Oxford, and he now teaches English language at the University of Pisa. He carried out the research for the exhibition *Ruskin and Tuscany*, held in London, Sheffield, and Lucca in 1993, co-authoring the catalogue with Jeanne Clegg. Together with Donata Levi, he has published a book on John Ruskin and the teaching of drawing, *Ruskin Didatta* (1997), and is currently working on an electronic edition of Ruskin's 1845 Italian notebooks.

NICHOLAS SHRIMPTON teaches English at Lady Margaret Hall, Oxford. He has recently published a selected edition of the poems of Matthew Arnold. He co-edited *The Whole Music of Passion: New Essays on Swinburne* (1993) and has also written on Ruskin, Dante Gabriel Rossetti, and Pater.

SHARON ARONOFSKY WELTMAN, Assistant Professor of English at Louisiana State University, has written articles on Ruskin for *Prose Studies, Nineteenth-Century Literature*, and the volume *Remaking Queen Victoria* (1997). She is the author of *Mythic Discourse and Gender Subversion: John Ruskin in Nineteenth-Century Context* (1998).

List of Plates

Figures 1–6, 10, 12, and 13 are from photographs taken for the editors of the Library Edition of Ruskin's *Works* (London, 1903–12). These are reproduced by courtesy of the Ruskin Foundation, University of Lancaster. Figures 7, 8, 9, and 11 are reproduced by permission of the Visitors of the Ashmolean Museum, Oxford.

Note on References

Quotations from Ruskin's published works are taken from the Library Edition, E. T. Cook and Alexander Wedderburn (eds.), *The Works of John Ruskin*, 39 vols. (London, 1903–12). References are given parenthetically in the text, thus '(*Works* 17. 318)' refers to vol. 17, p. 318.

Introduction

DINAH BIRCH

In recent years, the study of Ruskin has been transformed. A prominent factor has been the revaluation of his later writing. The works that followed the celebrated books of his youth and middle age used often to be slighted. They were cited as evidence of a great mind's decline into eccentricity. All that has changed. They are now increasingly likely to be prized for their literary and intellectual innovation. Modern scholarship has revealed the complexity of Ruskin's relations with late Victorian culture. The sustained creativity with which he responded to change has become apparent.

1869 may be seen as a turning point in his life. It was the year of his election to Oxford's first Slade Professorship of Fine Art—his first public appointment. In the same year, he turned 50. His life began again in many ways. Alongside his Oxford lectures, in January 1871 he started to publish *Fors Clavigera*, his monthly series of 'Letters to the Workmen and Labourers of Great Britain'. In the letter for August 1871, he announced the foundation of the St George's Fund, soon to become the Guild of St George. In the same month, he bought Brantwood, the house overlooking Coniston Water in the Lake District that was subsequently to become his home. His mother died in December 1871, and he sold the family home on Denmark Hill. These were the years in which Ruskin published his scientific texts. *Love's Meinie*, on ornithology, came out in 1873–81; *Proserpina*, on botany, in 1875–86; *Deucalion*, on geology, in 1875–83. Together they constitute an extraordinary challenge to scientific orthodoxy. The same years saw successive series of lectures on art at Oxford, and letters for the continuing series of *Fors Clavigera* (1871–84). Alongside these commitments, Ruskin published his thoughts on Turner, on Venice, on prosody, on music, on myth, and finally his autobiography, *Praeterita* (1886–9).

His refusal to limit himself to any single field of thought lies at the heart of his project as a mature critic. But it also became an important reason for the decline of his reputation in the twentieth century. Specialization and professionalization had come to dominate scholarship.

Ruskin was suspicious of both. 'The other name of death is "separation" ', he remarked in the final volume of *Modern Painters* (*Works* 7. 207), in a passage he chose to reprint in *The Ethics of the Dust*. His argument was always that knowledge connects; that theologians, scientists, artists, economists, historians, lawyers, and politicians must learn from one another, or perish in isolation. The twentieth century thought differently—until recently. Now, as the boundaries of professional disciplines shift and dissolve, what once made Ruskin seem a gentleman amateur makes him a pioneer in interdisciplinary thinking. In their variety of scholarly approach, the essays in this volume follow Ruskin's expansive model. The historians, art historians, and literary critics contributing reveal how his multifaceted writings relate to our own mixed culture.

As he grew older, Ruskin was increasingly inclined to see his life in elegiac terms. His parents' death affected him deeply. In 1875 Rose La Touche, the Irish girl that he loved, also died. Many of his later works have a retrospective cast, as he pondered a life that had begun in what seemed a lost world. The title of his study of flowers is characteristic: *Proserpina: Studies of Wayside Flowers, While the Air was yet Pure among the Alps, and in the Scotland and England which my Father Knew*. Other late works present themselves in similarly nostalgic terms. *On the Old Road*, for instance, is the title of the collection of essays and pamphlets edited for Ruskin by Alexander Wedderburn in 1885; *Our Fathers Have Told Us: Sketches of the History of Christendom for Boys and Girls Who Have Been Held at its Fonts*, is the full title of the series which Ruskin began in 1884 with the publication of *The Bible of Amiens*. The autobiographical impulse of much of Ruskin's later writing, together with his fiercely anti-progressive views, made it easy to see him as a writer enmeshed in the Victorian age, looking backwards rather than forwards. This was another reason for the neglect of his late work. It was interpreted as a denial of the modern world, if not as mere self-indulgent melancholy.

One feature of the recent revaluation of these works has been the growing recognition of the radical invention that accompanies Ruskin's conservatism. The construction of elegy does not preclude innovation. Ruskin's compound arguments developed into new and often unexpected directions in these crowded years. But these are also the years, especially as the composite productions of the 1870s gradually spiral down into the advancing silence and mental illness of the later 1880s, when Ruskin's active presence begins to move into the realm of influence.

It is not simply Ruskin, but Ruskinism and Ruskinians that now etch themselves on the pages of cultural history. The vigour and diversity of that legacy is beginning to be fully acknowledged. Looking seriously at the late works has helped to reveal how extensively, and in how many different areas, he helped to define the terms of the debates that we have come to take for granted as the foundation of twentieth-century culture. Science, education, social politics, aesthetics—all bear the marks of Ruskin's far-reaching influence. It is such a pervasive legacy, its results now taken for granted in so many diverse areas of thought, that it is easy to overlook its range and force. The century that has passed since Ruskin's death in 1900 would have been unrecognizably different without his seminal presence.

Some of the channels through which Ruskin's thought flowed have scarcely been mapped. Among the most significant has been the impact of his work on twentieth-century social reform. Though it comes as no surprise to learn that his social thought was of fundamental importance to the development of public policy, our understanding of how this influence impinged has often, as Jose Harris points out, been sketchy and uncertain. Points of contact investigated in her essay include a number that are unexpected—including, to take one telling example, the revelation of the extent to which William Beveridge's programme of social welfare reforms in the 1940s is rooted in his long-standing engagement with what Ruskin had thought and written. Francis O'Gorman's study of scientific education in late Victorian and early twentieth-century culture makes a comparable case. Challenging the prevalent idea that Ruskin's contribution to educational debate was confined to the eccentric margins of the scientific community, Dr O'Gorman shows how widely Ruskin's views affected those who were formulating the policies that were to place science in modern culture. Ruskin had argued that education was incomplete without a serious study of science, but had defined such study in moral and often mythopoeic terms that ran counter to prevailing orthodoxies. Yet influential educationalists like John Lubbock and Oliver Lodge, important in the early years of Birmingham University, Patrick Geddes, botanist and social campaigner, and Michael Sadler, a pioneer in the university extension movement in Oxford, and later prominent in the Universities of Manchester and Leeds before becoming Master of University College, Oxford, all showed clear traces of Ruskin's educational thought. Ruskin emerges as more central to the development of early twentieth-century educational policies than has been acknowledged. In his essay on Ruskin and the

Labour movement, Lawrence Goldman confirms the importance of educational theory and its implementation as a means of disseminating Ruskinian influence. Dr Goldman's focus is on the role of Oxford's university extension movement as one of the most significant channels by which Ruskin's ideas 'captured the imagination of intelligent working people for a generation'. This allows him to demonstrate how Ruskin's presence infiltrated the formation of the British Labour movement. Ruskin taught Labour to develop its ethic of anticapitalism.

The role of Oxford, Ruskin's institutional base throughout the later years of his active life, in the development and dissemination of his thinking is a theme to which this volume's contributors persistently return. Donata Levi and Paul Tucker scrutinize Ruskin's practices as an art teacher in Oxford. They examine how he reconciled the need for an effective scheme of instruction with his deeply felt views on the moral and spiritual implications of art in education. The 'search for fixed principles' led him to emphasize the ethical importance of the disciplines of line in the teaching of drawing. 'A line of absolute correctness' was more than a matter of technical accuracy. Characteristically, he presented this as a long-established consensus, and this has tended to distract attention from the novelty of his contribution to the debate about how art should be taught. Here again, the emphasis falls on Ruskin's work in education. The extraordinary diversity of this is one of the integrative themes of *Ruskin and the Dawn of the Modern*. His observations on the theory and practice of music, and the role of music in education, provides another example. Ruskin's contribution to musicology has been almost entirely overlooked. Delia da Sousa Correa's essay on his use of musical terminology in his aesthetic and social criticism illuminates a new dimension in the writing of the 1870s and beyond. Ruskin's insistence on the moral energy of music, and its primary role in education, is a further strand in the network communicating his reforming models of thought to the public.

It was as a 'graduate of Oxford' that Ruskin had announced himself as an art critic, publishing the first volume of *Modern Painters* as an aspiring 24-year-old. In that volume, he had begun to find his voice as an antagonist, asserting a sustained opposition to accepted cultural values. Reminding us that this 'prickly and provocative voice' often continued to locate itself in Oxford, the essays collected here emphasize that the Professor of Art and the Master of the Guild of St George had learned to see himself in terms very different from those adopted by the eager champion of Evangelicalism and of Turner who had made his debut in

1843. Nicholas Shrimpton's essay on Ruskin and the aesthetes demonstrates how far the cultural thought against which Ruskin defined himself had also been modified. It is not just that he was neither an advocate of aestheticism, nor in any simple way its enemy, but rather that the grounds of the argument were unstable—and unstable partly through his contribution to them. This is one way in which he altered the cultural status of art in the era that has generated our own. Ruskin again emerges as defining and developing the terms of cultural change.

Alongside radical innovations in the perception of art's social function in the late nineteenth century came new ways of understanding gender. Here too, Ruskin's legacy has often been seen in oversimple or reductive terms. Sharon Aronofsky Weltman's study of myth and gender in Ruskin's science suggests that the process through which science is feminized in Ruskin's later texts is fundamental to the challenge which his work posed to developing models of scientific practice and prestige. *Fors Clavigera*, standing outside the educational work in Oxford and yet closely bound up with its aesthetic and political aims, is another facet of Ruskin's work in which his innovation has been underestimated. Politics, social reform, and aesthetic invention come together in its pages, as Ruskin formulates patterns of writing that open possibilities for the modernist discourse. Here, as throughout this volume, Ruskin's thought both locates and motivates what were to become critical concerns of twentieth-century culture.

I

Ruskin and Social Reform

JOSE HARRIS

Fifty years ago Ruskin was widely and, with rare exceptions, approvingly regarded as a major moral and practical inspiration behind the public welfare reforms of wartime and post-war Britain. His influence, remarked the then Master of Balliol, A. K. Lindsay, was 'so far-reaching that today it is difficult for us to realise the perversity and the power of the economic teaching which he fought'.[1] Social security from the cradle to the grave, public ownership of key industries, state patronage of culture, planned new towns, and policies of full employment were all seen as clearly foreshadowed in Ruskin's writings on social philosophy of the 1860s and 1870s, particularly *Unto This Last* and *Fors Clavigera*.[2] Richard Titmuss, the leading creator of the academic discipline of 'social administration' that emerged in many British universities in the post-war years, was specifically committed to Ruskin's vision of seeing social problems 'as a whole', rather than from a purely economic

A remote ancestor of this chapter was given as a talk to Professor Michael Wheeler's Ruskin seminar at Lancaster University. It has evolved almost out of recognition, but I am very grateful to members of that seminar for helpful comments and encouragement. It draws upon a larger study of the intellectual origins of modern social policy, supported by the British Academy and Naffield Foundation.

[1] Lord Lindsay of Birker, 'The Social Conscience and Ideas of Ruskin', given as a BBC Third Programme talk, 1948, published in *Ideas and Beliefs of the Victorians* (London, 1949), 277–82.

[2] J. H. Whitehouse, *Ruskin's Influence Today* (London, 1945); *Ruskin Renascence* (London, 1946); J. H. Whitehouse (ed.), *Ruskin. Prophet of the Good Life* (London, 1948). For details of Ruskin's influence on wartime state patronage of popular culture I am indebted to an unpublished paper by Fram Dinshaw, on 'Sir Kenneth Clark: From the Few to the Many'. The omnipresence of Ruskinian ideas in wartime was acknowledged perhaps unwittingly by one of their few hostile critics, F. A. Hayek. Hayek's *The Road to Serfdom* (London, 1944) never mentioned Ruskin by name. But his nightmare vision of the collectivist state—peopled not by ruthless tyrants but by public-spirited businessmen, paternalist governments, and an industrial workforce conscripted into 'labour service on military lines'—bore a much closer relation to the model set out by Ruskin (mediated probably by Sidney and Beatrice Webb) than to that of leading British socialist theorists of the 1940s, such as Evan Durbin or Harold Laski. For Ruskin and the Webbs, see below, pp. 27–8.

perspective.[3] Ruskin thus took his place, along with the Benthamites and the Fabians, the evangelicals and the Christian socialists, Carlyle and Dickens, among the Victorian prophets and pioneers of collectivism and social reform. More recent studies of Ruskin's proposals have been more guarded and disenchanted about the merits both of Ruskin's social philosophy and of state social services, but have nevertheless endorsed the view that there was a direct line of paternity between the philosophy of *Unto This Last* and the growth of social welfare.[4] In the 1990s the video recording that introduces visitors to Brantwood proclaims the same message; Ruskin, the great critic and art historian, was also the moral godfather of the modern welfare state.

Yet from the historian's point of view there is much that is enigmatic about this assessment, not least the fact that Ruskin was in many instances profoundly hostile to the views of those (such as the Benthamites) with whom his name was bracketed. The reputation fits awkwardly with social and cultural reality at many points. The social services of the mid-twentieth century were widely supposed to have bypassed Victorian 'moralism' with 'the magic of averages' and quantitative social facts, whereas Ruskin's vision of welfare was deeply bound up with the building of individual moral character and the systematic imposition of 'social control'.[5] The welfare state is often viewed as an institutional embodiment of secular modernity, while Ruskin was notorious for his hatred of the 'mad dog's creed of modernism', and—despite his mid-life crisis of orthodox faith—his view of ethics and social relations was at all times inexorably religious. The full-employment policies of the 'classic welfare state'[6] were rooted in monetary expansionism and manipulation of interest rates, whereas Ruskin's economics hovered between strict monetarism, denunciation of interest as 'usury', and the belief that in any case mere 'money' did not matter. By the 1960s and early 1970s, when public enthusiasm for state welfare reached its apogee,

---

3   Richard M. Titmuss, *Social Policy: An Introduction*, ed. Brian Abel-Smith and Kay Titmuss (London, 1974), 59.

4   James Clark Sherburne, *John Ruskin or the Ambiguities of Abundance: A Study in Social and Economic Criticism* (Boston, 1972), esp. 237–62; P. D. Anthony, *John Ruskin's Labour: A Study of Ruskin's Social Theory* (Cambridge: Cambridge University Press, 1983), 44, 56–7, 123; George P. Landow, *Ruskin* (Oxford, 1985), 6.

5   There is a large, usually critical, literature on the history of 'social control', reviewed by F. M. L. Thompson in 'Social Control in Victorian Britain', *Econ. Hist. Rev.*, 2nd series, 34 (1981). But for earlier, more favourable, usage by Ruskinians, see M. E. Sadler, 'Applied Science and Social Control', *Saint George*, 6 (1903), 277–86.

6   A term coined by Anne Digby to characterize the social policies of the mid-1940s to early 1970s (Anne Digby, *British Welfare Policy: Workhouse to Workfare* (London, 1989)).

popular interest in Ruskin's theories both social and aesthetic had gone into steep decline: his ideas were widely deemed of mere antiquarian interest and 'deeply dull'.[7] In the late twentieth century, social services are run by bureaucrats, clerks, accountants, and social workers, whereas Ruskin's ideal community was peopled by kings and queens, captains and chieftains, bachelors and rosières, bishops and dukes. The construction of a welfare state was closely linked to goals of 'equality' and 'equality of opportunity', which Ruskin frequently dismissed as mere rhetorical rubbish (*Works* 17. 46–8, 112, 396–7, 429–45). For many of its supporters the welfare state was a manifestation of faith in historical 'progress', whereas for Ruskin the history of civilization (social, political, and aesthetic) was marked by brief flowerings of virtue followed by inevitable doom and decay (*Works* 8. 193–4; 28. 92). Moreover, despite his personal involvement in social improvement schemes, Ruskin had little permanent hope that they would do any good. In elated moments he had visions of his guild and community experiments as models for wider social reconstruction; but more often he viewed them as mere personal escape routes, 'mere raft-making amidst irrecoverable wreck' (*Works* 28. 264).

All these dichotomies (and others that will be discussed below) make the pedigree between Ruskin and the growth of state social services in many ways puzzling and problematic. Yet, surprisingly, there has been little serious historical writing that gives the problem more than transient attention. Historians have written extensively about the character and roots of Ruskin's social thought, but—except in the most general terms—very little about its practical influence.[8] The current revival of Ruskin studies has explored in detail Ruskin's impact on environmentalism and natural science,[9] but not his impact on policies for social welfare, either in his own day or more recently. And the vast body of research carried out since the 1950s by historians into the origins of state welfare, and into social reform more generally, has treated the real historical

7 N. Shrimpton, 'Economic, Social and Literary Influences upon the Development of Ruskin's Ideas to *Unto this Last (1860)*', D.Phil. Thesis (Oxford, 1976), 8.

8 Philippe Jaudel, *La Pensée sociale de John Ruskin* (Paris, 1973); Catherine Williams, *Ruskin's Philosophy* (Penzance, 1975). Sherburne, *Ambiguities of Abundance*, set out to analyse the impact as well as the content of Ruskin's social thought, but eventually confined himself to the latter. Martin Wiener, *English Culture and the Decline of the Industrial Spirit 1850–1980* (Cambridge, 1981) assumes Ruskin's influence at many points, but with conspicuous absence of specific evidence.

9 Michael Wheeler (ed.), *Ruskin and the Environment: The Storm Cloud of the Nineteenth Century* (Manchester, 1995); and Michael Wheeler (ed.), *Time and Tide: Ruskin and Science* (London, 1996).

Ruskin largely as a non-person (partly, perhaps, because his detailed ideas often clashed embarrassingly with the fictive persona ascribed to him in the 1940s). The fact that the very concept of '*social* welfare' (as distinct from the utilitarian concept of mere 'welfare') was introduced into English usage by Ruskin has gone unnoticed, alike by historians, social scientists, and etymologists.[10] In this chapter I shall explore some ways in which these gaps might be filled. The chapter will offer a brief account and an interpretation of Ruskin's social welfare thought; it will examine the multifarious and often surprising ways in which his ideas were received and interpreted by different individuals and audiences; and it will attempt to identify routes by which Ruskinian principles were absorbed into, or rejected or modified by, practical social policy.

The outlines of Ruskin's social welfare proposals are well known and can be summarized briefly. Although foreshadowed at many points in *Modern Painters*, *The Stones of Venice*, and *The Seven Lamps*, it was not until middle age that he turned his serious attention to social questions —driven partly by the view that art and society were inseparable, partly by a mounting sense of that 'class-consciousness of sin' which, according to Beatrice Webb, was not to afflict the rest of British society until thirty years later. In a long series of public lectures, literary essays, papers to learned societies, and letters to working men, delivered and published between the late 1850s and the 1880s, Ruskin continually challenged the view (which he ascribed to Smith, Mill, Fawcett, and the framers of the 1834 New Poor Law) that individual well-being could best be attained by private calculation within a self-activating market economy. He proposed instead the reconstitution of an integrated, pre-industrial, hierarchical 'citizens' economy', in which market relations would be totally replaced by an ethic of public service (*Works* 16. 9–10; 17. 17–23, 43–56). In place of a deterrent Poor Law and spasmodic private charity, there would be state old age pensions, steeply progressive taxes on income, subsidized people's housing, strict communal enforcement of 'the laws of health', and public provision for children of a combined liberal and vocational education (*Works* 16. 26–8; 17. 21–3; 27. xliv–l, 115–31; 28. 638–65). Social provision was to be administered in the community by pastoral 'bishops', responsible for knowing personally the needs, characters, and circumstances of the families under their

10   The second edition of the *OED* found the earliest usage of 'social welfare' in a legal citation of 1892; but Ruskin used the term, which he claimed to have found in a newspaper leader, in his lecture on 'War' to the Royal Military Academy, published in *The Crown of Wild Olive* in 1866 (*Works* 18. 485).

care, and acting as 'not only the pastors, but the biographers of their people' (*Works* 17. 378–9; 18. 72–3). Public endowments would assist young men and maidens (the 'bachelors and rosières') to marry and rear children; but this privilege would be strictly monitored by the community and confined to candidates who were economically and domestically competent and of sound moral character (*Works* 17. 419–22).[11] For those who could not find work the community would provide public employment at standard rates of pay, thus enabling them to buy goods and services from other producers; and in an economy run like a well-managed patrimonial estate, Ruskin contended, there need *never* be any shortage of useful occupation (*Works* 17. 44–6, 176–7, 540–6). Those who lacked productive skills would receive practical training in 'government schools'; and those who refused to work 'should be set under compulsion of the strictest nature, to the more painful and degrading forms of necessary toil . . . the due wages of such work be retained—cost of compulsion first abstracted—to be at the workman's command, so soon as he has come to sounder mind respecting the laws of employment' (*Works* 17. 22).

Underpinning all these policy schemes was a series of moral visions and values that sharply challenged many aspects of the social philosophy of mid-Victorian England (and indeed of many other periods and societies as well). Wealth was to be measured, not by its mass, but by the 'moral sign' attached to its method of acquisition (*Works* 17. 52). Public relief, instead of conferring automatic civil disability, was to be seen as a form of honourable civic entitlement; while manual labour should have the same status and security as 'sword, pen or lancet' (*Works* 16. 110–15; 17. 22–3). Workers were to be viewed not as contractual units of production, but as 'Soldiers of the Ploughshare' who sacrificed their lives for their country: employers of labour were to be, not anonymous owners of capital, but captains and chieftains bound to their subordinates by bonds of mutual fealty and love (*Works* 16. 26; 17. 33, 75). Statesmen and public office-holders were to be fathers of their people, actively willing on behalf of each citizen exactly the same privileges and levels of prosperity as they would will for their own sons (*Works* 17. 42). Well-run households and close-knit family relationships were to be treated, not as privatized bolt-holes from business and public life, but as ethical and practical models for the working of the national economy and for the

---

[11] The matrimonial arrangements described by Ruskin are still practised in many South American village communities to the present day. I owe this information to Dr Umberto Bullon.

wider body politic (*Works* 16. 20–4; 18. 66–8, 110–2, 135–9).[12] There was to be no absolute right of property; but small-scale ownership should be diffused as widely as possible throughout the community (turning workers into householders and 'minute squires'), while large landowners were to occupy their traditional estates merely as actively employed salaried officials managing a public trust (*Works*. 17. 436–43; 27. 380). Both property-ownership and income were to be subject, not to absolute equality but to 'restraint . . . within certain fixed limits' (*Works* 17. 322). All, whatever their rank and status, were to participate in manual labour; and work of all kinds (liberated from the slavery of machinery) was to be experienced, not as a burden and a pain but as a duty and a joy—both as dutiful acquiescence in nature's laws, *and* as the highest form of freedom, honour, self-fulfilment, and pleasure (*Works* 18. 401–3). Strong government and state interference were to be seen not as instruments of tyranny, nor even as necessary evils, but as preconditions of welfare and justice and 'the very root of all human progress or power' (*Works* 16. 26). Both the flourishing of individuals and the well-being of nations were to be evaluated, not by the abstract measuring-rod of money, but by the more sensitive indices of 'health' and 'life' (or their opposites 'illth' and 'death'), which Ruskin believed could be as precisely observed and identified as disease is diagnosed by a doctor (*Works* 17. 89, 473–4).[13] The goals of good social policy were in no sense merely to redistribute resources or to abolish poverty. They were to 'civilise' the body politic, 'to raise, as well as feed, the poor', and to transform parasites both high and low into disciplined, productive, public-spirited, and, above all, 'honest' citizens (*Works* 8. 264; 17. 347–8). Such goals, Ruskin himself acknowledged, might seem to many absurdly impractical and utopian; but, 'in a science dealing with so subtle elements as those of human nature, it is only possible to answer for the final truth of principles, not for the direct success of plans' (*Works* 17. 23).

The roots and lineages of these ideas can be traced in a wide variety of intellectual traditions, often coexisting rather uneasily with each other.

---

[12] Ruskin has often been viewed as exemplifying a 'Victorian vision' of 'home as a nest', and certainly he saw the well-ordered home as a refuge from the competitive chaos that he perceived around him. But in his ideal vision exactly the opposite was the case; the ethical and functional relationships of family life were to infiltrate, civilize, and eventually encompass the wider society.

[13] The medical analogy is perhaps a misleading one, implying to many modern readers merely another form of narrow scientism. But to Ruskin as to Aristotle the doctor's skill epitomized the faculty of viewing a problem from many angles, empirically as well as intuitively; it was both a science and an art.

Much of Ruskin's practical information about the 'condition of England question' appears to have been derived from the writings of the evangelical anti-Malthusian and critic of the New Poor Law, Robert Benton Seeley, published in many popular editions from the mid-1840s.[14] Ruskin's chivalric employers and captains of industry seem to have come from Carlyle and Saint-Simon, the wise and loving legislators from *The Republic* of Plato, the mistrust of abstract laws from Bishop Butler and Dr Whewell, the moral hatred of mechanization from the Romantic movement, the vision of guilds and gothic workmanship from medievalists like Toulmin Smith and from Ruskin's own studies of Switzerland and Venice. His view of property as a 'great entail' between the generations seems to be derived from Burke, while his conjuring-up of the national economy, not as a nexus of competition, but as a single 'firm' or 'farm', had echoes of both seventeenth-century mercantilism and eighteenth-century physiocracy (*Works* 8. 233; 16. 23, 65). The false shepherds of *Unto This Last* came from St Matthew and the prophet Nehemiah, the pastoral 'bishops' of *Time and Tide* from the Acts of the Apostles and from the 'Godly Commonwealth' experiments of Dr Thomas Chalmers;[15] while the exemplary, queen-dominated, multi-purpose household harked back to Homer and the Song of Songs. Despite Ruskin's fondness for kings and queens, there was a strong classical-republican strain in his idealization of small landowners and squires, in the conscription of male youth into a citizen's militia, in the quasi-military model of public works and provisioning commissars, in the stern policing of domestic morality, and in the vision of social policy as an instrument of civic virtue and public duty (*Works* 17. xvi–xx, 14–23, 31–3).[16] Despite his interest in applied biology, Ruskin would have nothing to do with the new Darwinian determinism that was becoming fashionable in social science in the 1860s and 1870s; instead his view was the strongly environmentalist one, that there was no intrinsically 'degenerate' class and that, if sound social policies were adopted,

[14] Robert Benton Seeley, *The Perils of the Nation: An Appeal to the Legislature, the Clergy, and the Higher and Middle Classes* (London, 1843); *Remedies Suggested, for some of the Evils which Constitute 'The Perils of the Nation'* (London, 1844). For the influence of Seeley on Ruskin's thought, and on the preparation of *Unto This Last*, see annotations to Michael Sadler's copy of *Perils* (library of Nuffield College, Oxford).

[15] On the social doctrines of Chalmers, see Stewart J. Brown, 'Thomas Chalmers and the Communal Ideal in Victorian Scotland', in T. C. Smout (ed.), *Victorian Values* (London, 1993), 61–80.

[16] For a visual representation of this theme, see the portrayal of 'Good Civic Government', from the fresco by Ambrogio Lorenzetti in the Palazzo Publico at Siena (*Works* 16, facing 54), discussed by Ruskin in his 1857 Manchester lectures.

within a few generations all traces of inherited physiological decay would have vanished (*Works* 16. 161–9; 17. 106–7, 405–6). There was also a major debt to his evangelical upbringing, not simply in his intimate familiarity with the social teaching of Old and New Testaments, but in the constant cross-referencing of widely dissimilar texts and in the extrapolation of layer upon layer of hidden spiritual meaning from the most unlikely objects, images, and events (exemplified by the discussion in letter 37 of *Fors Clavigera* on 'Why have our little girls large shoes?')

Despite Ruskin's high standing as an author and public lecturer, such complexity and eclecticism might have been expected to obscure rather than explain his message, both to listening audiences and to those who read his lectures in their published form; and certainly there is much evidence to suggest that the early response to his social policy strictures was one of bored and baffled bewilderment. This was true even of some of Ruskin's warmest admirers. 'Only a genius like Mr Ruskin could have produced such hopeless rubbish', was the oft-cited response to a chapter of *Munera Pulveris* published in *Fraser's Magazine*.[17] 'When Ruskin speaks of Nature and Art, he seems to me inspired', wrote Julia Wedgwood, in whose father's drawing-room Ruskin had first encountered the teachings of Christian socialism. 'When he turns to finance, to politics, to the social arrangements and legislative enactments of mankind, I can recognise neither sober judgment nor profound conviction'.[18] Others declared him 'womanish' and 'sentimental'. Such reactions were to continue throughout his life, in London, Manchester, Sheffield, Oxford, and elsewhere; but between the 1860s and the 1880s there was a gradual transformation in public responses to Ruskin's social doctrines. The quarter of a century after the publication of *Unto This Last* brought the onset of cyclical trade depression, the massive expansion of British finance capital, the onset of large-scale unemployment, the economic collapse of large areas of the countryside, and a tidal wave of mass migration to the slums of the great cities—all of which made Ruskin's critique of an unfettered market economy, and of the breakdown of mutual social obligations, seem much less opaque and capricious than it had seemed in 1859. The economic downturn of the late 1860s brought widespread disenchantment with, and reaction against, the mechanistic and impersonal

---

[17] W. G. Collingwood, *The Life and Work of John Ruskin* (London, 1892), ii. 17.
[18] Frances Julia Wedgwood, *Nineteenth Century Teachers and Other Essays* (London, 1909), 242.

structures of the 1834 Poor Law.[19] During the 1870s there was a major crisis of confidence in orthodox economic theory, not merely among philanthropically-minded reformers, but among the economists themselves; and there was also a marked shift towards communitarianism, organicism, and idealism among political philosophers.[20] The late 1870s brought the onset of the so-called 'Great Depression', and during the 1880s there was a traumatic housing, unemployment, and public order crisis in many of Britain's major cities.[21]

In the face of such changes, Ruskin's insistence on seeing social problems, not through the medium of the market but 'as a whole', began to make much more sense than it had done when first propounded; and, as had happened earlier in his career with respect to buildings and paintings, people found themselves beginning to look at the structure of society through Ruskin's eyes. Even the very eclecticism of Ruskin's thought began to stand him in good stead, as troubled people from many different backgrounds—Comtean positivists, Christian and secular socialists, civic reformers, organizers of charity, ethical idealists, organized working men, conscience-stricken wealthy men, and the large army of late-Victorian 'single-issue' campaigners and moral 'faddists'—all began to find in Ruskin an inspiration and sounding-board for new social programmes. By the 1890s Ruskin's social writings, once a drug on the market, were being reissued in popular editions, several of which became best-sellers. Although as a practical experiment the Guild of St George was an expensive failure, by the end of the century there were Ruskin societies devoted to promoting the ideas of the master in many provincial towns, and their federated journal *Saint George* was to be a significant organ of Edwardian social-reformist thought.[22] It is against this background that we should begin to look more closely for evidence of

[19] *Royal Commission on the Poor Laws, Majority Report*, Cd. 4499, (*Parliamentary Papers* xxxvii, London, 1909), 145–55.

[20] T. W. Hutchison, *A Review of Economic Doctrines, 1870–1929* (Oxford, 1953), 1–31. Ruskin's relationship to political philosophy, and to nineteenth-century philosophy more generally, remains inadequately explored. Given Ruskin's hostility to historical relativism, it seems difficult to accept R. G. Collingwood's claim that Ruskin was a 'Hegelian' without knowing it (R. G. Collingwood, *Ruskin's Philosophy* (Kendal, 1922)). But his attachment to Plato meant that his way of conceiving society was close to that of the Idealist school which emerged in the 1870s and 1880s. Bradley's famous account of 'My Station and its Duties' (A. C. Bradley, *Ethical Studies* (Oxford, 1875), 160–206) was remarkably close to Ruskin's position in e.g. *Works* 17. 319–23, 396–7, though both also echoed the Anglican catechism.

[21] Jose Harris, *Unemployment and Politics: A Study in English Social Policy 1886–1914* (Oxford, 1984 edn.), 51–8.

[22] On Ruskin's guild experiment, see Margaret E. Spence, 'The Guild of St. George:

Ruskin's direct or indirect influence upon ideas about social welfare and practical social reform.

Ruskin's personal involvement in schemes of social betterment dated back to the early 1850s, when he had begun to give lectures on art at F. D. Maurice's Working Men's College. In 1854 he had come into contact with the famous public health reformer, Dr John Simon, through the organization of a scheme of relief for the victims of cholera; and a close personal friendship ensued that was to be of lifelong importance to both Simon and Ruskin. The two men had much in common; both were self-torturing, depressive perfectionists, both suffered aesthetic as well as moral outrage at the ugliness and squalor of mid-Victorian London, and both saw personal and public cleanliness ('the speedy abolition of all abolishable filth') as a paramount, almost theological, virtue.[23] Simon's biographer, Royston Lambert, suggests that in practical terms Simon's influence on Ruskin was greater than vice versa; but the historian who reads Simon's reports on public health, written during and after his appointment as chief medical officer to the Privy Council, may perhaps question this view. Although Ruskin learned much from Simon about the nature of urban poverty, it was Ruskin who supplied the messianic note to Simon's writings on the theory of sanitation; and, in their combination of a grand, dramatic, almost apocalyptic vision of national well-being with minute attention to physical and human detail, Simon's public health reports strongly echoed Ruskin's rhetorical and literary style. Simon fully shared Ruskin's 'classical republican' vision of the inexorable decay of urban civic life, brought about by the disastrous estrangement between a privatized plutocracy and a filthy, diseased, ever-multiplying, proletarian rabble; and like Ruskin he believed that the statesman's model for 'the politics of poverty' should be preventive medicine rather than political economy.[24] Only by extensive use of the regulatory powers of the state, could 'Statesmanship' (the 'magnified art of medicine') replace disease, crime, poverty, and drunkenness by 'the interior forces of personal character, the faculties of activity and self-control, the thrift-powers of labour and frugality'; only thus could society realize the essence of the Ruskinian vision, that it was 'the strength and worth

Ruskin's Attempt to Translate his Ideas into Practice' (repr. from the *Bulletin of the John Rylands Library*, 40/1 (1957)).

[23] Royston Lambert, *Sir John Simon 1816–1904 and English Social Administration* (London, 1963), 198–9, 487–90, 553–4, 589–91; John Simon, *Public Health Reports*, vol. ii (London, 1887), 475: *Works* 28. 655.

[24] John Simon, *English Sanitary Institutions* (London, 1983), ch. 16.

and happiness of the people' which were 'the essential signs of civilization'.[25]

Simon was one of the two most important channels through whom
Ruskin's theories flowed into social practice during the 1860s, the other
being Octavia Hill, the granddaughter of another great Victorian health
reformer, Dr Southwood Smith. Octavia Hill had been one of Ruskin's
drawing-pupils, and had worked for him as a copyist of old masters, before she had embarked upon her life's vocation of charitable reform.
Since 1853 Ruskin had given generous financial aid to Miss Hill's
Working Ladies' Guild, which trained and found employment for unemployed single women,[26] and in the early 1860s he moved more fully
into the arena of practical reform by investing more than £10,000 in her
pioneering schemes for working-class housing management. Under these
schemes Miss Hill took over semi-derelict properties occupied by the
most desolate and degraded of the London poor ('wretched, dilapidated
cowsheds, manure heaps, old timber and rubbish of every description'),
and over a period of years transformed them into well-ordered and
hygienic business and community organizations.[27] Her properties were
supervised by highly trained 'lady rent-collectors' who extracted a limited profit of 5 per cent, exercised a 'tremendous despotism' over the
health and morals of tenants, and were instructed to act as 'QUEENS as
well as FRIENDS' to the communities under their charge.[28] In the late
1870s Ruskin and Miss Hill were to quarrel, she accusing him of utopian
extremism and total lack of capacity for any practical business; but it is
interesting to note that, in the earlier stages of their partnership, quite
the opposite appears to have been the case. Despite his objections in
principle to 'interest' and 'rent', it was initially Ruskin who impressed on
Octavia Hill the view that her schemes should not be purely charitable,
and that the public were much more likely to subscribe to a regime that
exacted a modest rent than to bottomless-purse philanthropy.[29] And
when Miss Hill fell into despair at the savagery of her tenants and the
hopelessness of her task, it was Ruskin who helped her out of it by

[25] Ibid. 478–81.

[26] Gillian Darley, *Octavia Hill* (London, 1990), 52.

[27] Ibid. 91–100; E. Moberly Bell, *Octavia Hill: A Biography* (London, 1942), 74–100.

[28] *Royal Commission on the Housing of the Working Classes*, Vol. ii, C. 4402, I
(*Parliamentary Papers*, xxx, London, 1884–5), evidence of Octavia Hill, Q. 8976; Octavia
Hill, *Letter to My Fellow Workers* (1874), cited by Jane Lewis in David Englander and
Rosemary O'Day (eds.), *Retrieved Riches: Social Investigation in Britain 1840–1914*
(Aldershot, 1995), 51.

[29] *Octavia Hill: Early Ideals* (letters ed. by Emily S. Maurice; London, 1928), 162–3; E.
Moberly Bell, *Octavia Hill*, 76–7.

proposing and financing numerous additional amenities that made the model apartment-blocks more humane and civilized—such as gardens, nurseries, playgrounds, summer outings, and communal Christmas and May-day festivities.[30] Ruskin was also closely involved with Miss Hill and others in the 1860s movement for organizing and harmonizing London's great mass of private voluntary charities; and in 1869 he became one of the first Vice-Presidents of the London Charity Organization Society—a body committed to promoting self-help, character, and 'civil duty' among the poor, and to opposing ill-thought-out schemes of charitable 'sentimentality'.[31] It was the Charity Organization Society that persuaded George Goschen, President of the Poor Law Board in Gladstone's first ministry, to modify the policy of mechanistic deterrence prescribed by the New Poor Law and to shift towards the principle of discrimination between applicants of 'good' and 'bad' character.[32] In this period too Ruskin became involved in the plans for cross-class contact and cooperation that were to develop into the university settlements movement; it was at Ruskin's house in Denmark Hill that the discussions took place in 1868 between Ruskin, Edward Denison, J. R. Green, Brooke Lambert, and Edmund Hollond that were the prelude to the foundation some years later of Toynbee Hall.[33]

In these activities of the 1860s there was little of the utopianism and sentimentalism that critics found in Ruskin's lectures and writings; and such activities may indicate that, initially at least, the social vision of *Unto This Last* was conceived as a parable or 'lay sermon' rather than a blueprint for practical reform. In the intense constitutional debates of the 1860s Ruskin's voice was largely a conservative one; prior to the 1867 Reform Act, he was urging working men not to bother with the vote, but to confine themselves to setting up their own industrial parliament (*Works* 17. 324–32). Towards the end of the 1860s, however, there were

[30]   Darley, *Octavia Hill*, 91–114.

[31]   Helen Bosanquet, *Social Work in London 1869–1914: A History of the Charity Organisation Society* (London, 1914), ch. 1.

[32]   Discrimination between 'deserving' and 'undeserving' poor is often ascribed to the 1834 Poor Law itself, and seen as the quintessence of Victorian moralism. But in fact officials under the Poor Law were legally prohibited from taking any account of personal character. Recognition of 'deservingness' was an innovation of the mid-Victorian era, intended to rescue the respectable poor from the policy of 'deterrence' that, in theory at least, was uniformly meted out to all members of the pauper class. The new policy seems initially to have had Ruskin's support, but he later turned strongly against it (Maurice (ed.), *Octavia Hill: Early Ideals*, 179–81; *Works* 17. 540; 28. 67).

[33]   J. R. Pimlott, *Toynbee Hall: Fifty Years of Social Progress 1884–1934* (London, 1935), 12–14, 30–2.

signs that the cautious, prudential character of Ruskin's practical interests of that period was giving way to something altogether more ambitious and subversive. One of the first public signs of his encroaching
mental illness came when he disrupted a meeting on industrial relations
that was being chaired by Gladstone at the Social Science Association,
by demanding instead a discussion on the so-called 'natural law of
wages' (*Works* 17. 536–9). In the early 1870s he began to take much more
seriously his own strictures about the moral evils of interest and rent. He
accused Octavia Hill of becoming 'too successful to be quite right'; and
he condemned her shift towards a strategy of 'Raising the poor without
gifts', arguing instead that the principle of the 'Gift' was a Heaven-sent
privilege and duty.34 He gradually withdrew from all personal contact
with her housing schemes, eventually transferring to her at a purely
nominal price all his share in the ownership of her model properties.
'My work is now, and must be, totally in another kind,' he wrote to her
in July 1875; 'not as you put it, that I want perfection, while you are content with the immediate possible—but that while your work is only mit-
igating of mortal pain, mine is radically curative.'35 His disenchantment
with gradual piecemeal reform was reinforced by the fate of his friend
Simon, who—after the triumphant success of his health schemes in the
mid-1860s—found himself in the 1870s outflanked and marginalized by
the Poor Law sector of the newly established Local Government Board,
which refused to allow public health schemes to be used as a cloak for a
more general war on poverty. The growing extremism of Ruskin's views
in the mid-1870s meant that he was increasingly estranged from bodies
like the National Association for the Promotion of Social Science,
through whom ideas about reform were mediated to politicians, civil
servants, and fashionable London; and his paper on social policy to the
Metaphysical Society in May 1875 simultaneously threw down the glove
to both the scientific and the theological establishments.36 In the mid-
1870s, however, Ruskin's election to the new Slade Professorship of
Art at Oxford opened up to him an entirely new audience, the rising

34 Darley, *Octavia Hill*, 145; Ruskin to Octavia Hill, 30 Aug. 1870, cited in Maurice
(ed.), *Octavia Hill: Early Ideals*, 180–1. Hill had moved in the opposite direction from
Ruskin, becoming convinced that subsidized rents were a mere 'rate in aid of wages, which
according to orthodox economic theory depressed rather than improved the standard of
living of recipients' (*Royal Commission on the Housing of the Working Classes*, Q. 8870).

35 Ruskin to Octavia Hill, 9 Apr. 1895 (Maurice (ed.), *Octavia Hill: Early Ideals*, 186–7).

36 *Works* 16. 161–9; Lawrence Goldman, 'The Social Science Association, 1857–1886:
A Context for Mid-Victorian Liberalism', *English Historical Review*, 101 (1986), 99–154:
Alan Willard Brown, *The Metaphysical Society: Victorian Minds in Crisis, 1869–1880*
(New York, 1973), 153–4, 328.

generation of undergraduates. This was to prove one of the most powerful conduits for the transmission of Ruskin's ideas into the spheres of social policy and public administration.

Much has been written about Ruskin's Oxford road-building experiments and his attempts to initiate undergraduates into the duty of manual labour. Many memoirs of the 1870s and 1880s suggest that, for stylish young men from Oscar Wilde downwards, breakfast with Ruskin followed by a working trip to the Hinksey road became a fashionable high-spot of Oxford life. More important as an influence on policy, however, was to be the use that Ruskin made of his lectures on art to propound his social doctrines; doctrines that made a profound impact on a small group of men who were later to become active in many areas of public life. Initially the most prominent was W. H. Mallock, who was later to recant his discipleship of Ruskin and become a militant defender of free-market economics; but his most famous book, *The New Republic* of 1877, portrayed Ruskin as the one teacher of wisdom in a world of canting hypocrites and false prophets.[37] More long-lasting Oxford disciples included men like Michael Sadler, Arthur Acland, and Hubert Llewellyn Smith, all of whom were to play a major role in late-Victorian and Edwardian reform movements. Michael Sadler, later to become the chief administrator of the Privy Council Committee on Education, was present at Ruskin's lectures on *The Art of England*, when Ruskin denounced the 'Great 800-year old Picnic Party of the Upper Classes', and called for the creation of a new popular national culture, made up of secure employment, decent housing, art and folk-song, public libraries, and village museums. 'To see the man is almost an exultation', Sadler recorded:

to hear him is to be inspired . . . . the sentence in which he told of the greatness of the past of England, & asked with profound scorn whether all that can now be said of a country where S. George fought and S. Augustine preached, which 'stands, the champion of all succour folded in the mantle of its seas', is that 'John Bull is guarding his pudding'—this one sentence quite made my hair stand on end.[38]

Sadler's conversion to Ruskinian ideas led directly to his involvement in the setting-up of the University Extension movement, and to a lifelong

---

[37] W. H. Mallock, *Memorials of Life and Literature* (London, 1920), 58–9, 64–5; D. J. Ford, 'W. H. Mallock and Socialism in England, 1880–1918', in Kenneth D. Brown (ed.), *Essays in Anti-Labour History* (London, 1974), 317–42.
[38] Michael Sadleir, *Michael Ernest Sadler, 1861–1943* (London, 1949), 32–3 and 45. See pp. 50, 64–5.

commitment to the promotion of art and manual skills within the curriculum of national education. As a senior civil servant attached to the Privy Council he was to be responsible for drafting the Revised Code of 1893, which introduced for elementary schools a Ruskinian programme of 'punctuality, good manners, cleanliness, duty, honour and truthfulness', in place of the 'mechanical and inflexible' code of rote-learning introduced at the time of the 1870 Education Act. A year later the code was extended to include school visits to museums and art galleries. Sadler also drafted a new curriculum for local authority Continuation Schools, which prescribed such Ruskinian ideals as truth, duty, citizenship, drawing, and gardening. The legislation that introduced these codes was introduced into parliament by another of Ruskin's disciples, Arthur Acland, with the words 'the great object of education is not merely knowledge but character'. As vice-president of the Privy Council Committee on Education Acland also reformed the Science and Art department, introduced grants for technical and craft education, and abolished the mid-Victorian system of 'payment by results'.[39]

A close friend and Oxford contemporary of Michael Sadler was Hubert Llewellyn Smith, who also heard Ruskin's Slade lectures and developed a lifelong commitment to promoting technical skills and the visual arts within the context of elementary and secondary education.[40] Llewellyn Smith's major impact on social policy, however, was to be in the sphere of unemployment and labour problems, where he was to become the most powerful public administrator of his age. He worked for several years as an investigator on Charles Booth's survey of London, lived and taught at Toynbee Hall, and in 1893 became head of a newly constituted Labour department in the Board of Trade: in this latter role he set about fulfilling Ruskin's dictum that the collection of detailed knowledge about its citizens was one of the first duties of good government. He also became a powerful advocate of the new Ruskinian 'social economics', which sought to supplement the older political economy with social, cultural, structural, and geographical analysis.[41] His evidence to the House of Commons Select Committee on Distress from Want of Employment in 1895 was a major landmark on three different

---

[39] Gillian Sutherland, *Policy-Making in Elementary Education 1870–1895* (Oxford, 1973), 330–1, 337; *Works* 27. lxi–lxviii; Michael E. Sadler, 'Compulsory Continuation Schools', *Saint George*, 10 (1907), 11–15.

[40] Hubert Llewellyn Smith, *The Economic Laws of Art Production* (London, 1924); *The Place of Economy in Art* (London, 1930).

[41] H. Llewellyn Smith, *Economic Aspects of State Socialism* (Oxford, 1887).

levels; in demonstrating his techniques of empirical social analysis, in bringing the newly forged concept of 'unemployment' to the forefront of public debate, and in arguing (as Ruskin had argued thirty years earlier) that the labour market was incapable of automatic self-adjustment, and that unemployment could only be cured by conscious processes of classification, discipline, and organization.[42]

Llewellyn Smith's influence may also have been important in attracting to Ruskinian ideas a slightly later generation of Oxford graduates and Toynbee Hall residents, who never heard Ruskin lecture in person. One of the most influential of these was Edward Urwick, a Balliol-educated idealist philosopher and lecturer at the Charity Organization Society's School of Sociology, who in 1912 became Professor of Social Philosophy and head of the Social Science department at the London School of Economics. Both as a member of the COS and as the architect of what was to become the leading centre for academic 'social policy' in Britain, Urwick insisted that the training of social workers and administrators should consist of 'citizenship' and 'social economics' rather than formal political economy; and his own writings on social philosophy drew heavily upon both Ruskin and Plato.[43] Other Toynbee-based Ruskinians were T. Edmund Harvey, organizer of the Toynbee Hall Enquirers' Club, who succeeded Samuel Barnett as warden of the settlement in 1906;[44] and J. Howard Whitehouse, a companion of the guild of St George and editor of the journal *Saint George*, who became the settlement's secretary in 1907. Whitehouse's mission as a social reformer was to extend to boys of the working classes the same facilities for culture, sport, leadership, and adventure that were available in the most progressive public schools; and he dreamt of replacing the 'selfish apathy' and 'thoughtless uniformity' of 'lonely lives in semi-slums' by a new popular order of Arthurian knighthood.[45] Whitehouse was elected a Liberal MP in 1910 and was to act as one of Lloyd George's parliamentary private secretaries during the passage of the National Insurance Act

---

[42] *Select Committee on Distress from Want of Employment, Minutes of Evidence*, House of Commons 365 (*Parliamentary Papers* ix, London, 1895), QQ. 4526–5019. See also *Report on Agencies and Methods for Dealing with the Unemployed*, prepared for the Controller-General of the Commercial, Labour and Statistical Department of the Board of Trade, by H. Llewellyn Smith, C. 7182 (*Parliamentary Papers* lxxxii, London, 1893).

[43] E. J. Urwick, *Luxury and Waste of Life* (London, 1908); *A Philosophy of Social Progress* (London, 1920); *The Message of Plato: A Re-Interpretation of the Republic* (London, 1920); *The Social Good* (London, 1927).

[44] T. Edmund Harvey, 'A London Boy's Saturday', *Saint George*, 9 (1906), 149–67.

[45] J. H. Whitehouse, 'The Work of the Boys' Club and its Place in Social Progress', three papers in *Saint George*, 7 (1904), 115–22; 7 (1904), 202–8; 7 (1904), 228–32.

in 1911.[46] He was later to become the founder of Bembridge school (run on Ruskinian principles), the owner of Brantwood, and a lifelong acolyte and memorialist of the Ruskinian tradition.[47]

An even more influential Toynbee Hall Ruskinian was William Beveridge, the future author of the social welfare reforms of the 1940s. With his rather hard-nosed, secular, bureaucratic, approach to welfare Beveridge appears at first sight a rather unlikely enthusiast for Ruskin; and there is no breath of a mention of Ruskinianism in his autobiography. Yet Beveridge was a frequent contributor to *Saint George*, and was an active member of its editorial board from 1906 until the journal's demise in 1911 (the same period in which he was assisting Llewellyn Smith to draft the labour exchange and social insurance reforms of the 'New Liberal' government).[48] There were in fact certain features of Ruskin's social thought that chimed closely with Beveridge's own ideas —particularly his concern with seeing concrete issues 'in the round', and his mistrust of axiomatic economic theory. Like Ruskin, Beveridge believed that the training of good citizens was an ultimate goal beyond the mere relief of poverty; and, as with Ruskin, there was in Beveridge an underlying streak of ruthlessness about the fate of work-refusers, weaklings, and wilful social failures.[49] There was also a close affinity with Ruskin's belief in a publicly controlled labour market, which throughout his life was to haunt Beveridge's vision of a properly regulated system of national social welfare.[50] The shade of Ruskin helps to explain the provenance of one of Beveridge's writings that historians have found most anomalous and puzzling. This was his paper to the Sociological Society in 1906, where he proposed that, after the labour market had been systematically reorganized, hopeless 'unemployables' should become 'the acknowledged dependants of the state, removed from free

[46] Whitehouse, *Ruskin Renascence*, 16.

[47] J. S. Dearden, *Ruskin, Bembridge and Brantwood: The Growth of the Whitehouse Collection* (Keele, 1994).

[48] W. H. Beveridge, 'Organized Remedies for Unemployment', *Saint George*, 9 (1906), 46–9; 'Labour Exchanges in the United Kingdom', ibid. 13 (1910), 161–82. The article on 'Insurance against Unemployment', in *Saint George*, 14 (1911), 38–43, signed 'Quintilius' was almost certainly also by Beveridge, and bore all the hallmarks of his style of thought ('we are now concerned more with social reconstruction than with mere measures of relief'). Jose Harris, *William Beveridge: A Biography* (Oxford: 2nd edn., 1997), 168–95.

[49] Compare Ruskin's 'I am not a saviour of sick men, but an organizer of strong men' (Philip Boardman, *The Worlds of Patrick Geddes: Biologist, Town Planner, Re-educator, Peace-warrior* (London, 1978), 33), with Harris, *Beveridge*, 119–20.

[50] W. H. Beveridge, 'Organised Remedies for Unemployment', *Saint George*, 9 (1906), 46–9: *Unemployment: A Problem of Industry* (London, 1909 and 1930); *Full Employment in a Free Society* (London, 1944), 110–93.

industry and maintained adequately in public institutions, but with complete and permanent loss of civil rights—including not only the franchise but civil freedom and fatherhood'. This paper has been read as a testimony to the prevalence of Darwinian thought in Edwardian social policy; but it may perhaps more accurately be heard as an echo of the stern treatment of idlers in *Unto This Last* and of the community regulation of marriages in *Time and Tide* and *Sesame and Lilies*.[51]

Ruskin's influence on the ideas and careers of his Oxford disciples is relatively easy to trace, but by the 1890s much of his popular following lay elsewhere—in provincial civic societies, in the Ethical movement and progressive nonconformity, in academic circles remote from Oxford, and in the various branches of socialism. The trail here is more elusive and patchy, and invites more detailed research than has been possible for this chapter. Both the Edwardian Garden City movement and the Town-Planning movement were full of people anxious to realize Ruskin's prescriptions about cottages, open spaces, low rents, craft-production, and healthy integration between the spheres of 'life' and 'labour'.[52] Despite the critical account of Ruskin's thought written by the leading British Positivist, Frederic Harrison, many aspects of Ruskin's thought were attractive to members of the Positivist movement and to people on its fringes who were influenced by positivist ideas.[53] Among them were the biologist and town-planner Professor Patrick Geddes; the neo-Malthusian secularist J. M. Robertson; the unorthodox economist and social theorist J. A. Hobson; and many other members of the first national Sociological Society, founded in London by Geddes and Victor Branford in 1904. J. A. Hobson, doyen of the Rainbow circle and a prominent theorist of 'New Liberalism' was to spend a lifetime in tireless (though not uncritical) pursuit of Ruskin's vision of a supra-economic calculus for measuring 'wealth' and 'well-being'.[54] In addition, Hobson

[51]   W. H. Beveridge, 'The Problem of the Unemployed', *Sociological Papers*, 3 (1906), 328–31. It should be added that, like Ruskin himself, Beveridge often expressed certain extreme opinions with an ironic tongue in cheek. The paper may perhaps be interpreted more as evidence of a certain intellectual cast of mind than of serious policy intentions.

[52]   Dean Kitchin, 'Man and His Tools', *The Garden City*, 2/15 (1907), 303–6; and ibid. 18. 364–5. *The Garden City* (renamed *Garden Cities and Town Planning* in 1911) ran from 1904 to 1932 and was the official journal of the Garden Cities Association. Until 1918 its cover portrayed a queen sitting in her garden, holding aloft what appeared to be a citadel (or possibly a king's treasury), as an image of civic life. See also Anthony Sutcliffe (ed.), *British Town Planning: The Formative Years* (Leicester, 1981), 80, 115–18, 156.

[53]   Frederic Harrison, *John Ruskin* (London, 1902); *Patrick Geddes*.

[54]   J. A. Hobson, *John Ruskin: Social Reformer* (London, 1898, 2nd edn. 1899); *Work and Wealth: A Human Valuation* (London, 1914); *Property and Improperty* (London,

invoked Ruskin's ideas about maldistribution of wealth, to support his own theory that inadequate demand and 'underconsumption' were the prime causes of unemployment (unemployment, not just of labour, but of land, savings and capital as well).[55] And Ruskin's argument that wealth production was quintessentially cooperative ('large fortunes cannot honestly be made by the work of any *one* man's hands or head') seems the obvious source for Hobson's claim that the community was 'organically' entitled to a share of private profits.[56] Ruskin's ideas were thus inseminated into the very heartland of the kind of advanced liberalism that he himself had so much distrusted and despised. Another unusual Ruskinian was William Smart, Professor of Political Economy at Glasgow University, who as a young man had written a long essay suggesting that Ruskin's writings should be seen as a moral meditation in the manner of Plato's *The Republic* rather than as a treatise on practical reform. Smart also composed a seminal article on 'The Old Economy and the New', which portrayed the narrowly technical economics of the past era as having given way to a much more synoptic 'Social Philosophy', whose focus was 'not Wealth but Labour'. Smart's subsequent research on national income and income distribution persuaded him that Ruskin had in fact been entirely wrong about the parasitism of the merchant class and the inherent injustice of capitalism; but he was nevertheless a founder member of the Ruskin Society of Glasgow, and remained throughout his life a strong supporter of Ruskin's moral, civic and 'public service' ideals, returning in his sixties to 'my old Ruskin and Carlyle faith'.[57]

1937); H. C. G. Matthew, 'Hobson, Ruskin and Cobden', in Michael Freeden (ed.), *Reappraising J. A. Hobson: Humanism and Welfare* (London, 1990), 11–30.

55 J. A. Hobson and A. F. Mummery, *The Problem of the Unemployed: An Enquiry and an Economic Policy* (London, 1896); Jose Harris, 'From Sunspots to Social Welfare: The Unemployment Problem 1870–1914', in Bernard Corry (ed.), *Unemployment and the Economists* (Cheltenham, 1996), 52–68. Ruskin's 'underconsumptionism' was of course very different from that of his heirs of the mid-twentieth century: it meant that all should have an adequate supply of long-lasting high-quality goods, rather than an infinite supply of the disposable products of mass production.

56 *Time and Tide*, 101. This point is missed in John Allett's *New Liberalism: The Political Economy of J. A. Hobson* (Toronto, 1981), 16 and 70–95, which otherwise offers an excellent account of Hobson's debt to Ruskin.

57 William Smart, *A Disciple of Plato: A Critical Study of Ruskin* (Glasgow, 1883); 'The Old Economy and the New', *Fortnightly Review*, 56 (1891), 279–91; William Smart, *The Distribution of Income: Being a Study of What the National Wealth is and of How it is Distributed* (London, 1899, 1923 edn.), 23–4, 307–40; A. M. McBriar, *An Edwardian Mixed Doubles: The Bosanquets Versus the Webbs 1890–1929* (Oxford, 1987), 187. Smart's main difference from Ruskin was that he thought a 'public service' or 'social service' ethic could be successfully superimposed upon a capitalist economy.

Among Ruskin's most dedicated nonconformist disciples were a father and son, Dr John Brown Paton and Dr John Lewis Paton, respectively the leading minister of the Congregational Union, and the High Master of Manchester Grammar School. Dr John Brown Paton was the founder and first president of the Nottingham Congregational Institute, built in the late thirteenth-century Gothic style, which his son later described as 'virtually a national temple' of Ruskinian civic idealism. The elder Paton was the originator of the National Home Reading Union, designed to raise standards of literary taste among the new mass reading public, to which all the local Ruskin societies became affiliated in the 1890s. He was also the founder of the Gateshead and Lingfield labour colonies: self-supporting subsistence farming schemes whose dual aim was initially to train and rehabilitate the urban unemployed, and ultimately to provide a model for non-profit-making, cooperative craft and agricultural production. In the 1890s and 1900s Paton was the dominant figure in the Christian Social Service Union, and a leading promoter of the numerous civic trusts, guilds of help, and councils of social service that sprang up throughout England and Scotland in this period—inspired partly by Ruskin's pastoral 'bishops', partly by the legacy of Dr Thomas Chalmers, and partly by the 'Elberfeld' schemes common in the cities of north Germany.[58] Paton's son, Dr John Lewis Paton, was if anything an even more dedicated Ruskinian than his father. A companion of the Guild of St George, he used his role as a headmaster to foster craft education and the moral worth of manual labour, campaigned for the introduction of 'progressive' principles throughout the public school system, and organized summer schools, camps, and boys' clubs that were designed to universalize Ruskinian artistic, civic, moral, and social ideals.[59] In 1906 both Patons were involved in the setting-up of the British Institute of Social Service, an organization dedicated to 'practical Platonism', 'social redemption', and cross-class civic culture, that provided a national focus and clearing-house for social reform and voluntary social work organizations in more than sixty towns and cities. Its

---

[58]   John Brown Paton, *Applied Christianity: A Civic League—Social and Educational —for our Cities and Towns* (Social Questions of the Day, no. 2, (London, 1906)); James Marchant, *J. B. Paton, M.A., D.D., Educational and Social Pioneer* (London, 1909); John L. Paton, *John Brown Paton: A Biography* (London, 1914); Norman Wyld, 'The Liverpool City Guild', *Town Planning Review*, 1/1 (1910), 84–6.

[59]   J. L. Paton, 'Chivalry Ancient and Modern', *Saint George*, 5 (1902), 189–201; 'Schoolboys as Navvies', ibid., 7 (1904), 54–7; 'The University and the Working-Folk', ibid., 11 (1908), 155–69; 'Cross-Fertilization in Schools', ibid., 13 (1910), 1–9; 'Civic Education', ibid., 13 (1910), 107–8.

representative emblem—engraved on stationery, leaflets, annual reports, and house journal—was a Gothic woodcut in the style of Durer, portraying the trials and triumphs of St George.[60]

Despite widespread genuflexion, Ruskin's influence on the social policies of British socialism remains inadequately explored. Bernard Shaw in 1920 suggestively remarked that a main cause of the weakness of Marxism in Britain was that those within the socialist movement who were inclined to violence and state terror had no need of Marx; they already had their prophet in Ruskin.[61] This aspect of Ruskin's thought found an echo in some of Ruskin's socialist admirers of the 1930s; but socialists of the 1890s and 1900s were much more inclined to emphasize his support for public welfare schemes, his idealization of the independent master craftsman, and his ethic of public service. Guild socialists of the 1900s, such as Maurice Reckitt and A. J. Penty, constantly cited Ruskin's views on the evils of usury and the intrinsic worth of labour, while conveniently ignoring his emphasis on the duty of obedience and the inexorable necessity of state power.[62] Members of the Christian socialist movement in the Edwardian era were perhaps less uncritically Ruskinian than their antecedents of the 1880s; they had a new moral philosopher in Hastings Rashdall, whose guiding social principle of 'equality of consideration' was markedly different from the parable-of-the-vineyard position adopted in *Unto This Last*.[63] In the sphere of social policy, Ruskin's major influence on socialists almost certainly came through Sidney and Beatrice Webb: a claim that may seem paradoxical, in view of the Webbs' reputation for 'mechanical' and 'utilitarian' reform, but one that is borne out at many points in their multifarious writings. Both the Webbs were admirers of Ruskin before they met each other; both shared Ruskin's conviction that the clue to social betterment lay not in relief but 'prevention', that the aim of policy was 'not to be *R*eformatory but Formatory'.[64] Sidney's notion of a 'rent of ability' was foreshadowed by Ruskin's defence of a residual profit for the energetic employer; and in an early article he ascribed to Ruskin the rise of an ethic of 'salaried public

[60] *Progress: Civic, Social, and Industrial: The Organ of the British Institute of Social Service*, 1/1 (1906).

[61] G. B. Shaw, *Ruskin's Politics* (London, 1921).

[62] Peter Grosvenor, 'A Mediaeval Future: The Social, Economic and Aesthetic Thought of A. J. Penty (1875–1937)', Ph.D. thesis (London, 1997).

[63] Hastings Rashdall, 'The Rights of the Individual', *Economic Review*, 6 (1896), 319–23.

[64] Beatrice Webb, *Our Partnership* (London, 1948, 3rd edn. 1975), 422–77; *Works* 17. 544.

service, with the stimulus of duty and esteem' rather than inheritance or profit, that he sought to make his own.[65] The Webbs' theory of the National Minimum, often perceived as the intellectual harbinger of the welfare state, also resounded with powerful echoes of Ruskin. It prescribed minimum standards of income, health, education, employment, and leisure, to be provided by government for all citizens whether they wanted it or not; accompanied by physical exercise, technical training, and conscription into a civic militia for all male citizens—and by compulsory discipline and re-education for those who were recalcitrant.[66] A key principle of the Webbs' famous Minority Report on the Poor Laws of 1909 was that all persons had an equal right to instant relief, regardless of character and past contribution ('even unto this last'); only *retrospectively*, if found to be defective in willingness to work or moral character, should they be disciplined and retrained, before being restored to full civic life—all of which again bore the indelible hallmark of Ruskin.[67] Writings by the Webbs on such themes as 'national housekeeping' and female citizenship were deeply reminiscent of Ruskin's thought, both in their conception of the national economy as a well-managed domestic household, and in their image of the omnicompetent mother-housekeeper, not as a servile drudge, but as the ideal type of skilled craftsman, moral guardian, and active citizen in the well-run modern state.[68] The same might be said of the Webbs' lifelong admiration for the 'vocation of leadership', and of their idealized vision of the 'soldiery', not as warriors but as uniformed public servants, benevolent commissars, and guardians of civil society (a central theme of their ill-fated *Soviet Communism: A New Civilisation?* of 1936).[69]

What, if anything, do these links and lineages tell us about Ruskin's overall impact upon the history of social policy and the emergence of the 'welfare state'? Ruskinian language and Ruskinian ideas resonate

---

[65] *Works* 17. 319–23; Sidney Webb, 'The Difficulties of Individualism', repr. in Sidney and Beatrice Webb, *Problems of Modern Industry* (London, 1902), 249.

[66] Sidney and Beatrice Webb, *Industrial Democracy* (London, 1897, 2nd edn. 1902), pp. liv–lvi, 766–84; Sidney Webb, 'Social Movements', in *Cambridge Modern History*, xii: *The Latest Age* (Cambridge, 1910).

[67] E. J. Urwick, 'The Reports of the Poor Law Commission', *Saint George*, 12 (1909), 79–90.

[68] S. and B. Webb, 'What is Socialism?', eight articles in *The New Statesman*, May–July 1913, especially 'National Housekeeping', 31 May 1913, 236–8; B. Webb, 'Motherhood and Citizenship', *The New Statesman*, Supplement, 16 May 1914, 10–11.

[69] *Works* 17. 462–3; Sidney and Beatrice Webb, *Soviet Communism: A New Civilisation?* (London, 1935, 3rd edn. 1944), 94–8, 842–5, 973.

throughout large areas of early twentieth-century public policy: in the introduction of national insurance and old age pensions, in attempts to 'organise the labour market', in the discovery of 'underconsumption', and in the vision of injured workmen as the 'wounded soldiers of industry'.[70] His influence can be traced in embryonic ideas about town-planning, in battles over educational reform, in the passion of British sociologists for empirical measurement of nutrition, disease, and poverty, and in the systematic extension of the regulatory powers of the state. The long line of schemes for 'decasualization' of labour, put forward by Charles Booth, Llewellyn Smith, Beveridge, and the Webbs, all echoed Ruskin's argument in 'The Roots of Honour' that regular hours and fixed wage-rates should replace the cycles of overwork and unemployment, irregular wages and destitution, that characterized the lives of the unskilled casual poor (*Works* 17. 68–71).[71] Disciples of Ruskin were to the forefront of the turn-of-the-century campaigns for land and taxation reform ('the duty of the State . . . is to re-acquire by taxation that share of value which is the community's by right').[72] They were found also in large numbers within the vast network of Edwardian and inter-war civic and voluntary organizations, dedicated to instilling habits of 'good citizenship' and to transforming 'disorganized' private charity into a form of supplementary public service. Key documents in the growth of public welfare were written by reformers in the Ruskinian tradition, such as the two reports of the Royal Commission on the Poor Laws (the Minority Report composed by the Webbs, the Majority Report largely drafted by Professor William Smart[73]). Major actors in the history of social policy, from Octavia Hill and John Simon through to William Beveridge and Richard Titmuss, were personally close to Ruskin, or acknowledged a debt to the influence of his social thought. Beveridge's insistence in his old age that what he had intended to create

[70] A term used by Earl Fitzwilliam in a Lords' debate on industrial accident legislation in 1904, cited in P. W. J. Bartrip and S. B. Burman, *The Wounded Soldiers of Industry Industrial Compensation Policy 1833–1897* (Oxford, 1983), 5. On Fitzwilliam's links with Ruskinian circles, see Sadleir, *Michael Sadler*, 393–4.

[71] Harris, *Unemployment and Politics*, 15–22.

[72] H. Rose, 'The Politics of the Street and the Philosophy of the Study: Professor Huxley and the Land Question', *Isdragil: Journal of the Ruskin Reading Guild*, 1 (Jan.–Sept. 1890), 12.

[73] On Smart's contribution to the Majority report, see McBriar, *An Edwardian Mixed Doubles*, 283 and 299. Like the Minority, the Majority envisaged reformatory training camps for those who refused to work; but they baulked at the Minority's Ruskinian stance, that all who applied for support should be relieved without question in the first instance, and only subsequently classified as willing or unwilling to work.

was not a 'welfare state' but a 'social service state' was a direct echo of the language of Ruskin; while Titmuss's conception of the ethical imperative of the 'Gift Relationship' was an exact secular replication of the theory of the 'Gift' that Ruskin had urged upon Octavia Hill a hundred years before.[74]

Yet the evidence marshalled above needs to be treated with some caution. The very fact that the inspiration of Ruskin was claimed by reformers in such widely varying and often conflicting traditions suggests that the nature of Ruskin's influence was rather different from what interpreters of the 1940s supposed. And it suggests also that the intellectual roots of modern social welfare are themselves much more diverse than is often imagined. People frequently found what they looked for in Ruskin; and over a period of a hundred years, different reformers found legitimation for social strategies of many different kinds: for individual moral reformation, inter-class paternalism, urban and civic renewal, rural retreatism, fascist-style regeneration, self-governing workshops and craft-production, universalist social services, redistribution of wealth and income, and comprehensive social control by an authoritarian administrative state. Vegetarians, purity reformers, and animal rights campaigners all embellished their arguments with Ruskinian texts.[75] As with his writings on art and aesthetics it was, and still is, possible to read Ruskin's social thought and prescriptions on social policy *both* as archaic and anti-modernist, *and* as profoundly 'modern' (although conceptions of what constitutes 'modernity' tend to differ between the aesthetic and social spheres[76]). By the 1920s and 1930s the outer extremes of Ruskin's followers embraced those who hailed him as a prophet of Marxist-Leninist revolution, and those for whom he meant May Queen coronations in upper-class girls' boarding-schools.[77] More-

74 Harris, *Beveridge*, 452; Richard M. Titmuss, *The Gift Relationship: From Human Blood to Social Policy* (London, 1970); above, p. 19.

75 See e.g. *Herald of the Cross* (1905–); *The Shield: A Review of Moral and Social Hygiene* (1916–); *Excalibur: The Chronicle of the Fellowship of the Round Table* (1929–). One should, however, resist the temptation to discover Ruskin in everything: I am unconvinced, for example, by the frequent claim that Ruskin was a serious precursor of marginal utility. The opposite view of Hobson, that the Ruskinian quest for a more broadly-based, humanistic economics was *undermined* by the rise of marginalism, with its exclusive focus on a utilitarian calculus, seems much more plausible. (J. A. Hobson, *Free-Thought in the Social Sciences* (London, 1926), 95 and 119.)

76 For example, the shattering of conventional representation often associated with modernism in the arts seems to have little in common with the search for impersonal social 'laws' often associated with modernism in the social sciences.

77 e.g. Anthony Blunt, 'Art under Capitalism and Socialism', in C. Day Lewis (ed.), *The Mind in Chains: Socialism and the Cultural Revolution* (London, 1937); Elsie J.

over, for many of the writers and reformers mentioned above, Ruskin's social writings were less a blueprint for action than simply a form of personal inspiration and moral enlightenment. Like his writings on art, they opened people's eyes to a new way of looking at society, but did not necessarily give detailed instruction on how things should be done. Some, like William Smart, saw *Unto This Last* and the other 'social' texts primarily as a series of allegorical meditations, an inner city of the mind. Michael Sadler, in recalling the experience of hearing Ruskin lecture, suggested that in his calmer moments Ruskin himself really held this view—a meaning conveyed by the irony and humorous gestures of his lecturing style but not necessarily transmitted in the cold light of print.[78]

Another important point is that few of Ruskin's admirers agreed with him on every point, or were exclusively influenced by Ruskin. As mentioned above, Octavia Hill openly quarrelled with Ruskin; but to her dying day she continued to revere his ideas on citizenship and moral character, whilst insisting upon the sovereignty of market economics. William Beveridge throughout his career hankered after the model of a state-directed labour market, but saw it as regrettably incompatible with other desirable, *non*-Ruskinian goals, such as representative democracy and personal freedom. J. A. Hobson, deeply indebted to Ruskin for his theory of underconsumption, nevertheless criticized his mentor for glossing over 'the vital difference between the "money-lender" and the "investor" ', thus affording an easy target for hostile critics.[79] Virtually none of Ruskin's major disciples seriously believed in the possibility or even the desirability of reversing industrialization. Many who revered Ruskin's wider social philosophy were nevertheless critical of ways in which his doctrines were being interpreted; within the town-planning movement, for example, there was much questioning of the merits of decanting city-dwellers into green-field sites, and of building Gothic cottages as the ideal people's dwelling-house of the twentieth century (criticisms with which Ruskin himself would almost certainly have

---

Oxenham, *Queens of the Abbey Girls* (London, 1926). In fact the two extremes were less remote than one might imagine. The original May Queen ceremonies at Whitelands College were presided over by Anthony Blunt's uncle, the Revd Gerald Blunt (*Saint George*, 1 (1898), 147–51); while Elsie Oxenham's father, the novelist John Oxenham, was a founder of the White Knight Crusade and a pioneer of public works schemes for the unemployed (O. K. Parr, *My Chief Knight: John Oxenham*, (London, 1944); Erica Oxenham, *Scrapbook of J.O.* (London, 1946), 25–41).

[78] Smart, *A Disciple of Plato*; Sadleir, *Michael Ernest Sadler*, 32–3; *Works* 27. lix–lx; 28. 13–24; 29. 254.

[79] Hobson, *John Ruskin: Social Reformer*, 144–53.

concurred).[80] There was much exaggeration of Ruskin's anti-urbanism, and corresponding neglect of his view that modern cities did not *have* to be like those of mid-Victorian industrial Britain: 'They *may* be vast with Christian splendour, greater and more beautiful than even Babylon— and have gardens with green currents through them like the sea at Venice.'[81] And there was also, complained J. A. Hobson, much gentri- fication and emasculation of Ruskin's ideas even among his most dedic- ated followers; much 'planeing down' of 'the barbed sayings of the master into smooth conventional platitudes'.[82]

A final and perhaps obvious point is that the practical purchase of Ruskin's ideas has ebbed and flowed according to context, class, and cir- cumstance. W. G. Collingwood's biography of 1893 remarked that Ruskin's social theory was 'to most readers nowadays as comprehensible as, twenty years ago or less, it was incomprehensible . . . Ruskin's teach- ing is essentially modern. Its atmosphere is that of the time coming.'[83] But the character of 'the time coming' was in turn to be much more com- plex and contingent than Collingwood supposed. Michael Sadler, whose Ruskinian approach to education was influential in the 1890s, found himself only a few years later outflanked and outmanœuvred by more traditionalist views; policy-making within the Education department retained 'its essentially conservative, defensive character'.[84] Ruskin's ideas on women as queens in their households, on public endowment of the early years of parenthood, and on well-run households as models for the wider 'civic economy', seemed liberating and status-conferring to many late-Victorian and Edwardian women, and were closely replicated in the welfare demands of the 'domestic feminist' movement of the inter- war years. But they have come to be viewed as impenetrably obscurantist and repressive by many career feminists attuned to the free market of the late twentieth century.[85] Ruskin's far-famed influence within the

---

[80] C. H. Reilly, 'The City of the Future', *Town Planning Review*, 1/3 (1910), 191–7; A. T. Edwards, 'A Criticism of the Garden City Movement', ibid. 4/2 (1913), 150–7; *Works*, 17. 525–7.

[81] Ruskin to Octavia Hill 8 July 1868, in Maurice (ed.), *Octavia Hill: Early Ideals*, 177.

[82] 'The Social Economics of Ruskin', *Saint George*, 4 (1901), 65–76.

[83] W. G. Collingwood, *The Life and Work of John Ruskin*, ii. 155, 253.

[84] D. N. Chester, 'Robert Morant and Michael Sadler', *Public Administration*, 28 (1950), 106–16; and 'Morant and Sadler—Further Evidence', ibid. 31 (1953), 49–54; Sutherland, *Elementary Education*, 343.

[85] Annie Cobden Sanderson, 'Domestic Economy and the Ideal Home', *Humane Review*, (July 1901), 127–34; Emily H. Smith, 'Freedom and British Womanhood', *Saint George*, 10 (1907), 187–96; Dinah Birch, 'Ruskin's "Womanly Mind"', *Essays in Criticism*, 38/4 (1988), 308–9.

Edwardian labour movement appears to have been largely eclipsed by the massive devaluation of craft skills and shift to mass production brought about by the First World War; but a decade later Amabel Williams-Ellis recorded that Ruskin's reputation as a patron of working-class welfare was not 'merely a petrified and inanimate one':

Ruskin lives on obscurely in the memory of the people. Visit an English manufacturing town, and you may quite likely find that the Labour club is called Ruskin Hall. Here not only are meetings held, but billiards are played and beer is drunk in his name, much as the stalls and side-shows of an old English fair were set up in the name of Virgin or Saint.[86]

Ruskin himself frequently made the point that people would understand his ideas better at moments of acute social crisis or dire physical danger, like being adrift with a shipwrecked party in an open boat; only then would the virtues of leadership, altruism, discipline, obedience, and the invisible reality of absolute mutual dependence, become starkly apparent.[87] It was thus no coincidence that Ruskin's social welfare schemes made their greatest impact and enjoyed their greatest reputation in the midst and immediate aftermath of the Second World War: no coincidence also, that in the current era of competition and affluence, all but the vaguest awareness of their precise character and influence has largely faded away.

[86] Amabel Williams-Ellis, *The Tragedy of John Ruskin* (London, 1928), 10.
[87] *Political Economy of Art*, 71–2; *Unto This Last*, 36–7; *Time and Tide*, 80–1.

2

Ruskin's Science of the 1870s: Science, Education, and the Nation

FRANCIS O'GORMAN

A portion of Ruskin's creative energy in the 1870s was engaged in the writing of science. Three books emerged from this: *Love's Meinie* (1873–81), which concerns birds, *Proserpina* (1875–86), which concerns flowers, and *Deucalion* (1875–83), which is a more recognizably orthodox book about geology. As was Ruskin's familiar practice, each of these three 'texts' was published initially in serial parts, a fact which must be borne in mind when thinking of them as separate volumes.[1] *Love's Meinie* began life as part of Ruskin's 1874 Oxford lectures and *Deucalion* also includes material from the Oxford lectures for the same year as well as material from London lectures, though Ruskin comes to describe it in chapter 8 (volume i) as 'an absolutely trustworthy foundation for the geological teaching in St. George's schools' (*Works* 26. 197). *Proserpina*, the text which has attracted most of those modern critics of Ruskin who have looked at his science, did not begin as lecture material and was conceived more straightforwardly from the start as a serviceable serialized textbook for the St George's Schools proposed in *Fors Clavigera*.[2] All three of the texts, however, came eventually to be imagined by Ruskin as fulfilling this role.

It has been customary to dismiss these three volumes of Ruskin's late work as eccentric or self-indulgent. Certainly, Ruskin's tone when

This chapter is a version of a paper first given at the '*Ruskin in the 1870s*' conference at Trinity College, Oxford, 6 July 1996. I am grateful to Dr Dinah Birch and Prof. Jose Harris. A first draft of my discussion of Lubbock and Lodge appeared in *The Ruskin Gazette*, 1 (1996), 9–18.

[1] For a consideration of Ruskin as a periodical writer, see Brian Maidment, 'Readers Fair and Foul: John Ruskin and the Periodical Press', in Joanne Shattock and Michael Wolff (eds.), *The Victorian Periodical Press: Samplings and Soundings* (Leicester, 1982) 29–58.

[2] For details of the whole St George's enterprise, see Margaret Spence, 'The Guild of St. George: Ruskin's Attempt to Translate his Ideas into Practice', *Bulletin of the John Rylands Library*, 40 (1957–8), 147–201.

addressing children, as in, particularly, *Proserpina*, does not travel well into the present, as the fate of *The Ethics of the Dust* testifies more forcibly.3 And Ruskin's resistance to Darwinism which is, as Robert Hewison says, no more than a rearguard action,4 tends to make us think of the science books as intellectually a backwater and thoroughly different from the more engaging literary negotiations with science which have recently been explored in the work of, for instance, George Eliot, Thomas Hardy, George Meredith, or Gerard Manley Hopkins. Some early Ruskin biographers certainly found difficulty in handling the science: W. G. Collingwood could not find a frame of reference for the botanical work, saying politely 'this was not science, strictly so called, it was a field of work which no one but Mr. Ruskin has cultivated'.5 Ruskin's disputes in *Deucalion* and in *Fors Clavigera* with John Tyndall, the Royal Institution's prominent Professor of Natural Philosophy, prompted stronger words of criticism from some contemporary writers such as the positivist Frederic Harrison. And in 1884, W. Clement Ley, though himself only an amateur scientist, wrote in nothing less than *Nature* to deplore Ruskin's bad empiricism, this time in the *Storm-Cloud* lectures of the same year. Ruskin, he said, like all literary men who try to talk about science, will continue to produce scientific nonsense until they 'master the simplest elementary primers'.6 E. T. Cook found that Ruskin's criticism of modern men of science grated awkwardly against his own more liberal agenda. 'Ruskin chaffed men of science', he complained in the Introduction to volume 25, '. . . and sometimes allowed himself in passages, destined to stand, a freedom of contemptuous comment which his admirers must deplore' (*Works* 25. xlvi).

Some modern critics of Ruskin have approached the science more productively. Edward Alexander, Dinah Birch, Frederick Kirchhoff, Beverly Seaton, and Paul Sawyer, for instance, have illuminated a variety of more significant and important features of Ruskin's work in science, prompting more sensitive critical reading.7 Most recently, Michael

---

3 *The Ethics* has nonetheless recently received more rewarding readings. See Dinah Birch, '*The Ethics of the Dust*: Ruskin's Authorities', *Prose Studies*, 12 (1989–90), 147–58 and Sharon Aronofsky Weltman, 'Gender and the Architectonics of Metaphor: Ruskin's Pathetic Fallacy in *The Ethics of the Dust*', *Prose Studies*, 16 (1993), 41–61.

4 Robert Hewison, *John Ruskin: The Argument of the Eye* (London, 1976), 176.

5 W. G. Collingwood, *The Life and Work of John Ruskin*, 2nd edn. (London, 1893), ii. 172.

6 W. Clement Ley, 'Mr. Ruskin's Bogies', *Nature*, 29 (1883–4), 354.

7 See Edward Alexander, 'Ruskin and Science', *Modern Language Review*, 64 (1969), 508–21; Dinah Birch, 'Ruskin and the Science of *Proserpina*', in Robert Hewison (ed.), *New Approaches to Ruskin: Thirteen Essays* (London, 1981), 142–56; Frederick

Wheeler's multi-contributor *Time and Tide: Ruskin Studies* for 1996 was partially devoted to the topic of Ruskin and science.[8] The purpose of this chapter, however, is not to examine the puzzled or censorious contemporary responses nor to suggest how we might read the specific texts of *Love's Meinie, Proserpina,* or *Deucalion* more rewardingly today, but to inquire into the whole question of Ruskin and science within some more diverse interstices of late Victorian and early twentieth-century culture. I want to look at ways in which Ruskin's ideas about science, or Ruskin's ideas which could be seen to impact upon science, were understood within the last decades of the nineteenth century and the first years of the twentieth in a variety of different cultural locations. I shall examine how different scientists—a term I use for convenience though conscious of its ahistoricality[9]—read and deployed Ruskin in various ways and for various reasons, and also how Ruskin's ideas about science and education moved from the pages of his own texts into the language of others, to be reconstituted within the terms of others' arguments. For Ruskin's ideas about science broadly defined, or ideas about science thought to be Ruskin's, were not stillborn in the years I examine; they moved within the culture in a number of spaces, facilitating and propagating a range of discourses.[10]

Cook, as part of his effort to refashion Ruskin as a man of more liberal outlook, stressed the personal relationship of Ruskin and Darwin. He recounted a meeting arranged by Charles Eliot Norton in which Ruskin and Darwin's 'animated talk afforded striking illustration of the many sympathies that underlay the divergence of their points of view and of their methods of thought' (*Works* 19. xlv). Although the depiction of such friendly relations conceals the depth of Ruskin's antagonism towards the theory of evolution, it serves as a reminder that we must

Kirchhoff, 'A Science against Sciences: Ruskin's Floral Mythology', in U. C. Knoepflmacher and G. B. Tennyson (eds.), *Nature and the Victorian Imagination* (Berkeley, Calif., 1977), 246–58; Beverly Seaton, 'Considering the Lilies: Ruskin's "Proserpina" and Other Victorian Flower Books', *Victorian Studies*, 28 (1984–5), 255–82 and Paul Sawyer, 'Ruskin and Tyndall: The Poetry of Matter and the Poetry of Spirit', in James Paradis and Thomas Postlewait (eds.), *Victorian Science and Victorian Values: Literary Perspectives* (New Brunswick, NJ, 1981), 217–46.

[8] Michael Wheeler (ed.), *Time and Tide: Ruskin Studies—Ruskin and Science* (London, 1996).

[9] See Sydney Ross, '*Scientist*: The Story of a Word', *Annals of Science*, 18 (1962), 65–85.

[10] For a general essay on the reception of Ruskin's ideas during the period I address, see Brian Maidment, 'Interpreting Ruskin 1870–1914', in John Dixon Hunt and Faith M. Holland (eds.), *The Ruskin Polygon: Essays on the Imagination of John Ruskin* (Manchester, 1982), 159–71.

not think in terms of an absolute divide between Ruskin and Victorian men of science. Henry Acland's important and long-enduring friendship with Ruskin, threatened only by the vivisection question, is another example of close relations with professional men of science.[11] Ruskin's disagreement with Tyndall over the glacial controversy caught the eye of many of his early biographers but a hitherto unpublished letter in the Royal Institution in London reminds us that Tyndall was capable of holding Ruskin in high regard. The letter, sent from Dover on 9 October 1873 to Carlyle, follows Ruskin's attack on Tyndall in the *Fors Clavigera* letter of that month for apparently misrepresenting the work of the geologist James Forbes (*Works* 27. 635–43). Tyndall writes:

> Last Sunday I was down at Sir John Lubbock's country residence. While her husband and I were out for a ramble Lady Lubbock entered into conversation with a Mr. Allen of Keston, who I believe is in some sense the publisher of Mr. Ruskin. From him she learned many things to my disadvantage, as set forth by Mr. Ruskin . . . To shorten matters I am told that Mr. Ruskin has made a bitter attack upon me appropos [*sic*] of Principal Forbes and the glaciers.
>
> This I did not merit at Mr. Ruskin's hands; for over and over again when in private conversation he has been subjected to far graver attacks than he could possibly direct against me, I have defended him.[12]

Tyndall, a fellow member with Ruskin of the Metaphysical Society, may be overemphasizing his defence of Ruskin to Carlyle in order to point up what he sees as the injustice of the attack but his claim of such habitual support is still another form of warning against the perception of Ruskin and modern science simply in two hostile camps.

Ruskin attracted support and interest from scientists in a variety of ways. Some of his most severe criticism of modern science was directed against developing theories of plant reproduction which stressed the role of insects in pollination. The 'unclean stupidity' of these 'materialisms' (*Works* 25. 263) appalled and distressed Ruskin's sense of the purity and divinely created nature of the flower. When he says of Oxford in *Praeterita* that 'though I think she might also have told me that fritillaries grew in Iffley meadow, it was better that she left me to find them for myself, than that she should have told me, as nowadays she would, that

---

[11]   On Acland and vivisection, see Robert Hewison, *Ruskin and Oxford: The Art of Education* (Oxford, 1996), 40–2.

[12]   Royal Institution, MSS.T.6/F7.8 The extract is published by courtesy of the Royal Institution of Great Britain. For Carlyle's reply, see Francis O'Gorman, 'Ruskin's *Fors Clavigera* of October 1873: An Unpublished Letter from Carlyle to Tyndall', *Notes and Queries*, NS 43 (1996), 430–2.

the painting on them was only to amuse the midges' (*Works* 35. 261), it is to such scientific work that he refers. One figure important alongside Darwin in work on insect pollination was John Lubbock FRS (1834–1913) whose *On British Wild Flowers Considered in Relation to Insects*, published in 1875, was a significant contribution to the topic. In April of the same year Ruskin confessed to Susan Beever to being 'made so miserable by a paper[13] of Sir J. Lubbock's on flowers and insects': 'the man really knows so much about it', he said, 'and has tried so many pretty experiments, that he makes me miserable' (*Works* 37. 165). But it would be wrong to think that the gap which Ruskin establishes between himself and Lubbock here was the only aspect of the story. In fact, Lubbock, later Lord Avebury, was a dedicated Ruskin enthusiast: he called himself an 'intense admirer of his writings',[14] and in 1902 he served as President of the Ruskin Society of Birmingham. Lubbock's dedication to Ruskin was neither shallow nor marginal to his own intellectual and professional concerns. In fact, he perceived a striking contiguity between Ruskin's work and some of his own convictions and aspirations for science. Periodically, he was to use Ruskin, during the course of his own public career, to articulate his sense of what science was about and from time to time to employ Ruskin's words strategically in the formulation of his determined argument within the increasingly important and urgent debate in later Victorian England concerning the legitimacy, necessity, and function of science in school education.

Lubbock's career involved a series of campaigns concerning the place of science both within school education and to a lesser extent within university curricula. Consistently, as Michael Sadler later noted, 'he pleaded the claims of physical science to a place in the programme of what is taught'.[15] The language that he repeatedly chose for this campaign formulated science as an activity with a clear aesthetic dimension, which was, at its most appealing level, knowledge of the beautiful. In Lubbock's 1903 lecture to the new Birmingham University, he argued that science must be part of a broad curriculum taught by schools

[13] Presumably, as Cook and Wedderburn indicate (*Works* 37. 165 n.), John Lubbock, 'Common Wild Flowers Considered in Relation to Insects', *Nature*, 10 (1874), 402–6, 422–6.

[14] J. H. Whitehouse (ed.), *Saint George*, 6 (1903), 1. Whitehouse's connections with the Birmingham Ruskin Society and *Saint George* are discussed in James S. Dearden, *Ruskin, Bembridge and Brantwood: The Growth of the Whitehouse Collection* (Keele, 1994), 15–25.

[15] Michael Sadler, 'Education and Letters', in Mrs Adrian Grant Duff (ed.), *The Life-Work of Lord Avebury (Sir John Lubbock) 1834–1913* (London, 1924), 197–8.

currently too heavily weighted in favour of the classics. 'Nobody wishes
—' he said, 'scientific men would certainly not wish—to exclude classics. What we plead for is that science, the knowledge of the beautiful
world in which we live, should not be excluded.'[16] This formulation of
science as knowledge of beauty is a feature of Lubbock's whole rhetoric
about science and education which aspires to fuse fact with value, to
familiarize and demystify the idea of science by articulating it in terms
already familiar to, and validated by, the culture. Similarly, he said to the
fledgling University, 'Science . . . stimulates the imagination, in which,
perhaps, we English are just a little deficient'.[17] A science which quickens
the imagination was intended to seem more humanly attractive, a discipline addressed to wider faculties of the mind.

In 1876, while Ruskin was writing his own science textbooks, Lubbock employed Ruskin's words to express a feature of his own conception of school science. In 'On the Present System of Public School
Education', Lubbock reflected upon the findings of the Devonshire
Commission, of which he had been a member, which had so forcefully
and devastatingly declared to Parliament that ' "the present state of scientific instruction in our schools is extremely unsatisfactory' ".[18] It is
against the immediate backdrop of this public diagnosis—the *Devonshire Report* was published 1872–5—that Lubbock endeavours to signify the profits and pleasures straightforward, accessible science may
bring to the school pupil. Using Ruskin he indicates what is wrong with
contemporary school science and implicitly what science teaching at its
best should address:

Our eloquent countryman, Mr. Ruskin, has truly said that

'The whole force of education, until very lately, has been directed in every possible way to the destruction of the love of nature . . . every liking shown by children for simple natural objects has either been violently checked . . . or else
scrupulously limited to hours of play: so that it has really been impossible for
any child earnestly to study the works of God but against its conscience; and the
love of nature has become inherently the characteristic of truants and idlers.'[19]

This is a situation which, Lubbock says, must be reversed in favour of a
'more enlightened system of education'.[20] He allows us to believe that
proper school science is the opposite of the merely abstract and dry-as-

---

[16] Lord Avebury, *Essays and Addresses 1900–1903* (London, 1903), 247.
[17] Ibid. 255.
[18] Quoted in John Lubbock, *Addresses, Political and Educational* (London, 1879), 48.
[19] Ibid. 49.   [20] Ibid. 50.

dust and something which, instead, directly addresses a 'love of nature' and encourages the examination of 'simple natural objects'. He offers a science filled with life and love, of which Ruskin himself might approve.

In 1909 Lubbock suggested that ordinary, easily approachable science was engaged in a core task with which Ruskin had also been preoccupied. He wrote of the pleasure and reward human beings lost through knowing nothing of science: 'I often grieve', he remarked, 'to think how much happiness our fellow-countrymen lose from their ignorance of science.'[21] Science, he continued, teaches men about the beauty and wonder of the world and because of this is engaged in a shared enterprise with Ruskin for whom 'the love of beauty was almost a religion, and I need not say how much he has done to educate others to enjoy it'.[22] In *The Pleasures of Life*, Lubbock offered science again, via Ruskin, as revelation of beauty and wonder which, properly used, could transform for the ordinary person the quotidian into the marvellous: 'Where the untrained eye will see nothing but mire and dirt, science will often reveal exquisite possibilities. The mud we tread under our feet in the street is a grimy mixture of clay and sand, soot and water. Separate the sand, however, as Ruskin observes—let the atoms arrange themselves in peace according to their nature—and you have the opal.'[23] Lubbock endeavours to promote science in a succession of books and essays as a matter of 'living interest'[24] for all who would learn, especially the young. Dedicated to explaining, demystifying, and validating the place of science principally within the national schemes for education and by extension within society more generally, Lubbock periodically finds in Ruskin an authority and a language, already culturally familiar, through which to voice his aims. Lubbock may have thought little of Ruskin's often aired criticisms of scientists[25] but this did not mean he would relinquish Ruskin's words in articulating and further authorizing some of his own claims for science.

As Victoria's reign ended and the twentieth century began, Ruskin's work was employed by scientists with other professional and social priorities. In October 1905, the eminent physicist Oliver Lodge (1851–1940), who had chosen as a student a leatherbound edition of Ruskin's works as a prize, published the first of two articles in Whitehouse's *Saint George* entitled 'Mr. Ruskin's Attitude to Science'. Lodge's articles were

---

[21] Lord Avebury, *Peace and Happiness* (London, 1909), 238.
[22] Ibid. 239.
[23] John Lubbock, *The Pleasures of Life*, 3rd edn. (London, 1887), 156–7.
[24] Ibid. 190.   [25] See *Saint George*, 6 (1903), 4.

an effort to demonstrate that the fashionable idea that Ruskin's 'attitude to scientific investigation was one of loathing' was 'to some extent a popular fallacy'.[26] Ruskin's mental powers were, Lodge says, 'analytic and perceptive to an extraordinary degree' and:

The same extraordinary powers of observation and analysis which admittedly he brought to bear in the domain of Art generally—the same minute accuracy of observation and patience of study which he bestowed on the pediment of a pillar or the tracery of a window—were equally available when dealing with the outlines of mountain ranges, and with such productions of Nature as crystals, or leaves, or feathers, or clouds.[27]

Lodge here, via Ruskin, indicates his own perception of a community between art and science as commencing with accurate observation. By publishing in his first article a series of letters upon wave movement and molecular motion which Lodge and Ruskin had exchanged from January 1885, Lodge attempted to illustrate his thesis that Ruskin, when properly informed, was fascinated by modern physics and willingly its student. 'On the whole', Lodge remarked, 'these letters seem to me likely to be of distinct interest, by reason of the light they throw upon the undeveloped scientific side of his mind—a side naturally unrecognised, save perhaps by his closest intimates: a side not even by them fully realised'.[28] Lodge's point is also about being properly informed. He does not disguise the fact that Ruskin's own scientific learning was sometimes lacking, that in volume v of *Modern Painters*, for instance, 'his notable observations of cloud-form and cloud-phenomena were accompanied by vague hypotheses concerning the cause of the phenomena, and by guesses which in a few particulars were definitely below the standard of the scientific knowledge of the time'.[29] Lodge presents Ruskin as in need of scientific instruction, willing to acquire it when confronted by it (at least when in the form of Lodge himself), and having a fundamental intellectual aptitude for scientific work.

Lodge's Ruskin articles need to be seen within his own broader ambitions for scientific education itself. Lodge is particularly disposed, in 1905, to counter the prevalent view of Ruskin as the crotchety antagonist of modern science because this reveals something important about Ruskin within the context of Lodge's own concerns as an educationalist. Lodge, in 1900, became the first Principal of the newly founded Birmingham University—Lubbock, who was Warden of the Guild of

26 *Saint George*, 8 (1905), 279, 280.   27 Ibid. 280.
28 Ibid.   29 Ibid. 281.

Undergraduates at Birmingham, may well have accepted the position and addressed the University with the lecture referred to above at his invitation—and thus a man ostensibly in a peculiarly powerful position to determine the course of a new university curriculum, different from that of either Oxford or Cambridge. In his article 'A Modern University', published in the high-profile *Nature*, in 1900, Lodge argues that the function of a new university is not, like the ancient institutions of Oxford and Cambridge, to provide scholarly, specialized courses based on the classics but to present a curriculum which offers a broad education and a serious programme of basic science:

> The modern university must aim for a long time not at depth so much as at breadth. Depth for the few, breadth for the many. It must seek to turn out all-round men, and not specialists only.
>
> Its graduates should not one of them be illiterate, not one of them ignorant of the fundamental principles of science. Trained scientific men they cannot be, in any numbers—the idea would be absurd—but they should have sufficient education to understand a scientific question and know where to go for the answer. They should have lived for a time—even a short time—in the atmosphere of science, and thereafter it will never be quite strange to them.[30]

The aim of Birmingham University should be to educate broadly, to give an undergraduate a basic grasp of what Lodge calls, with a problematic certainty, the fundamental principles of science. He was brisker and briefer in private correspondence. 'I notice . . . you seem doubtful about a mixed B.A. partly Arts and partly Science', he chided his friend Silvanus Thompson a few years later: 'I regard this as the proper function of the B.A.'[31]

Given the ideas expressed in *Nature*, aspects of Lodge's later Ruskin article come more sharply into focus. By emphasizing that Ruskin, the great art critic, was also an interested student of the physical sciences, Lodge finds a culturally familiar example relevant to his own aims for a broader education. Lodge detects in Ruskin, for whom he had organized a testimonial in 1885,[32] a man whom he believes from personal experience to have been fundamentally interested in the exactitudes of scientific study and presents him to the readers of *Saint George*—published

---

[30] *Nature*, 62 (1900), 185.

[31] Lodge papers, University College Library, London, letter of 22 Apr. 1907, MS. Add. 89/104 II. Every effort has been made to locate the copyright holder but without success; any reader with information is invited to write to the publishers with details.

[32] For details of this, see the collection of printed papers in the Bodleian Library, Oxford, catalogued as BOD.17006 d.9.

in Birmingham and initially the journal of the Birmingham Ruskin Society—whilst Lodge himself was endeavouring, by this time against much opposition, to steer his own Birmingham University towards a broader curriculum hospitable to science. In simultaneously indicating Ruskin's ignorance of scientific theories, moreover, which impinged directly upon his work as an art critic, Lodge is also presenting a case for the importance of scientific education for all, even for as great a man as Ruskin, thus obliquely emphasizing the necessity and importance of his own increasingly embattled (and ultimately unsuccessful) designs for his University.[33] The culturally prestigious figure of Ruskin served Lodge— as he had served Lubbock—within a campaign for the promotion and broadening of a particular form of science education.

Other serious and committed Ruskin readers thought about science during the period I am examining, and their activities and careers were influenced by that thinking. Two specific examples demonstrate different but related ways in which readers thought on the particular matter of science's relation to other cultural practices. The first is William Marwick, editor of the *Ruskin Reading Guild Journal* and the other ephemeral Ruskinian journals *Igdrasil* and *World-Literature*. Marwick made an effort to produce all his journals with a breadth of cultural coverage, embracing under one cover, for instance, articles or notes on art, social questions and educational questions, reviews of books from a range of disciplines, and reports from Ruskin Associations and events such as the Whitelands May Day celebrations. He also endeavoured to incorporate a number of pieces relating to science, including reports from the meetings of the British Association for the Advancement of Science. His intention was clearly to gesture towards a form of cultural conspectus and to indicate, amongst other things, that science remained within the fold, that it was a peculiarly Ruskinian duty to keep pace with as wide a range of society's activities as one could, including science. The Carlylean title of *Igdrasil* itself embodied something of this intention. Explaining the journal's purpose in 1891, Marwick said that it was 'to look at Literature, Science, Art, Music and Social Philosophy in relation to the progress of the human race'[34] and that the Norse myth of the

---

33　W. P. Jolly observes that, in his time at Birmingham, Lodge was not only 'unable to broaden the degree syllabus, he did not even manage to alter the examination timetable', W. P. Jolly, *Sir Oliver Lodge* (London, 1974), 136.

34　*Igdrasil*, 3 (1891), p. i. For some bibliographical details of Marwick's Ruskinian journals, see James S. Dearden, *Facets of Ruskin: Some Sesquicentennial Studies* (London, 1970), 130–1.

tree of Igdrasil would symbolize its ambitions by representing compre-
hensiveness, ' "the past, the present and the future: what was done, what
is doing, what will be done." '[35]

Marwick's journals comprised, in however circumscribed a way, an
attempt to offer an overview and an effort to retain science within the
orbit of the Ruskinian reader. Another more prominent Ruskin reader
whose professional work was much more explicitly concerned with science but who nonetheless felt the creative pressure of Ruskin's plural cultural interests was Patrick Geddes, whose Edinburgh Summer Schools of
Art and Science were, appropriately enough, praised by Marwick's
World-Literature. Geddes was, from 1889 to 1914, Professor of Botany
at University College, Dundee. He was active throughout his life in a
variety of other fields including sociology, education, town-planning,
and art criticism[36] He was also the author of *John Ruskin, Economist*
(1884). Geddes's diversity of interests was described as early as 1940 in a
propaedeutic essay by F. D. Curtin as bearing testimony to his enthusiasm for Ruskin.[37] The Edinburgh summer schools tried to systematize
such diversity: they provided lectures in a range of subjects and hoped
that the querying of compartmentalization between science and other
disciplines such as sociology would prove educationally fruitful and
would 'be readily understood on consideration of that parallelism and
interdependence of the "humanities" and the natural sciences, which are
being demonstrated on all sides by thinkers of the most widely separate
schools'.[38] Geddes's plans for a many-sided school education, moreover,
drew explicitly upon what he understood to be a Ruskinian programme.
Schools, he wrote in 1884, should aim to offer the kind of completeness
in liberal education that, he thought, Ruskin had described in *Fors
Clavigera* and, in the future, 'when schools at once really classical and
modern have arisen to give that genuine knowledge of nature and literature which make alike scientist and scholar, that genuine discipline in
arts coarse and fine which makes the worker, and that factual grip of history and society which makes the citizen, we shall after all only be having in more systematic form the essential curriculum of a St. George's

---

35 Ibid. p. iii.

36 See Patrick Geddes, *Every Man His Own Art Critic at the Manchester Exhibition,
1887* (Manchester, 1887).

37 See Frank Daniel Curtin, 'Aesthetics in English Social Reform: Ruskin and His
Followers', in Herbert Davis, William C. DeVane, and R. C. Bald, *Nineteenth-Century
Studies* (Ithaca, NY, 1940), 227–36.

38 Patrick Geddes, *A Summer School of Science* (Edinburgh, 1890), 4–5.

School'.[39] Geddes found in Ruskin a figure of cultural stature whose breadth of concern from art to economics to science itself was coincident with the spirit of his own philosophy.

Various readers employed Ruskin or responded to Ruskin in ways which involved their conceptions of science in the modern world. Many of their ideas were very closely related to theories of education and it is to this topic that I want now to turn more fully. Ruskin's work in science in the 1870s was part of his serious thinking about education. His intentions for the St George's Schools, his Sheffield museum project,[40] his teaching as Slade Professor and the writing of, not least, *Love's Meinie*, *Proserpina*, and *Deucalion*, which he came to describe in 1876 as 'three grammars—of geology, botany, and zoology—which will contain nothing but indisputable facts in those three branches of proper human learning; and which, if I live a little longer, will embrace as many facts as any ordinary schoolboy or schoolgirl needs to be taught' (*Works* 28. 647), are all aspects of Ruskin's resourceful, many-sided project in the 1870s to restore the nation's moral health through proper education. *Love's Meinie*, *Proserpina*, and *Deucalion* envisaged, as Ruskin himself came to envisage them, as textbooks for the new schools, are features of his educational undertaking in this decade of prolific and proliferating activity; they are series which come to bear explicitly the duty of transmitting the kinds of knowledge, values, and beliefs Ruskin wished to impart to the children of the present and thus to the adults of the new century. They are teaching texts which at their boldest aspire towards the improvement of national welfare. Placing Ruskin's science books within this wider educational programme necessitates asking a more extensive question about the reception of Ruskin's ideas upon education. For, within the ampler environment of Ruskin's wider contribution to educational debate, it is possible to determine whether or not aspects of the aspirations of *Love's Meinie*, *Proserpina*, and *Deucalion*, however indirectly, do succeed in achieving intellectual currency.

A number of related points stand out in the science books as particularly pertinent for subsequent discussions or reappearances of Ruskin's educational ideas during the period at which I am looking. But they are all related to the fact that his plans for education in ornithology, botany, and geology seek the assimilation of knowledge with values, forming a study which, as even Ray Lankester was to say of his professional

---

39 Patrick Geddes, *John Ruskin, Economist* (Edinburgh, 1884), 41.
40 See Janet Barnes, *Ruskin in Sheffield* (Sheffield, 1985).

conception of science in 1915, 'satisfies man's soul'[41] as well as his mind. Whilst Ruskin demands that his students should know names, be able to recognize different species, and have a solid grasp of basic facts—such as what a root or a flower is—his whole method interprets the natural world, principally through extensive and involved mythological language, as morally relevant to human life. It is, as Frederick Kirchhoff says, a truly 'moral science'[42] well exemplified in the following words from the 'Leaf' chapter of *Proserpina*:

> Now as Mercury is the ruling power of the hill enchantment, so Daphne of the leafy peace. She is, in her first life, the daughter of the mountain river, the mist of it filling the valley; the Sun, pursuing, and effacing it, from dell to dell, is, literally, Apollo pursuing Daphne, and *adverse* to her (not, as in the earlier tradition, the Sun pursuing only his own light). Daphne, thus hunted, cries to her mother, the Earth, which opens, and receives her, causing the laurel to spring up in her stead. That is to say, wherever the rocks protect the mist from the sunbeam, and suffer it to water the earth, there the laurel and other richest vegetation fill the hollows, giving a better glory to the sun itself. For sunshine, on the torrent spray, on the grass of its valley, and entangled among the laurel stems, or glancing from their leaves, became a thousandfold lovelier and more sacred than the same sunbeams, burning on the leafless mountain-side.
>
> And farther, the leaf, in its connection with the river, is typically expressive, not, as the flower was, of human fading and passing away, but of the perpetual flow and renewal of human mind and thought, rising 'like the rivers that run among the hills'; therefore it was that the youth of Greece sacrificed their hair— the sign of their continually renewed strength,—to the rivers, and to Apollo (*Works* 25. 244–5).

Ruskin's understanding of myth's relationship to natural phenomena dictates the terms of his discussion of mountain form and of the habitat of the laurel; his conviction that nature was created for human beings likewise determines his interpretation at the end of the passage of the human significance of the leaf, in its connection with water, as an emblem of 'the perpetual flow and renewal of human mind and thought'.

Within this general desire to teach a science which was human centred, moral in the broadest but most fundamental of terms, Ruskin's pedagogic project aimed to produce specific mental attitudes and forms of ethical behaviour from his pupils. In the *Fors Clavigera* letter most dedicated to the discussion of Ruskin's educational plans—letter 95 for October 1884—Ruskin declared that 'The laws of virtue and honour are

---

[41] Sir Ray Lankester, *Diversions of a Naturalist* (London, 1915), p. vi.

[42] Frederick Kirchhoff, 'A Science against Sciences', in Knoepflmacher and Tennyson, *Nature and the Victorian Imagination*, 253.

. . . to be taught compulsorily to all men' (*Works* 29. 499). In the science books, Ruskin's whole mode emphasized a particular law: reverence for the natural world was vital to the child's development. Part of the function of myth for Ruskin was to restore a sense of the mystery and sacredness of the natural world which he believed, in common with so many of his contemporaries, early societies had expressed through narratives of divine presence.[43] Ruskin's effort to educate children into reverence for nature generates condemnation, not least, of the 'vile industries and vicious curiosities of modern science' which have, he says in *Love's Meinie*, 'robbed the fields of England of a thousand living creatures' (*Works* 25. 56) and betrayed what should be humanity's proper attitude to nature, a betrayal most grievously evidenced in vivisection. A reverent child, living by the Wordsworthian virtues of admiration, hope, and love, will not grow into an adult capable of such a betrayal. By restoring a sense of responsibility towards nature, Ruskin seeks to improve the prospects for England's future moral health.

Love's Meinie, Proserpina, and *Deucalion*'s efforts to promote a moral education also involved an insistence on a particular way of thought, a mental posture with distinctive political overtones: obedience to authority. Ruskin expresses the essence of this demand in explicitly political terms in *Fors*, requiring that all members of the Guild obey 'the dictation of necessary law' with an obedience which is 'absolute, and without question; faithful to the uttermost,—that is to say, trusting to the uttermost' (*Works* 28. 649). In the science texts, and particularly in *Deucalion*, a version of that requirement for obedience reappears as Ruskin periodically warns his readers to accept the authority of trustworthy knowledge without question. Let 'the facts at least be clear', he says in the very first chapter of *Deucalion*, '. . . but all debate declined' (*Works* 26. 106). 'I urge [my pupils]', he says later in 'The Iris of the Earth' chapter of the same book, 'to know as many [facts] as they can thoroughly know,—not more; and absolutely forbid all debate whatsoever' (*Works* 26. 166). *Deucalion*, it is no surprise to find, was to be the book given as a prize in the Ruskin May Day celebration at Whitelands College to the girl who ' "is not ashamed to do as she is told by those in authority over her" '.[44] Controversy, questioning, arguing, and debating are unwanted at the stage of education to be addressed in St George's Schools; dispute is a commotion 'idler than the chafed pebbles of the wavering beach' (*Works*

43 An extensive study of Ruskin and myth is to be found in Dinah Birch, *Ruskin's Myths* (Oxford, 1988).
44 *Saint George*, 1 (1898), 150.

26. 154) and assent to the unequivocal, dependable, and trustworthy is imperatively required. Ruskin uses science to teach not only reverence but respect, not only affection but obedience, offering a politically and socially committed pedagogy through which he seeks to mould the minds of future citizens.

As an educationalist, Ruskin's work found, in the period I am examining, a wide readership. Of the sizeable number of individuals who wrote or lectured upon Ruskin in the last years of the nineteenth and early years of the twentieth century a significant proportion chose education as their theme, including J. Marshall Mather, Henry Rose, William Jolly, Churton Collins, Michael Sadler, Julia Firth, and the Revd J. P. Faunthorpe. These were men and women from a diversity of backgrounds, and some were or came to be in positions of considerable responsibility and influence with regard to education. In their various interpretations and emphases, they found Ruskin's work a source of ideas and guidance in education at a time of unprecedented interest in the issue at all levels. They responded warmly to Ruskin's demands, central to the science textbooks, for a broadly moral education, and approved his strong sense of education's leading role in fashioning behaviour and belief appropriate for citizens of a just and moral society. Through their work, and that of others, the didactic aspirations of the science books, in various reconfigurations, attained, however indirectly, a distinct degree of purchase.

Many Ruskin readers stressed the importance of education as moral as opposed to merely technical, factual, or skill-based. (There was to be much the same emphasis upon the centrality of morality amongst those readers who were concerned, during the period this essay addresses, with Ruskin's conception of economics.) Professor Churton Collins, in a lecture on 'Ruskin as an Educationalist' to the Birmingham Ruskin Society on 21 November 1906, told his audience that, alongside and part of aesthetic education, an essential feature of Ruskin's scheme was 'moral education'. 'Moral education', he said, picking up also on Ruskin's requirement for obedience, 'begins by making the educated one clean and obedient. And this must be done thoroughly and at all costs, and with any kind of compulsion that may be necessary.'[45] One of Michael Sadler's 'great heroes', as Lynda Grier remarks, was Ruskin (though she spends no time discussing him).[46] Addressing the

[45] *Saint George*, 10 (1907), 101. See below, pp. 66–7.
[46] Lynda Grier, *Achievement in Education: The Work of Michael Ernest Sadler 1885–1935* (London, 1952), 1.

Birmingham Ruskin Society on 13 December 1899, Sadler said, following Ruskin, that 'the highest function of education, the necessary note of all education worthy of a free people, is the training of the judgment and the strengthening of the moral will'.[47] He continued: 'No purely intellectual test is a just criterion of educational excellence. The highest intellectual outcome of educational discipline must have a moral side as well.'[48]

Sadler's argument about the moral dimension of education was often expressed in terms of education as training for citizenship. He believed that educational policy should have a clear view of what kind of person it is seeking to produce, what kinds of values, attitudes, and convictions it desires to foster. This he associated directly with Ruskin. 'All the current educational theories', he told the Educational Science Section[49] of the British Association in York in 1906, 'lay stress upon the social aspects of education; upon the importance of making the schools prepare the children for citizenship'. This, he noted, was the view 'taken by all the profounder English writers on education' including Ruskin.[50] Michael Sadler (1861–1943) was to attain an eminent position as an educationalist: a graduate of Trinity College, Oxford, he was appointed Secretary of the Extension Lectures of the Oxford University Examinations Delegacy; he served on the Bryce Commission (March 1894 to August 1895), becoming Director of Special Inquiries and Reports in the Department of Education in 1895. He was Professor of Education at Manchester University, Vice-Chancellor of Leeds from 1911, and Master of University College, Oxford, from 1923. His words, with their Ruskinian dimensions, circulated within significant educational structures.[51]

William Jolly was certainly not as highly placed as Sadler but nevertheless held a professional position in education as a schools inspector in Scotland. He was the author of a book entitled *Ruskin on Education* (1894) in which he too declared the importance of the broadly moral

---

[47] *Saint George*, 3 (1900), 102.

[48] Ibid. 113.

[49] On the formation of this section of the British Association, see Richard R. Yeo, 'Scientific Method and the Rhetoric of Science in Britain, 1830–1917', in John A. Schuster and Richard R. Yeo (eds.), *The Politics and Rhetoric of Scientific Method: Historical Studies* (Dordrecht, 1986), 283.

[50] M. E. Sadler, *Address to the Educational Science Section*, British Association for the Advancement of Science, York, 1906 (London, n.d.), 3.

[51] Further discussion of Michael Sadler's contribution to educational debate will be found in Lawrence Goldman, 'Ruskin, Oxford, and the British Labour Movement 1880–1914', below pp. 64–5.

nature of teaching. He wrote: 'With Ruskin, the moral aim of Education is vital, central, and all-embracing—"it is the leading of human souls to what is best, and making what is best out of them,"—an admirable, unsurpassed statement at once of its purpose and its material.'[52] It is a sign of how audible and indeed controversial a force Ruskin was deemed to be within educational debate at the end of the century that Jolly's book prompted a strong riposte from Robert James Muir, likewise an inspector of schools, who, in his *Ruskin Revised* (1897), criticized Jolly's *Ruskin on Education* and looked unfavourably at a whole series of Ruskin's specific and practical proposals for educational reform, arguing against Ruskin's often stated insistence that competitive examinations in education were undesirable.[53]

At other times, writers indicated the importance of reverence, care, or love for the natural world as part of Ruskin's specific legacy to a morally aware education. Churton Collins said that part of the 'epitome [of] Ruskin's educational ideas' was the definition of 'Education [as] the reverend and earnest study of nature and man to the glory of God, the better teaching of what is for the future benefit of our country and the good of mankind'.[54] John Faunthorpe, the Ruskinian Principal of Whitelands College, London, and editor of an *Index to Fors Clavigera* (1887), gave a lecture entitled 'Ruskin's Educational Ideals' again to the Birmingham Ruskin Society in December 1898 in which he told his audience that Ruskin believed 'The purpose of education consists half in making children familiar with natural objects, and the other half in teaching the practice of piety towards them'.[55] J. Marshall Mather, who had announced himself simply as a 'Member of the Ruskin Society' on the title-page of his *Life and Teaching of John Ruskin* (1883), wrote that 'Reverence and Compassion'[56] were central to Ruskin's ideas about the development of a child's mental graces. Mather went on to say that Ruskin desired specifically to teach a child science but definitely 'not in order to make it a cold and cruel spectator, or a listless observer of the wonders of the universe';[57] part of the very purpose of *Love's Meinie, Proserpina*, and *Deucalion*, on the contrary, was in keeping with all of Ruskin's teaching to 'cultivate sight *and sentiment*'.[58]

---

[52] William Jolly, *Ruskin on Education: Some Needed but Neglected Elements* (London, 1894), 106.

[53] See R. J. Muir, *Ruskin Revised and Other Papers on Education* (Edinburgh, 1897), 1–56.

[54] *Saint George*, 10 (1907), 93.   [55] *Saint George*, 2 (1899), 24.

[56] J. Marshall Mather, *Life and Teaching of John Ruskin* (Manchester, [1883]), 85.

[57] Ibid. 87–8.   [58] Ibid. 88. My emphasis.

Ruskin's ideas about education provided matter for discussion after he himself had ceased to speak in public. Some of the terms of his own arguments about proper education found a reception amongst a variety of writers, some of whom were strategically placed within structures of institutionalized education. Later in the twentieth century, other educationalists were to remark upon the significance of Ruskin's ideas: at a Ruskin celebration in 1919 Viscount Bryce, head of the Bryce Commission, was to say that 'The memory of such a genius as Ruskin's cannot but endure'[59] whilst John William Mackail, the classical scholar who also, as Assistant Secretary to the Board of Education, was prominent in the implementation of the 1902 Education Act, declared rather more boldly at the same event that even as he spoke 'The State [was] inaugurating a great constructional work in what Ruskin had so deeply at heart, National Education'.[60]

The science books belong to the whole corpus of Ruskin's writing on and schemes for education in the 1870s, in which themes of moral instruction aside from the merely factual learning of data, of the formation of admirable citizens and of reverence for the natural world are important. These themes live beyond the pages of Ruskin's own multifarious educational writing, finding a life in a variety of different spaces within the culture when Ruskin himself was more or less silent or indeed dead. In an assessment of the wider significance of Ruskin's efforts to write science text books for St George's Schools, we must survey this wider context of the reception of Ruskin's ideas on education and there we will find ideas which relate to the didactic concerns of *Love's Meinie, Proserpina*, and *Deucalion*.

Ruskin's entry into the argument about education in the 1870s placed him, not least in the context of the University of Oxford, within an increasingly high-profile national debate in which major cultural issues as well as specifically educational ones were at stake. In the particular case of science education in schools, the matter was gaining peculiar urgency. There were certainly examples of innovative institutions in the first half of the century with a forward-looking approach to science teaching: Charles Pritchard's prospectus for Clapham Grammar School in 1840, for instance, announced that it differed 'from that afforded at the great public schools of the country, principally in the greater infusion of sound mathematical and scientific instruction into the general plan of

---

59 J. Howard Whitehouse (ed.), *Ruskin Centenary Addresses: 8 February 1919* (London, 1919), 7.
60 Ibid. 24.

tuition'[61] and Coleridge, after all, had presciently planned in 1796 to include science teaching (optics, chemistry, anatomy) in the school he
wanted to found after returning from Germany. But such schools, at least
those under the aegis of the Established Church, were exceptions. More
characteristic was the complaint by the Reverend William Tuckwell,
Headmaster of Taunton College School, to the British Association in
August 1871, that the number of schools which taught science 'fairly and
systematically, which honour it with separate masters and with due ap-
pliances, and which accord to it its proper time and worthy rank in relation to other subjects taught, can be counted on the fingers of one
hand'.[62] Some of the conclusions of the Devonshire Commission—including 'We regret to observe that in many of the Larger Schools the
number of Science Masters is totally inadequate'[63]—added the weight
of officialdom to Tuckwell's point. F. W. Farrar, later another President
of the Birmingham Ruskin Society, whilst at Harrow as a master addressed the Royal Institution 'on the scandalous neglect of science in the
schools'.[64] In the ancient universities a debate about the place of science
teaching was growing louder; Acland and Ruskin's University Museum
had been a good step in the formation of proper resources for science
teaching in Oxford but as the end of the century approached, the ancient
universities came increasingly under pressure to advance their commitment to science, not least by thinking afresh about the seemingly ring-
fenced status of Classics. Men of the stature of Tyndall and Huxley had
found difficulty in securing permanent scientific appointments in the
middle of the century and it was a source of great frustration that Ray
Lankester could still complain to the Biological Section of the British
Association at Southport in 1883 that 'In England, with its 25,000,000
inhabitants, there are only four universities which possess [scientific] endowments and professoriates—viz. Oxford, Cambridge, Durham, and
the Victoria (Owens College [Manchester])'.[65]

The movement to establish science within the educational curricula of
the nation was partly motivated, particularly as the century neared its

[61] Charles Pritchard, 'Prospectus' published as an appendix to his *An Address
Delivered at the Opening of a Proprietary Grammar School*, 3rd edn. (London, 1840), 3–4.
I thank Dr Percy M. Young for lending me a copy of this.

[62] The Revd W. Tuckwell, *The Obstacle to Science Teaching in Schools* (London, 1871), 4.

[63] The *Devonshire Report* (1872–5) quoted in J. Stuart Maclure, *Educational Documents England and Wales: 1816 to the Present Day*, 3rd edn. (London, 1973), 107.

[64] R. H. Super, 'The Humanist at Bay: The Arnold-Huxley Debate', in Knoepflmacher
and Tennyson, *Nature and the Victorian Imagination*, 234.

[65] E. Ray Lankester, *The Advancement of Science: Occasional Essays and Addresses*
(London, 1890), 80.

close, as others have argued, by perceptions of the increasing economic and industrial power of Germany.[66] Efficient and effective science teaching became a matter which concerned the very prospects of the empire, for technical advance, only possible with men better trained in science, was urgently necessary for success in international commercial competition. The place of science in education was also a broader debate which involved nothing less than the whole issue of negotiating spaces and roles for science itself within the wider culture, a matter which became increasingly complex as the century moved on just as, in print, the scientist's task of relating to non-specialist readers became more involved.[67] Education and the place of science within the curricula at all levels was a topic which pertained to the shaping of cultural consensuses towards science in general terms. Frank Turner has added that science education, from more or less the halfway point in Victoria's reign, proved an arena in which science endeavoured to procure cultural authority in its usually abrasive relationship with religion.[68]

These contextual points frame the increasing interest in science's place in education in the 1870s and onwards and enable one to see the historical place of Ruskin's own endeavours with *Love's Meinie*, *Proserpina*, and *Deucalion* more clearly and to identify more successfully the distinctive shape of their contemporaneity. As Ruskin's mainstream scientific contemporaries increasingly turned their minds to the schools and universities, to the encouragement of science teaching within those institutional structures, Ruskin, far more alive to the immediate issues of his day than he is customarily believed to have been, was, in his own way, already there. Ruskin in the 1870s had already perceived the landscape of a developing debate and was vigorously attempting to provide, with a sense of urgency, his own characteristically radical and challenging answers to the questions of the place of science in education. These answers comprised nothing less than his own alter-

[66] See, for instance, Brian Simon, *Education and the Labour Movement 1870–1920* (London, 1965), 165 ff.

[67] On the relationship between science and audience within the popular press at the end of the century, see Peter Broks, 'Science and the Popular Press: A Cultural Analysis of British Family Magazines 1890–1914', Ph.D. thesis, Lancaster University, 1988 (British Library microfiche DX-86305).

[68] See Frank M. Turner, 'The Victorian Conflict between Science and Religion: A Professional Dimension', *Isis*, 69 (1978), 372. Turner has noted elsewhere the increased emphasis amongst public advocates of science in the last years of the nineteenth century upon the civic values of science and its use in education for training for citizenship: see Frank M. Turner, 'Public Science in Britain, 1880–1919', *Isis*, 71 (1980), 589–608. Ruskin would have recognized this development.

native definitions of science and science teaching arising from his conviction that the dissemination of a reverent and humanely attuned science which was faithful both to the particularities of the external world and to its spiritual and moral aspect was essential within any serious endeavour to construct the terms of proper education. John Morley was able to describe in 1887 'the present extraordinary zeal for education in all its forms'[69] but to lament the upper hand he saw science claiming in its bid for a dominant place within education.[70] Ruskin assailed what he perceived to be modern science in a variety of different ways but in the plans for science education suggested in *Love's Meinie*, *Proserpina*, and *Deucalion*, he sought to negotiate with it in a cultural space of increasing national significance and, with audacity, to attempt his own interpretation of what he believed to be the rightful place and nature of science teaching.

The late Victorian and early twentieth-century resonances of the topic 'Ruskin and science' are, within a variety of different spaces within the culture, more ample than might have been expected. Ruskin's words are put to use by those endeavouring in different ways to negotiate a space for science, as they wished to represent it, within that culture or more specifically within modern education. Ruskin's own ideas about education, central to the science textbooks of the 1870s, manage to find a hearing and to attain a degree of circulation within different and sometimes significant strata of society. And Ruskin's efforts to write those textbooks reveal a particular dimension of contemporaneity in his plans for education in St George's Schools, his alert sense that he must provide an answer to the particularly modern question of the nature and scope of school instruction in science. Ruskin's prickly, provocative, and mythopoeic science, then, was a sign that his eye was more on the map of the modern world in the 1870s than he is often given credit for, and of more consequence than has customarily been asserted.

---

[69] John Morley, 'The Study of Literature' (1887) in Lord Playfair *et al.*, *Aspects of Modern Study: Being University Extension Addresses* (London, 1894), 59.

[70] See ibid. 64–5.

3

Ruskin, Oxford, and the British Labour Movement 1880–1914

Lawrence Goldman

Ruskin's influence over the working class in Britain was at its most pronounced during the last years of his life. In the mid-1880s Tom Mann 'quoted Ruskin and Thorold Rogers more often than any other authorities' in his speeches.[1] At a 'labour meeting' in London in 1890, when John Burns relied on Ruskin's authority for an answer to a query from the floor, his questioner demurred: he did not 'want to know what Mr. Ruskin says. He has read him at home.'[2] In 1894, a survey of London public libraries revealed that Ruskin was 'the most popular author who deals with political economy and sociology'.[3] Five years later, an article in the labour press marking Ruskin's eightieth birthday described him as 'more widely read to-day by thoughtful men and women than any other writer.'[4] In a labour movement held together in the 1890s by ethical and spiritual commitment as well as by material interest, Ruskin, along with certain other 'teachers and prophets of the nineteenth century' as Keir Hardie called them in 1893—and his list included as well Carlyle, Mazzini, Whitman, Tennyson, and William Morris—was a guide and an inspiration.[5] When two itinerant Americans, Walter Vrooman and Charles Beard, decided to found a college for the education of working men in Oxford in 1899, they named it Ruskin Hall.[6]

---

[1] Tom Mann, *Tom Mann's Memoirs* (London, 1923), 50–2.

[2] W. G. Collingwood, *The Life and Work of John Ruskin* (2 vols., 1893), ii. 253.

[3] 'What London Reads', *London*, 19 Apr. 1894, 243, cited in Alan Lee, 'Ruskin and Political Economy: *Unto this last*', in Robert Hewison (ed.), *New Approaches to Ruskin: Thirteen Essays* (London, 1981), 83.

[4] A. E. Fletcher, 'Mr. Ruskin's Birthday', *The New Age*, 2 Feb. 1899.

[5] Keir Hardie writing in *The Labour Leader*, Jan. 1893, quoted in Henry Pelling, *The Origins of the Labour Party 1880–1900* (1954, 2nd edn., Oxford 1965), 140.

[6] Ellen Nore, *Charles A. Beard: An Intellectual Biography* (Carbondale, Ill., 1983), 14–27; Paul Yorke, *Education and the Working Class: Ruskin College 1899–1909* (Oxford, 1977), 1–11.

Ruskin's prominence is nowhere more evident than in the famous article of June 1906, 'The Labour Party and the Books that Helped to Make It', published soon after the election of the first twenty-nine Labour MPs.[7] The piece is mentioned frequently, though has rarely been accorded the serious consideration it deserves.[8] W. T. Stead, the campaigning journalist and editor of the *Review of Reviews*, asked the Labour MPs, and also a variety of 'Lib-Lab' MPs who represented labour interests within the Liberal Party in the House of Commons, to provide information on the writers and books that had shaped them. He contacted fifty-one MPs in all, of whom forty-five replied, and of these, forty-three mentioned at least one author or work. Stead interpreted the responses as evidence of the thirst for knowledge and self-improvement among the autodidacts who led emergent Labour.[9] For the historian, the piece is interesting for what it reveals about Labour's consciousness.

As might be expected, sixteen of the forty-five mentioned the Bible as a formative influence, though it is legitimate to suspect its importance to other members of the group who did not mention it specifically, but who probably took its influence for granted. The author mentioned most often—some seventeen times—was Ruskin, with eight MPs referring specifically to *Unto This Last*.[10] Next in prominence were Carlyle and Dickens, both mentioned thirteen times, followed by Henry George (11) and John Stuart Mill (10). Alongside Dickens, the most prominent literary figures were Shakespeare and Scott (10 each). Bunyan was mentioned by eight of the group; Burns by six, and William Morris by three. Marx was mentioned by two Labour MPs, Will Thorne and James O'Grady. Because Stead did not attempt to standardize his inquiries, the responses he received and printed verbatim take varied forms and can hardly be held reliable. In the circumstances, it is the very crudest empiricism to count references and draw simplistic conclusions from the results. But it is noteworthy that without prompting, and given space to express them-

---

[7] 'The Labour Party and the Books that Helped to Make It', *Review of Reviews*, 33 (June 1906), 568–82.

[8] An exception to this is Frank Bealey and Henry Pelling, *Labour and Politics 1900–1906: A History of the Labour Representation Committee* (London, 1958), 276–7. It is noteworthy that many entries on the first Labour MPs in the *Dictionary of Labour Biography* refer to the 1906 article. See *Dictionary of Labour Biography*, eds. John Saville and Joyce Bellamy, 7 vols. (London, 1972–84).

[9] 'The Labour Party and the Books that Helped to Make It', 568.

[10] The seventeen were Thomas Burt, John Burns, Richard Bell, W. Brace*, J. R. Clynes, Will Crooks*, C. Duncan*, Walter Hudson, Fred Jowett,* J. Johnson*, John T. Macpherson*, James Parker, Fred Richards, W. C. Steadman, J. W. Taylor*, G. J. Wardle*, John Williams. (Those marked with an asterisk mentioned *Unto This Last*.)

selves in their own words, a third of the total sample mentioned Ruskin. And it is also interesting that in some cases, they did so with unconcealed emotion. Ruskin 'seized and possessed' Thomas Burt. Walter Hudson found Ruskin's works 'invaluable'. It was *Unto This Last* that apparently made Fred Jowett 'a socialist' and a group of Ruskin's works occupied 'the place of honour' on his bookshelf. To Fred Richards, Ruskin's works provided the same inspiration as the New Testament. He compared them to the Sermon on the Mount and added, enigmatically (but also characteristically) that 'a wish to live such a life is to me divine'.[11]

Accurately assessing intellectual influences is always difficult, and lists of authors given in such circumstances are prone to reflect the fashion of the moment, as much as the reading habits of a lifetime, though there is no need to descend to the cynicism of one attempt to discredit Ruskin as an economic thinker which has also tried, unsuccessfully, to minimize his influence over the working-class movement at the turn of the twentieth century by dismissing the 1906 article.[12] Stead's piece, for all its imperfections, provides an authentic account of the inspiration of the founders.

Why was Ruskin so prominent? Of the fifty-one MPs surveyed by Stead, only one, John Macpherson, who represented Preston, had studied at Ruskin College, as Ruskin Hall was later renamed.[13] Of the rest, little evidence can be found to link them with Ruskin himself, or with any of the organizations which sought to spread Ruskin's messages. The efforts of Ruskin himself to reach a working-class audience during the 1860s and 1870s were unsuccessful. Whatever the influence of *Unto This Last* in the late Victorian era, it sold less than a thousand copies in the

---

[11] 'The Labour Party and the Books that Helped to Make It', 569, 575, 578.

[12] Alan Lee's analysis of Ruskin as an economic thinker is part of a long and reasonable tradition of criticism, dating back to the first responses that followed publication in 1860 of the essays which became *Unto This Last*. But Lee's attempt to diminish the significance of Ruskin's influence over the labour movement is uncharacteristically captious. It misses the point to question whether labour men 'could have gleaned much of an understanding of economics from Ruskin', since he was not read primarily as a teacher of economics, but as the articulator of the moral revulsion felt by sections of the working class for the economic system in which they laboured. And because Lee is insensitive to Ruskin's appeal to working-class readers as a moral critic of capitalism, he ascribes the otherwise inexplicable popularity of *Unto This Last* to 'the added ingredient' of style, as if readers were gulled by Ruskinian rhetoric. At the very end Lee accepts that it was Ruskin's 'call to justice not his claim to have set the science of political economy on a new footing that appealed to his readers'. The contradictions suggest confusion, and a purposeful attempt to diminish Ruskin and his influence, that is not historically sensitive to either the man or his context. Lee, 'Ruskin and Political Economy', 83–5.

[13] *Dictionary of Labour Biography*, v. 150.

decade after its publication in 1862.[14] *Fors Clavigera*, Ruskin's 'letters to the workmen of Great Britain' published monthly between 1871 and 1884, and distributed privately at Ruskin's direction, was ignored by the class for which it was intended, and found only a small and privileged readership.[15] Hence the interest in Ruskin among the British working class at the end of the nineteenth century, and the means by which Ruskin's ideas were spread among them, present an acknowledged and puzzling historical problem: as Ruskin retired to Brantwood in the late 1880s and ceased all public activism, so his influence increased.

One indication and perhaps also cause of that increasing influence can be found in the range of organizations established from the 1880s to spread knowledge of Ruskin's principles. Ruskin had himself established the Guild of St George as a practical exemplification of his ideas. His followers established Ruskin Reading Guilds and also Ruskin Societies, and the cheap editions of his works published by George Allen in the 1890s also contributed to Ruskin's prominence by making it easier for workers to read him.[16] There was an interval of fifteen years between the first edition of *Unto This Last* in 1862 and the second in 1877, but thereafter it was never out of print, and sold around 2,000 copies in each of the remaining years of the nineteenth century.[17]

Yet this activity may not have amounted to much, and may not, in itself, explain the rising interest in Ruskin in the late Victorian era. As early as 1893, Ruskin's secretary and biographer, William Gershom Collingwood, noted that the formation of such groups demonstrated the remarkable enthusiasm of Ruskin's readers, but he nevertheless questioned 'the usefulness of their meetings, lectures and publications'.[18] The majority of members of the Ruskin Societies were 'well-intentioned professional people' rather than workers. And both the Societies and Guilds, though initially successful, seem to have lost their influence and focus as they broadened into general associations for ethical uplift.[19] Brian Maidment, taking a sceptical view of the impact of

[14] Clive Wilmer, 'Introduction', in *John Ruskin: Unto This Last and Other Writings* (Harmondsworth, 1985), 29.

[15] Brian Maidment, 'Ruskin, Fors Clavigera and Ruskinism, 1870–1900', in Hewison, *New Approaches to Ruskin*, 196. J. A. Hobson, *John Ruskin Social Reformer* (London, 1898; 2nd edn., 1899), 282–3.

[16] 'Appendix II. Ruskin Societies and Their Work', Hobson, *John Ruskin*, 326–8; L. T. Dodd and J. A. Dale, 'The Ruskin Hall Movement', *Fortnightly Review*, NS 73 (Feb. 1900), 325; Maidment, 'Ruskin, Fors Clavigera and Ruskinism', 195.

[17] Wilmer, 'Introduction', 29.

[18] Collingwood, *Life and Work of John Ruskin*, ii. 252.

[19] Maidment, 'Ruskin, Fors Clavigera and Ruskinism', 206–7.

these organizations and publications, also doubts whether 'publishing policy alone' can explain Ruskin's importance around 1900, and has pointed out that many of Ruskin's books on social and economic questions had long been available 'in relatively cheap form'.[20] Meanwhile, Ruskin's recent biographer, Tim Hilton, has confessed enigmatically that he 'no longer believe[s] that Ruskin had any real connection with the Labour movement', though the meaning of 'connection' here is uncertain, and we must await clarification in a forthcoming volume.[21]

Given these caveats, it might seem foolhardy to put forward another means by which Ruskin's ideas were transmitted to the working class. Ruskin had been unsuccessful in reaching workers in the 1860s and 1870s during the long mid-Victorian economic boom; *pace* Hilton, he seems to have been much more successful at the end of his life, during the so-called Great Depression from the mid-1870s, when greater economic uncertainty made his ethical critique of Victorian capitalism more relevant. It may be as simple as that. Nevertheless, there may still be interest and purpose in tracing a new route that has not been mapped before— one that starts with Ruskin, as Slade Professor of Art, lecturing in Oxford in 1883–4, considers his influence on the University at that time, and traces the way in which a group of adherents, some of whom had heard him lecture in person, took his ideas to the nation through the new enterprise of University Extension, reaching in the process many thousands of working-class students over the course of the next generation. The claim is not that this can account by itself for the growing interest in Ruskin, for the process of influence is much more complex, but that it adds to our understanding of the place of Ruskin in the thought and affections of both intellectuals and workers, and explains how Ruskin became a point of contact between these groups. As Collingwood recognized, 'Some Ruskin missionary-preaching has been done by the University Extension. Undergraduates who listened to him in spite of their tutors' criticisms are lecturers in their turn; and they find Ruskin a subject for the masses, who eagerly listen to his social doctrines.'[22] That was written in 1893, though university extension probably had its greatest success in spreading interest in Ruskin in the following fifteen years or so. And in the process, it called upon the services of a varied group of lecturers of some note, including among them the leading educationalist, Michael Sadler; the Liberal MP, imperial administrator and scholar,

[20] Ibid. 195, 211 n.
[21] Tim Hilton, *John Ruskin: The Early Years 1815–1859* (New Haven, 1985), p. xiv.
[22] Collingwood, *Life and Work of John Ruskin*, ii. 254.

Charles Mallett; the novelist, John Cowper-Powys; the economist, J. A. Hobson; and one of the greatest Ruskinians of them all (though he is now forgotten), the Revd G. W. Hudson Shaw.

Ruskin was the first Slade Professor of Art in the University of Oxford from 1870 to 1879. A first bout of mental illness forced his resignation, but in 1882 he indicated his desire to resume the chair, and was re-elected in January 1883. In the Hilary, Trinity, and Michaelmas terms of that year, Ruskin delivered a series of lectures on 'The Art of England' largely in praise of nineteenth-century British painting, to enthusiastic audiences.[23] So great was the interest that the crowd for the first lecture 'had begun to assemble an hour and a half beforehand', and each lecture had to be delivered twice (*Works* 33. 259). Conscious that he was addressing an audience on the verge of adult life, Ruskin's theme was moral upliftment in and through art. But Ruskin's next set of lectures, given in Michaelmas 1884 and called 'The Pleasures of England', was far less successful. The lectures had not been planned and written in advance, and Ruskin, whose relations with 'the institutions' of Victorian Britain were generally fraught, as Robert Hewison has pointed out, was by now at odds with Oxford itself.[24] He deprecated the growing presence of natural science in the University, which he associated with the victory of the malign spirit of materialism. He was also in dispute with the university authorities, who had accepted his endowments for an Art School but who were reluctant to increase the accommodation and facilities for the teaching of art. They had also accepted his gift of several drawings by Turner, but were resisting Ruskin's pleas that they purchase two more Turner drawings that were then for sale.[25]

'The Pleasures of England' were supposed to survey the history of Christian England, illustrated at each stage by the popular art of the era. The pressures overcame Ruskin, and his lectures degenerated into incoherence and eccentricity, punctuated by vehement asides against the host of demons besetting him.[26] After the fifth lecture, on Protestantism, in

[23] For the text and accounts of Ruskin's lectures in 1883–4 see *Works* 33. li–lvii, lxvii–lxxi, 257–408, 411–537; E. T. Cook, *The Life of John Ruskin* (2 vols., London, 1911), ii. 475–82; G. W. Kitchin, 'Ruskin at Oxford, as an Undergraduate and as Slade Professor' in id., *Ruskin in Oxford and Other Studies* (London, 1904), 1–54.

[24] Robert Hewison, 'Afterword: Ruskin and the Institutions', in id., *New Approaches to Ruskin*, 214–29.

[25] Robert Hewison, 'A Graduate of Oxford', in id., *Ruskin and Oxford: The Art of Education* (Oxford, 1996), 40.

[26] Cook, *Life of John Ruskin*, ii. 476.

which Ruskin had assaulted the spirit and aesthetic style of reformed Christianity, and scandalized not only his audience but the London press, he was prevailed upon by friends to alter his plans and 'postpone' two further lectures on science and atheism in which he had intended to attack the drift he now saw in Oxford. He settled instead for readings from his earlier work. Ruskin left Oxford for the last time in December 1884. Subsequently, the University's decision to establish a chair and laboratory in physiology some weeks later led him to tender his resignation as Slade Professor.

This was hardly an auspicious episode, and might be thought an odd way to inspire the young. Nevertheless, the first series of lectures was an undoubted academic success. And there were those ready to act on Ruskin's message. For Ruskin's lectures in 1883–4 were delivered at a singular moment in the history of Oxford when some, at least, were becoming aware of the duties and obligations Ruskin described, and were seeking an enlarged role in a society suddenly more aware of want and inequality. As J. A. Hobson later explained, 'there was a deep inner propriety of time and place in the earnest prophetic voice' which used the Slade chair to protest against 'engrossing commercialism' and 'coldhearted intellectualism'.[27] The early 1880s saw the 'rediscovery' of Victorian poverty, symbolized by the publication in 1883 of the famous pamphlet, *The Bitter Cry of Outcast London*. The same year saw the premature deaths of two of the most influential figures in late Victorian Oxford: T. H. Green, the moral philosopher, and Arnold Toynbee, the pioneer of university extension lectures who had been foreman among the undergraduates who had dug the Hinksey Road under Ruskin's direction in 1874. Their examples of social engagement had pronounced, if only brief influence. In the following year, Oxford heeded the 'Bitter Cry' in its own fashion when it established the first university settlement at Toynbee Hall in Whitechapel. As one student later recalled, 'poetry and the arts for a while gave place in discussion to philosophy (notably that of T. H. Green) and social philanthropy—the bitter cry of outcast London, Toynbee Hall, the crusades of W. T. Stead etc.—a backwash from the prophetic preachings of Carlyle and Ruskin'.[28] The recognition of the enormous extent of urban poverty in a society that had grown steadily more wealthy in the nineteenth century lent weight and authority to the criticisms of Victorian capitalism and morality that Ruskin had launched, and which had been ignored in the 1860s. Now, in a more

[27] Hobson, *John Ruskin*, 263.
[28] Q [Sir Arthur Quiller Couch], *Memories and Opinions* (Cambridge, 1944), 73–4.

unstable economic situation, and in a less confident culture, where the failings of industrialism were being openly acknowledged—not least in Toynbee's *Lectures on the Industrial Revolution in England* which were published posthumously in 1884—Ruskin's assault on the commercial system seemed relevant, not to say inspirational.[29] One of those in the audience for Ruskin's lectures in 1883–4 later reflected that though his influence 'over the grown-up University was not great', he had considerable impact on some of the undergraduates.[30] For a group of student admirers soon emerged to reinvigorate Oxford's programme of extension lectures in the mid-1880s and spread Ruskin's message in the process.

At their centre was the Secretary of the Oxford Delegacy for the Extension of University Teaching—the chief administrative officer of the university body charged with organizing extension lectures between 1885 and 1895—Michael Sadler. Sadler was a product of Rugby, and an undergraduate at Trinity College between 1880 and 1884, an acknowledged leader among his generation of students, who took a first in Greats, and presided over the Oxford Union Society. He became the pre-eminent educationalist of his generation as an adviser to governments, as the first Professor of Education in Britain at Manchester University, as Vice-Chancellor of Leeds University, and, at the end of his career, as Master of University College, Oxford. Sadler's letters and memoirs preserve a record of Ruskin's influence in the early 1880s and help explain the respect in which he was then held. Sadler recalled the 'excitement' at Ruskin's first lecture—the crowds inside and outside the lecture theatre —the very clothes he wore, his mannerisms and eccentricities. 'His voice was entrancing. You could have listened to it for hours. The pronunciation was exquisite and the modulations of his tone like music.' But the message was not lost: 'Nominally these lectures of Ruskin's were upon Art. Really they dealt with the economic and spiritual problems of English national life. He believed, and he made us believe, that every lasting influence in educational systems requires an economic structure of society in harmony with its ethical ideal.'[31] As Sadler wrote to his mother, 'To see the man is almost an exaltation: to hear him is to be inspired . . . he has a most marvellous character & insinuating touch of influence—a quiet refinement and gaiety of mind—& an occasional power, which he cannot command at will, of unique eloquence.'[32] To

---

[29] Arnold Toynbee, *Lectures on the Industrial Revolution in England* (London, 1884).
[30] Kitchin, 'Ruskin at Oxford', 43–4.
[31] Michael Sadleir, *Michael Ernest Sadler: A Memoir by his Son* (London, 1949), 32–3.
[32] Ibid. 45 (10 Nov. 1883).

another correspondent he wrote of 'inexpressibly splendid' lectures: 'you can't have any idea what it is to hear the man'.[33]

Sadler took up his position organizing Oxford's programme of extension lectures a few months after Ruskin's last lectures as Slade Professor. The idea of extending the university—which meant, initially, the broadening of its social intake so that poorer men could study there—had been discussed in Oxford since the late 1840s, and had formed a secondary theme in the mid-Victorian reforms of the structures of the ancient universities. While Oxford debated how best to spread its influence, and how to bring deserving scholars to the university, Cambridge began an experiment in peripatetic lecturing in 1873 in which university men went regularly to teach groups in provincial towns and cities, and thereby 'extended' the university in another sense. In 1878 Oxford followed suit, though its efforts initially depended on individual initiatives, notably the lectures on economic history given by that ardent Ruskinian, Arnold Toynbee.[34] But Sadler's appointment marked a change, and for the next ten years he built up Oxford's programme, sending lecturers to ever more places, and drawing into the work a range of dedicated teachers, many of whom shared Sadler's ethical mission.[35] Several of Sadler's colleagues evidently shared his admiration for Ruskin: some of them had also heard Ruskin in Oxford. They shared Sadler's desire to reach working-class communities through university extension and offer them access to higher learning, simultaneously drawing them into the national culture. Extension lecturing was seen as a means of breaking down class antagonism and class isolation by many of those involved. Lectures and courses on Ruskin proved to be enormously popular and successful: instruction in his ideas affirmed the instinctive hostility of working-class communities to the economic system; substantiated and broadened the deep current of idealism (in the sense of anti-materialism) that ran through the educated working class at this time; and allowed university men from another experience to emphasize their solidarity with workers in the appreciation of a mutually revered authority.

Ruskin first formed a subject for lectures in Oxford's revived programme in 1886. Thereafter, he was lectured on in almost every year until the First World War. It was the custom for each extension lecturer to prepare a

33 Ibid. 50.

34 Lawrence Goldman, *Dons and Workers: Oxford and Adult Education Since 1850* (Oxford, 1995), 11–60.

35 Ibid. 61–87.

printed syllabus for each course, and many have survived. They generally included a précis of each lecture, relevant quotations, suggested
reading, and essay questions.[36] Taken together, they present a composite interpretation of Ruskin, telling us something about the way he was
understood by university men of this era, and about the transmission of
his ideas to a wider audience.

While there were some lecturers who offered courses of six or twelve
lectures wholly devoted to Ruskin, he was more frequently discussed in a
variety of contexts: in courses that considered Ruskin with Thomas
Carlyle; as one of several 'Prose Writers of the Nineteenth Century'; in
lectures on 'Victorian Literature' or 'English Essayists'; as one of several
'English Social Reformers'; as a thinker and writer on economics. In
such courses Ruskin's ideas were presented in one, two, or three lectures,
and he took his place alongside other writers and critics. The sheer range
and scope of Ruskin's productions over such a long and fertile writing
career allowed for this pluralism, as it also allowed for a diverse range of
interpretations of his thought and place in history. Few lecturers failed to
advert to Ruskin's style—he was, in the words of Cosmo Gordon Lang,
the future Archbishop of Canterbury, who lectured in the late 1880s, 'the
greatest word-painter of the period'. It was also accepted, in Lang's
words, that he was 'the greatest art-critic of modern times'.[37] Yet few
courses were given on Ruskin's teachings on art alone: perhaps the only
example was a course offered by Ruskin's secretary, Collingwood, in
1889.[38] Most lecturers, if they generally began with remarks on the first
stages of Ruskin's career, moved on to consider Ruskin as a social
thinker. Many sought to substantiate the '*essential connexion* between
his contributions to Art Criticism and his works in relation to Social
Science and Political Economy' in the words of one of the earliest

[36] The syllabuses were printed in Oxford and distributed to students on the relevant
courses. They are preserved in bound volumes in the Oxford University Archives, arranged
chronologically, and hence in the form in which the course was first delivered. Most were
unpaginated.

[37] C. G. Lang, *Syllabus of a Course of Twelve Lectures on Victorian Literature*, Lecture
x, 'Newman and Ruskin', Oxford University Archives, DES/SB/3/1/4 (1890–1).

[38] W. G. Collingwood, *Syllabus of a Course of Lectures on Ruskin's Art-Teaching*,
DES/SB/3/1/3 (1889–90). There is no evidence that this course was ever given to a group,
though Collingwood did lecture for Oxford on 'Great Schools of Art' in Matlock in the
autumn of 1891, and on 'Venetian Art' in 1892–3 at Halifax, Matlock, Rugby, and Ilkley.
Interestingly, in the autumn of 1886 he lectured under Oxford's auspices on a typically
Ruskinian subject, 'The Structure of Mountains', at The Institute, Coniston. 'The audi-
ence consisted chiefly of working people of the village'. Lecturers' and Examiners'
Reports, Oxford University Archives, 1886–7, DES/R/3/1, fo. 50. See also Historical
Register of Lecturers, 1885/6–1905/6, Oxford University Archives, DES/EP/1/8.

professional scholars of English literature, John Churton Collins.[39] E. H. Spender's lecture on Ruskin, dating from 1892–3, did this most successfully. Starting from Ruskin's contention that 'there can be no true art which is not based on true morality' Spender showed the derivation of Ruskin's principle that 'the art of any country is the exponent of its social and political virtues'. He also showed how Ruskin's thinking then turned to his own age and nation: 'The fundamental fault he finds in English life is that Art is divorced from Industry, and Industry from Art. The consequence is squalor and brutality on the one side, dilettantism and luxury on the other.'[40]

There were some notorious aspects of Ruskin's social thought which were either ignored, or openly disavowed. J. A. Hobson referred delicately in 1888 to Ruskin's views on 'the ideal woman's life' as 'far removed from possible practice, and . . . not quite intelligible'.[41] G. W. Hudson Shaw, who was a partisan for women's causes in a movement that did much for the higher education of middle-class women, did not mince his words, writing of 'the narrowness and limitations of his teachings as to women's position' as set out in *Sesame and Lilies*.[42] In a movement dedicated to bringing into being 'an educated democracy' and staffed by so-called 'democratic dons', Ruskin's contempt for liberal social forms and his attraction to aristocracy and hierarchy were set down as errors, and generally brushed aside in favour of a concentration on his economic ideas. Several lecturers, in treating of these, recognized that although Ruskin had thrown off the formal Christianity of his youth, his thought was still imbricated with Christian ethics. As E. H. Spender expressed it in 1892, Ruskin sought to 'Christianize our social relations'.[43] According to Hudson Shaw, 'Ruskin's main position was that our present social and industrial organization is a negative of Christian ethics.'[44] As another lecturer expressed it slightly later, 'Ruskin is a specifically moral,

---

39 J. Churton Collins, *Syllabus of a Course of Ten Lectures on Ruskin, Emerson and Matthew Arnold*, Lecture ii, DES/SB/3/1/21 (1904–5).

40 E. H. Spender, *Syllabus of a Course of Lectures on Victorian Writers, Pt. II*, Lecture viii, DES/SB/3/1/8 (1892–3).

41 J. A. Hobson, *Syllabus of a Course of Lectures on Prose Writers of the Nineteenth Century* (London, 1888), Lecture v, DES/SB/3/1/2 (1888–9). The syllabus was for a course of lectures under the auspices of the London Society for the Extension of University Teaching which had been founded in 1875.

42 G. W. Hudson Shaw, *Syllabus of a Course of Six Introductory Lectures on the Life and Teaching of John Ruskin*, lecture v, 38, DES/SB/3/1/19 (1902–3).

43 Spender, *Victorian Writers*, Lecture viii.

44 Hudson Shaw, *Life and Teaching of John Ruskin*, Lecture v, 37.

almost a specifically religious writer throughout.'[45] He was thus understood as more than just a great Victorian critic. According to Charles
Mallet, he was 'a visionary'.[46] According to others he was 'a social prophet and preacher',[47] a 'prophet and teacher',[48] a 'modern prophet'.[49]

In providing a context for his thought, lecturers frequently presented
Ruskin alongside other sages of the nineteenth century. In the Oxford
extension syllabus on Ruskin prepared by the most prominent member
of the Birmingham Ruskin Society, J. Ernest Pythian, a final lecture considered him in relation to Mazzini, Carlyle, Whitman, Tolstoy, and
William Morris.[50] In a course delivered by Hobson in 1895 Ruskin took
his place with Carlyle, Emerson, Mazzini, Browning, and Tolstoy.[51] In
these cases, Ruskin was associated with other idealist thinkers for whom
mind, soul, and instinct were paramount categories, and who rejected
materialism and utilitarian ethics. Of all these figures, it was Carlyle to
whom Ruskin was most frequently compared: the pairing was also evident in the reading of the first Labour MPs, for Carlyle was the second
most-mentioned author after Ruskin. But it is clear that Carlyle, though
admired by many of the lecturers, was a less sympathetic figure, thun-
dering against the remoter evils of early Victorian capitalism in a style
they found antipathetic. In Lang's shorthand of 1888, Carlyle was 'the
great scavenger of nineteenth century shams . . . of no "practical" use—
an avalanche of negative truths'.[52] To Lang, Carlyle's 'vehemence, his
wilful eccentricity' were defects, as were 'his exaggeration and turgid
rhetoric' to Mallet.[53] Some lecturers were evidently disturbed by
Carlyle's doctrine of the hero, and his contempt for democracy; others
took him to have validated might against right. Hobson could see the

---

45 D. W. Rannie, *Syllabus of a Course of Six Lectures on Carlyle and Ruskin*, Lecture
vi, DES/SB/3/1/21 (1904–5).

46 C. E. Mallet, *Syllabus of a Course of Lectures on English Essayists Political and
Social*, Lecture vi, DES/SB/3/1/4 (1890–1).

47 Spender, *Victorian Writers*, lecture viii.

48 Rannie, *Carlyle and Ruskin*, lecture vi.

49 Revd G. W. Hudson Shaw, *Syllabus of a Course of Lectures on Carlyle and Ruskin*,
Lecture iv, DES/SB/3/1/1 (1886–7).

50 J. Ernest Pythian, *Syllabus of a Course of Lectures on John Ruskin*, Lecture ix,
DES/SB/3/1/11 (1894–5).

51 J. A. Hobson, *Syllabus of a Course of Lectures on Modern Thinkers upon Life*,
Lecture ii, DES/SB/3/1/12 (1895–6).

52 C. G. Lang, *Syllabus of a Course of Six Lectures on Victorian Literature*, Lecture v,
DES/SB/3/1/3 (1889–90).

53 C. G. Lang, *Syllabus of a Course of Twelve Lectures on Victorian Literature*, Lecture
ix, DES/SB/3/1/4 (1890–91); C. E. Mallet, *Syllabus of a Course of Lectures on English
Essayists Political and Social*, Lecture v, DES/SB/3/1/4 (1890–1).

parallels between Ruskin and Carlyle: both opposed 'selfish material-ism', repudiated 'the philosophic method' and appealed 'to the emo-tions', and understood 'the importance assigned to the investigation of words', for words, when misused, were powerful agents of moral cor-ruption. Nevertheless, Ruskin's conception of life was 'more joyous', his remedies 'less stern'.[54] In Carlyle, 'the spirit of revolt against the char-acter of his age overpowered the creative instinct'.[55] Carlyle thundered against the dismal science, but Ruskin sought to set in its place a moral-ized political economy. This was the essential difference, and it was Ruskin's economic thought that attracted most attention. It was a mark of his impact on Oxford in the 1880s that the first extension lecture courses on political economy, given by young graduates like L. R. Phelps, L. L. Price, and Hubert Llewellyn Smith, who were to make their careers in the new, professionalized discipline of economics, included *Unto This Last* in their lists of recommended reading.[56]

For most lecturers, it was Ruskin's sheer audacity in seeking to redefine the concepts and aims of political economy that made him such an attractive and compelling figure. As one lecturer, A. M. D. Hughes, formerly of St John's, Oxford, expressed it in 1900, 'the principles must be restated with reference to human nature as it is, and the true ends of man's life'.[57] Hence the line of Ruskin's that was most often printed in these syllabuses, and which worked itself into the consciousness of so many in this period: 'There is no wealth but life'. *Unto This Last*, the source of this definition which fast became an aphorism, was the central text for almost all lecturers. It was understood as pivotal in Ruskin's career, marking the change in his focus from art to society. Ruskin de-scribed the essays at the time as 'the best, that is to say the truest, right-est worded and most serviceable things I have ever written', and later described it as 'the central work of my life . . . it contained at once the substance of all that I have had since to say'.[58] On its original publica-tion as essays in the *Cornhill Magazine* in 1860 it had ignited con-troversy, and dramatized Ruskin's position in the culture as a prophet without honour; it was short in length, and hence easily read; by the

54 Hobson, *Prose Writers of the Nineteenth Century*, Lecture v.

55 Hobson, *Modern Thinkers upon Life*, Lecture i, 3.

56 L. R. Phelps, *Syllabus of Six Lectures on the Making and Sharing of Wealth*; L. L. Price, *The Making and Division of Wealth, Trades Unions, Co-operation and Free Trade*; Hubert Llewellyn Smith, *Wealth and Industry*, DES/SB/3/1/2 (1888–9).

57 A. M. D. Hughes, *Syllabus of a Course of Six Lectures on Carlyle and Ruskin*, Lecture v, 7, DES/SB/3/1/17 (1900–1).

58 *Works* 17.17; Cook, *Life of John Ruskin*, ii. 2.

1880s it was widely available; and it was the single most cogent exposition of his economic ideas.

Unto This Last was written to provide, as Ruskin explained in the preface, 'an accurate and stable definition of wealth' and to show that its acquisition was possible 'only under certain moral conditions of society'. He attempted to redefine all the basic categories of political economy—not only wealth but value, labour, and capital as well. By so doing, he hoped to lay down a theoretical foundation for the reconstruction of society on the basis of cooperation, justice, and hierarchic order, rather than competition, avarice, and flux. The four essays that comprised the work were a sustained assault on political economy as an abstraction which had deliberately excluded all questions of morality, which caricatured human nature as selfish, and which spread doctrines inconsistent with Christianity. Political Economy sanctioned speculation, the taking of interest on invested capital, the policy of laissez-faire. In practice it led to the intensification of social divisions, and the dehumanization and degradation of work through the division of labour and the divorce of mental and manual tasks.[59] To all of this Ruskin was implacably opposed, and so, it would seem, were those who lectured about him, and also those to whom they lectured. The syllabuses present an almost uncritical account of the ideas in *Unto This Last*, and an endorsement of Ruskin's commentary on the inadequacies of conventional economics. That men are not self-interested only and that 'moral considerations' cannot be ignored were oft-repeated themes in these lectures. As one lecturer explained to an audience in Halifax in 1904–5, *Unto This Last* 'is on the one hand a plea for a more human science of economics, and on the other a denunciation of the inhumanity of the industrial system'.[60]

Of all the lecturers who dealt with Ruskin in this period—and there were several dozen of them—two stand out and deserve closer attention. The Revd G. W. Hudson Shaw was not only the most successful and popular of all the Oxford lecturers, but he did more than anyone to spread Ruskin's ideas, taking them with him into the communities of the English working class. Meanwhile, J. A. Hobson did most with the ideas themselves, using them to underpin the heterodox political economy he developed in the 1880s and 1890s—notably his underconsumptionist

[59] Lawrence Goldman, 'John Ruskin', *The New Palgrave: A Dictionary of Economics* eds. J. Eatwell, M. Milgate, and P. Newman, 4 vols., (London, 1987), iv. 228–9.

[60] J. A. Dale, *Syllabus of a Course of Six Lectures on Ruskin*, Lecture iv, DES/SB/3/1/21 (1904–5).

thesis—which has secured him a place in the pantheon of the most important economic thinkers.

Ruskin's impact on Hobson was profound. He described himself as 'engaged in the Ruskinian service' in the 1890s, and remained constant in his praise for Ruskin's economics to the end of his life.[61] From Ruskin he 'drew the basic thought of [his] subsequent economic writings, viz., the necessity of going behind the current monetary estimates of wealth, cost, and utility, to reach the body of human benefits and satisfactions which gave them a real meaning.'[62] Hobson was a little older than Sadler, having been at Oxford in the late 1870s. There is no record that he encountered Ruskin as an undergraduate, but by the time he embarked on university extension lecturing, first in London in the late 1880s, and then in Oxford, Hobson had engaged with Ruskin's ideas and was set on the course that would result in publication in 1898 of one of the very finest studies of the master, *John Ruskin: Social Reformer*. There is some confusion over Hobson's interest in Ruskin, and it has been suggested that Hobson's friends steered him from the exposition of his underconsumptionist heresies, which had caused him to be ostracized by conventional economic opinion, towards the 'safer subject' of a study of Ruskin.[63] But Hobson had been lecturing on Ruskin for many years before the book was written, and Ruskin was in no sense a safe subject: indeed, a close reading of Hobson's book shows how his underconsumptionist ideas were actually confirmed by Ruskin's economics. For according to Hobson,

The doctrine of the social utility of unlimited saving, the assumptions that industry is limited by capital, and that the demand for commodities is not demand for labour, are successfully exploded by Mr. Ruskin in various skilful analytic passages . . . [He] rightly insisted that if any order was to be put into the current teaching it must definitely accept consumption as the economic goal.[64]

Hobson's 'friends', moreover, or to be more precise, Charles Mallet, who encouraged him to write the book, were hardly neutrals: Mallet, later a Liberal MP, had given several courses of lectures on Ruskin for Oxford extension in the 1880s and 1890s himself, and shared Hobson's deep commitment to Ruskin's revolutionary ideas.[65] Hobson described himself in the 1890s as 'fumbling after the conception and expression of an

---

[61] J. A. Hobson, *Confessions of an Economic Heretic* (1938) (Hassocks, 1976 edn.), 43. For evidence of Hobson's enduring respect for Ruskin, see J. A. Hobson, 'Ruskin as Political Economist', in J. Howard Whitehouse (ed.), *Ruskin the Prophet* (London, 1920), 83–98.

[62] Hobson, *Confessions*, 42.

[63] Peter Clarke, *Liberals and Social Democrats* (Cambridge, 1978), 48.

[64] Hobson, *John Ruskin*, 121.   [65] Hobson, *Confessions*, 38.

economics which was more art than science, and therefore, more qualit-
ative than quantitative in its estimate of value, wealth, cost, and utility'.[66] This had been Ruskin's project throughout, and Hobson, as he
freely acknowledged, followed in his path.

Hobson devised six different courses on political economy as an
Oxford lecturer in the 1890s. He also lectured on Ruskin as one of six
'thinkers upon modern life'. But he first discussed Ruskin in a course
on 'prose writers of the nineteenth century' arranged by the London
Society for the Extension of University Teaching in 1888—and this first
engagement with Ruskin was critical. Ruskin's ideas on cooperation as
opposed to competition were described by Hobson as 'visionary and incomplete'. He made much of Ruskin's failure to provide a 'real measure
of value', describing Ruskin's time measure as 'futile'. He called Ruskin's
criticism of economic theory 'fallacious', though he conceded that 'his
passionate appeal for a higher conception of "Wealth" is a noble effort
at reform'.[67] But Hobson's ideas evidently evolved from this position.
For in 1892 his syllabus on 'The Making of Wealth' included a strikingly
Ruskinian passage notable for its focus on human welfare and behaviour
as the measure of true wealth: 'The old political economy non-moral.
Its unscientific treatment of human nature. Modern scientific view of
wealth builds on the basis of human desires and ideas. Human satisfaction as the ultimate measure of wealth. Wealth changes in quality and
quantity with the needs and desires of men.'[68] The syllabus he published
in the following year, the second part of a course he had been giving on
'Problems of Poverty', culminated in a final lecture for which *Unto This
Last* was recommended reading, and with Ruskin's famous aphorism
from the book, 'Government and Co-operation are in all things the laws
of life: Anarchy and Competition the laws of death.'[69] Two years later
his lecture on Ruskin as one of the 'Modern Thinkers upon Life' expressed his recognition that the point of origin of Ruskin's critical political economy, and his greatest single service as a social theorist, was his
emphasis on the dignity and quality of work itself.[70]

[66] Ibid. 43.

[67] Hobson, *Prose Writers of the Nineteenth Century*, Lecture v.

[68] J. A. Hobson, *Syllabus of a Course of Lectures on the Making of Wealth*, Lecture i,
DES/SB/3/1/8 (1892–3).

[69] J. A. Hobson, *Syllabus of a Course of Lectures on Problems of Poverty, Pt. II*,
Lecture vi, DES/SB/3/1/9 (1893–4).

[70] Hobson, *Lectures on Modern Thinkers upon Life* (1895–6). On Hobson as an exten-
sion lecturer see Alon Kadish, 'Rewriting the Confessions: Hobson and the Extension
Movement', in Michael Freeden (ed.), *Reappraising J. A. Hobson: Humanism and Welfare*
(London, 1990).

It was Ruskin as scientist—as a systematic thinker on economics—that Hobson emphasized subsequently in his celebrated study of *John Ruskin: Social Reformer*. It was a singular argument: no other lecturer or author had tried to vindicate the 'unity and consistency of conscious design in Mr. Ruskin's work.'[71] As Hobson 'fumbled' with Ruskin's ideas for a decade, Ruskin's 'futile' definitions and 'fallacious' criticisms of 1888 were reinterpreted, and the book's claim in 1898 was that Ruskin had demonstrated 'consistency of thought and feeling' and 'intellectual unity and order'.[72] Ruskin's work amounted to 'the first serious attempt in England to establish a scientific basis of economic study from the social standpoint'.[73] Hobson did not ignore Ruskin's suggestions on social organization. Like other extension lecturers he took issue with Ruskin for his distrust of democracy, and his faith in the beneficent intent of the upper classes. Nor did he believe that a social strategy premissed on the moral reform of individuals was adequate to deal with the complexities of modern capitalism.[74] He also accepted that Ruskin's denial of 'the productiveness of exchange' and his moral opposition to the taking of interest—points which conventional economists had used consistently in order to discredit Ruskinian economics—were both misguided doctrines.[75] Nevertheless, Ruskin's attempt to ground political economy in moral behaviour and to redefine its key concepts so that they reflected human rather than material values, won his admiration: 'By thus vitalising and moralising every term and every process Mr. Ruskin forms the outline of a Political Economy which is primarily concerned with the production of healthy life, the manufacture of "souls of good quality"'.[76] This was true wealth. That Hobson agreed with Ruskin, and presented him as a pioneer of the true economics, could only have confirmed his reputation as an intellectual maverick who belonged outside the new economics profession. But with the benefit of hindsight, knowing the significance of the underconsumptionist argument and of Hobson's subsequent work on the economic theory of imperialism to twentieth-century economic thought, his own respect for Ruskin's insights, which confirmed him in his unorthodox views and approach at the outset his career, deserves our respect in turn.

G. W. Hudson Shaw was one of Hobson's colleagues in the 1890s. A contemporary of Sadler's as an undergraduate, who also presided over the Union Society, he was also touched by Ruskin and by the special atmosphere of the University in the early 1880s. Hudson Shaw was

[71] Hobson, *John Ruskin*, vi.   [72] Ibid. v.   [73] Ibid. 107.
[74] Ibid. 196–209.   [75] Ibid. 140–153.   [76] Ibid. 84.

ordained after graduating in 1884, but was soon lured back to Oxford when Sadler became Secretary of the Extension Delegacy, where he became Senior Lecturer in History, and, in the 1890s, a Fellow of Balliol, his undergraduate college.[77] He later recalled that he entered the movement 'unwillingly, more or less a disbeliever, under pressure from Prof. M. E. Sadler, attracted mainly by the hope held out of close contact with working people and possible opportunity of aiding the ideals of T. H. Green and Arnold Toynbee. My scepticism regarding University Extension disappeared during the first year's work in Lancashire.'[78] In 1895 he described his aims in university extension in the manner of Green and Toynbee: 'to train good citizens, to extend high ideals from the few to the many', and to help form 'a true, cultured, educated, democracy'.[79] He soon emerged as the most successful of Oxford extension lecturers, whether judged by the number of invitations he received from local lecture centres, the size of his audiences, or his special rapport with working-class students and communities. Between 1886 and 1912 he lectured in many of the great cities and smaller industrial towns of England on a variety of historical subjects, but his special love was John Ruskin. In his first years as an extension lecturer, Hudson Shaw lectured on 'Carlyle and Ruskin'. He also worked up a more ambitious course on 'English Social Reformers', which included a lecture on Ruskin, and which he gave in over fifty different locations. And from 1901 until 1908 he gave a hugely successful course on 'The Life and Teaching of John Ruskin' to appreciative audiences all over industrial England. To give some sense of his success, 'English Social Reformers' drew an average attendance of 420 students at Huddersfield in the autumn term of 1887; 400 students at Barnsley in spring 1888; 500 at Sowerby Bridge in spring 1890; 250 in Halifax in autumn 1898; and 300 at Wigan in autumn 1900. The course on Ruskin's life and teaching enrolled 500 students at Heaton Chapel in the autumn term of 1902; 500 at Rochdale in spring 1906; 600 at Oldham in the autumn of the same year; and 520 at Preston in 1908.[80]

---

77 Stuart Marriott, 'George William Hudson Shaw', in J. E. Thomas and Barry Elsey (eds.), *International Biography of Adult Education* (Nottingham, 1985), 533–40; Goldman, *Dons and Workers*, 72–6.

78 G. W. Hudson Shaw, 'The University Extension Movement', Ministry of Reconstruction, Adult Education Committee 1917–19, Notes No. 75, Public Record Office, London, RECO 1 894, fo. 1.

79 Quoted in Marriott, 'George William Hudson Shaw', 539.

80 Historical Register of Lecturers, 1885/6–1905/6, and Oxford University Extension. List and Particulars of Courses to 1942, DES/EP/1/8 and DES/F/3/2/Z.

The syllabus that Hudson Shaw prepared for his Edwardian courses on 'The Life and Teaching of John Ruskin' ran to 55 pages.[81] Each lecture was given in précis, alongside relevant quotations from Ruskin, and from authorities on him. Hudson Shaw's interpretation of the master was not distinctively different from that presented by most lecturers, though as a churchman he gave himself more space to discuss the Christian basis of Ruskin's political economy, and the changes in Ruskin's religious belief across his life. He also gave more prominence to Ruskin's works on architecture in the late 1840s and 1850s in explaining his transition from a concentration on art to one on society. In what must have been a brilliant lecture on 'Ruskin: Venetian Historian', Hudson Shaw explained the connections between Ruskin's views on art, architecture, history, and morality, and showed how a focus on the quality and nature of work, as set down in the famous chapter on 'The Nature of Gothic', led him, inexorably, to a consideration of the social and economic organization of Victorian England.

Hudson Shaw took his courses on Ruskin to all the great working-class centres on the Oxford circuit. According to Sadler, his fame was 'almost mystical' among the working men of the north.[82] According to another lecturer, 'he was a great favourite with the working class audiences' in the North of England, 'and there is no doubt that he did more than any man to firmly establish working class centres in that part of the country'.[83] Albert Mansbridge, the founder of the Workers' Educational Association, described Hudson Shaw as 'a self-sacrificing inspiring force throughout the land'.[84] In 1903 Hudson Shaw became the first chairman of the WEA, though he remained a proponent of the grand public extension lecture, rather than the more intimate and academic tutorial class which the Association promoted, and he was uncomfortable with its overt political project. When Hudson Shaw's health broke down in 1909, Sadler wrote to him to express his appreciation of Shaw's achievement in spreading the ideas of the figure who had influenced them both so profoundly as undergraduates:

For more than twenty years you have been one of the great moving forces for good in English life. Very much of the change which has come over political

[81] G. W. Hudson Shaw, *Syllabus of a Course of Six Introductory Lectures on the Life and Teaching of John Ruskin*, DES/SB/3/1/19 (1902–3).

[82] Maude Royden, *A Threefold Cord* (London, 1947), 34. Maude Royden was Hudson Shaw's third wife.

[83] George Edens to Maude Royden, Mar. 1952, Royden Papers, Box 222, Fawcett Library, London Guildhall University.

[84] Albert Mansbridge to Maude Royden, 26 Jan. 1952, Royden Papers, Box 222.

thought is, in fact, the direct result of your teaching. You have been the link between Ruskin and the labour movement. More than any other man, you have made Ruskin's words live and bear fruit. You have added much of your own. Like all good interpreters, you are yourself a creator of ideals.[85]

What did the worker-scholars make of Hudson Shaw, and of Ruskin as mediated by Oxford extension lecturers in general? In addition to course syllabuses, brief reports on the classes themselves have survived, written by the tutors, and also by the class secretaries, usually students charged with local administration. It was customary for the most committed students to sit examinations at the end of a course which were sent to Oxford to be marked, and the examiners' reports are also extant. In addition, in one or two cases, prominent students of this period left records of what they studied and thought about John Ruskin. Taken together, the material is richly suggestive of working-class interest in Ruskin in late Victorian and Edwardian England.

The combination of subject and lecturer in Hudson Shaw's case seem to have made his courses on Ruskin singularly successful. F. Yorke Powell, later Regius Professor of History in Oxford, read the scripts written by students who attended Hudson Shaw's course on 'Carlyle and Ruskin' at Ilkley in the spring of 1888. He observed that 'the subject of this course of Lectures has clearly been attractive, there is great interest and thoughtful care shown in the answers sent me . . . There are few courses better adapted (as the examination has shown) for *getting students to think* than this on Carlyle and Ruskin'.[86] During the course of Hudson Shaw's lectures on 'English Social Reformers' in Newcastle-under-Lyme in autumn 1887, numbers actually increased, with 'by far the greatest interest being shown in the Ruskin subject'. On that evening, some 200 attended.[87] In the spring term of the following year the same subject and lecturer at Barnsley drew an average attendance of 350 students, 'composed entirely . . . of working people with a few National School Teachers', and they were described as 'singularly attentive & sympathetic'.[88] At Hebden Bridge the highly successful course on English Social Reformers in 1887–8, which enrolled 240 students, was followed by the establishment of a reading circle there, which began work on Carlyle's *Past and Present*.[89]

---

[85] Michael Sadler to G. W. Hudson Shaw, 7 Oct. 1909, Royden Papers, Box 222.

[86] Oxford University Extension. Lecturers and Examiners' Reports 1887–8, Oxford University Archives, DES/R/3/2, fo. 167.

[87] Ibid. fo. 73.

[88] Ibid. fo. 153. (This course was taught jointly by Hudson Shaw and Revd William Danks who wrote the report cited.)   [89] Ibid. fo. 50.

Hudson Shaw's course on 'The Life and Teaching of John Ruskin' in the Edwardian period was, if anything, even more inspiring. In many cases his reports describe the lectures as the most successful he had given at centres he had visited regularly in the past. At Wigan, where courses were organized and financed by the local cooperative society, in the autumn of 1901 'the attendance was excellent and maintained to the end. The audience, of all classes, was the best worth addressing I have encountered since the days of Oldham . . . This is the *real thing*. Here is represented that active, intelligent, artisan element of Univ. Extension work.' The local secretary concurred: 'The interest taken in the University Lectures by our Wg. class people is Progressive. The stimulus given by the course on "Social Reformers" followed by "Ruskin" has engrafted the future demand for similar courses'.[90] At Bolton in the same year, Hudson Shaw remarked that though he had lectured in the town for many years, he had never seen his audience (of some 220 students) 'more genuinely interested, more ready to read'.

A great many students have been led to examine thoroughly, not one book or one aspect of Ruskin's teaching, but his work as a whole. Many will continue their study. Some have found a prophet whose entire views they can accept heartily, some have discovered a new theory of modern life—which they feel at least bound to take into account.[91]

At Heaton Moor in the autumn of 1902, the course on Ruskin drew 500 students and the local committee declared it to have been 'the best course of Extension lectures we have ever had'.[92] At Rochdale—a town with a long tradition of working-class education, as well as cooperation —in the spring of 1906 the local secretary noted 'a marked advance in the number of working people (especially men) in regular attendance' to hear Hudson Shaw on Ruskin, and remarked on 'the keen discussion carried on at the close of each lecture'. The Oxford examiner was also impressed: 'The Rochdale papers are full of enthusiastic, but discriminating, praise of Ruskin's aims and ideals. In all the papers there is evidence of a thorough study of Ruskin's books; and in most the views of Ruskin are stated in great detail. The best papers combine clearness with thoughtfulness.'[93] During the same term (and at the very time when W. T. Stead was inquiring about the reading habits of the first Labour MPs) Hudson Shaw was also lecturing in Grimsby:

[90] Lecturers and Examiners' Reports, 1901–2, DES/R/3/30, fos. 66, 68.
[91] Ibid. fo. 25.
[92] Lecturers and Examiners' Reports, 1902–3, DES/R/3/31, fo. 7.
[93] Lecturers and Examiners' Reports, 1905–6, DES/R/3/34, fos. 560, 563, 564.

There is always a splendid audience filling the Town Hall at Grimsby, but I have not, in my experience, known such enormous & well-sustained attendances at this centre before, nor seen such deep and earnest interest manifested in any previous subject. All classes were represented, teachers and artisans not excepted.[94]

At Preston in autumn 1908, Hudson Shaw's course on Ruskin was put on for free, and over 500 enrolled. According to the local secretary, 'the general audience showed deep and unbroken interest in the lectures, which they enthusiastically applauded.'[95]

Some of this interest was a tribute to Hudson Shaw himself. And we must be aware of the natural tendency on the part of all concerned in these courses to write them up as successful. But it is clear that wherever and whenever Ruskin was taught, and particularly in working-class districts, the results were notable. In 1894, J. Ernest Pythian taught his only course for Oxford on Ruskin at Barnsley, and reported on a 'large, regular & attentive audience' which had shown 'so much interest'.[96] In the spring of 1905 a young Oxford graduate, J. A. Dale, was teaching a course on Ruskin in Halifax. He wrote of 'very good' discussions and essays which 'were among the most careful & conscientious I have ever had'. The Oxford examiner agreed: 'This is one of the best set of papers I have had for a long time. All the candidates show a keen interest in Ruskin's work and a contagious enthusiasm about some of his ideals. The treatment of questions is luminous; and, in some of the papers, exceedingly incisive and definite.'[97] Even John Cowper Powys—surely an unlikely figure to have been lecturing to earnest audiences in working-class areas on these subjects—enjoyed success. At Stoke in the autumn of 1907 his course on 'Carlyle and Ruskin' enrolled 286 students, and he reported that 'in no centre of his experience have the discussions in the class after the lecture been more interesting or more provocative of thought.'[98] His report on the same course given in the following year in Huddersfield, for which 280 were enrolled, deserves full quotation:

This course of lectures has proved in many ways one of considerable interest to both lecturer and audience . . . In fact the lecturer cannot recall ever having met with so much enthusiasm for Ruskin and so much interest in his work in any place as he encountered here. The final discussion aroused by the last lecture upon Ruskin's social theories in which many of the leading gentlemen of the

---

94 Ibid. fo. 558.
95 Lecturers and Examiners' Reports, 1908–9, DES/R/3/38, fo. 24.
96 Lecturers and Examiners' Reports, 1894–5, DES/R/3/19, fo. 355.
97 Lecturers and Examiners' Reports, 1904–5, DES/R/3/33, fos. 568–9.
98 Lecturers and Examiners' Reports, 1907–8, DES/R/3/37, fo. 472.

town took part and with surprising freedom expressed their views, suggested a new conception of Extension work of almost unbounded possibilities. The lecturer, at any rate, was profoundly impressed by the good humour with which men of absolutely opposite views expressed their personal convictions under the cover of this academic discussion.[99]

The lecturer's irony barely conceals an occasion that appears to have given an added meaning to 'class warfare'. Such was the immediacy and relevance of Ruskin that he could attract the burghers of Huddersfield to join the local artisans in vibrant argument. Ruskin's ideas were a terrain across which real social and political battles were fought out in the early years of the century.

Ruskin, as mediated by these lecturers, inspired myriad individuals, and two examples are offered: Edward Stuart Cartwright, of Longton in North Staffordshire, and T. W. Price of Rochdale. Both were exceptional: they were keen students of university extension; they were both members of the first two WEA tutorial classes, taught by the historian and socialist thinker R. H. Tawney in Longton and Rochdale from early 1908—indeed in each case they served as class secretary. Both men made adult education into a career, Price as Secretary of the Midlands District of the Workers' Educational Association from 1908, and then Assistant Secretary of the national WEA, and Cartwright as Organizing Secretary of the Oxford Tutorial Classes Committee from 1912 to 1945. Before this translation, Cartwright had been a clerk in local government employment in Longton, while Price, a member of the Independent Labour Party, had worked in a local bleaching works. Price was later to write the best history of the early years of the WEA.[100]

Cartwright left his papers to the University of Oxford, and they include beautifully written essays composed when Hudson Shaw came to lecture on Ruskin at Longton in 1906. The first essay, in October 1906, was a biographical account, focusing on Ruskin's childhood and background.[101] The second considered Ruskin as a writer of prose—as 'a

<hr/>

99 Lecturers and Examiners' Reports, 1908–9, DES/R/3/38, fo. 286.

100 H. P. Smith, 'Edward Stuart Cartwright: A Note on his Work for Adult Education, *Rewley House Papers*, 3/1 (1949–50), 8–24; R. H. Tawney, 'Mr. E. S. Cartwright: A Leader in the Adult Education Movement', *Manchester Guardian*, 16 Aug. 1950, 3; E. S. Cartwright, 'T. W. Price—An Appreciation', *The Highway* 37 (Dec. 1945), 47–8; T. W. Price, *The Story of the Workers' Educational Association from 1903–1924* (London, 1924).

101 'Heredity or Education: Which had the greatest influence on Ruskin?' in Notebooks, Essays and Miscellaneous Pamphlets Illustrating His Interests and Work as an Early Tutorial Class Student, E. S. Cartwright Papers, Oxford University Archives, DES/F/13/7.

master of the harmony of language', as Cartwright put it.[102] But it was the third essay—' "There is no Wealth but Life". Explain fully what Ruskin meant by this'—which reveals most about Ruskin's impact on the students of university extension. Cartwright noted how Ruskin came to political economy as a consequence of 'his conclusion that all good art was the outcome of sound national life'. He found not a true science of political economy, but 'a science of getting rich and of buying in the cheapest and selling in the dearest market, regardless of the effects upon producer & worker'. This was 'Mercantile Economy', indicted by Ruskin because 'it leaves out of account the effects of man's feelings and affections upon his capacity for work, and treats him as a mere machine'. In opposition, Ruskin developed an alternative science that 'was not only a noble but also a convincingly logical one' which ordered 'the forces and activities of life so that the best conditions for its development shall prevail'. But the prophet was without honour: 'Unable to reason Ruskin out of Court, they laughed him out. Avarice, selfishness and pride were all against him. It was as when Christ bade the young man leave all and follow him. The sacrifice was too great.' There is something of Hobson in this interpretation, for Ruskin is presented as a logical thinker. There is also a kind of Fabian rationalism here, so characteristic of the Edwardian period, in which Ruskin is presented as the reasonable voice of order and efficiency in the allocation of work and rewards. According to Cartwright, 'The true political economy would regulate industrialism and the incidence of production and consumption so as to bring about a harmony of worldly possessions throughout all orders of society'. And there is also a strong identification of Ruskin with Christ —of Ruskin as a Christian thinker, spreading Christ's message, and also suffering for his pains.[103]

Price published his interpretation of Ruskin in three articles in some of the earliest monthly numbers of the *Highway*, the journal of the WEA, in the spring and summer of 1909. The second, on 'Ruskin and Social Reform', and the third on 'Ruskin and Politics' rehearsed the universally acknowledged failings in Ruskin as a 'constructive' rather than 'critical' thinker. Much of his 'social teaching' was 'fantastic and crude', wrote Price: he was 'a master of diagnosis' but 'his attempts at prescription are anything but happy'. *Unto This Last* in its 'swift but accurate

---

[102] 'What are the chief characteristics of the best prose and how far are these exhibited in Ruskin's writing?', DES/F/13/7.
[103] ' "There is No Wealth But Life"—Explain fully what Ruskin meant by this', Dec. 1906, DES/F/13/7.

analysis' showed Ruskin at his best as critic; conversely, 'the fantastic provisions of Ruskin's scheme of land reform, with the landed gentry retained as national ornaments at a fixed salary' was an example of Ruskin at his worst. While Price understood Ruskin's fear of democracy—'that men are not wise merely by virtue either of their numbers or their poverty'—his authoritarianism 'was wholly wrong'. But in his first article, on 'Ruskin and the Workers', he explained lucidly why such a misguided social thinker was still a persuasive influence in working-class circles. Workers distrusted and doubted the doctrines of conventional economics which seemed designed to buttress existing social evils. In Ruskin they found an economist who looked beyond this false science to its human consequences. And the humanity of Ruskin's political economy was its attraction: 'Man he describes as "an engine whose motive power is a soul," and the hearts of the workers are uplifted, because, strange to say, they have a deep-rooted preference for being regarded as men and women rather than as "units of labour".' Ruskin's appeal was instinctive and experiential: 'the workers know that he speaks the truth, no matter what the economists may say', wrote Price. It was 'because they have suffered' that they appreciated 'the unanswerable logic of his indictment of modern industrial methods'.[104]

Price pitted Ruskin against the 'University trained-economist'. Indeed, he began his first article with an anecdote about the reaction of a 'famous economist' when Price told him 'of a little band of working men and women' who had read *Unto this Last* 'to improve their knowledge of Sociology, Economics, History': 'The effect upon the great man was remarkable, his eyebrows went up and his face took on a smile half of pity, half of sarcasm. He evinced no further interest in the matter, and abruptly changed the subject.'[105] By 1909 there were many intellectuals who could not share this enthusiasm for Ruskin, though they were sympathetic to the working class. It has been suggested by Hilton that 'the nadir of Ruskin's reputation' was reached in the Edwardian period, but this hardly accords with the argument being advanced here: among working people it actually appears to have reached its zenith, at least until about 1910.[106] Rather, as Colin Matthew has suggested, Ruskin was losing his relevance among the intelligentsia specifically.[107] To a new

[104] T. W. Price, 'Ruskin and the Workers'; 'Ruskin and Social Reform'; 'Ruskin and Politics', *Highway*, 1/6,7,10 (Mar., Apr., July 1909), 93–4, 107–8, 151–2.

[105] Ibid. 93.

[106] Hilton, *John Ruskin*, xi.

[107] H. C. G. Matthew, 'Hobson, Ruskin and Cobden', in Freeden (ed.), *Reappraising J. A. Hobson*, 16.

generation of progressive thinkers emerging from the universities, Ruskin meant little. One such was R. H. Tawney who was born in 1880, the year in which Sadler and Hudson Shaw went up to Oxford. Tawney may even have been the 'famous economist' to whom Price referred. Certainly, he dealt incisively with Cartwright when his initial essay, written in Tawney's first Oxford-WEA tutorial class in Longton in early 1908, strayed over familiar ground. Tawney had set his new students an ambitious task: 'If you were going to devote six months to the study of Economics, what branch should you select and why; and how should you set about it?' Cartwright launched into an explicitly Ruskinian definition of the nature and scope of political economy, and discussed the argument of *Unto This Last*. He concluded that he would 'choose for study that branch of Economics which deals with Social Conditions, and at the same time should look forward to the realization of Ruskin's noble ideal when other ideas of wealth than mere possessive ones may hold sway in economic thought.' This cut little ice with Tawney. His lengthy comment vindicated 'the isolation of wealth as a separate object of study' by Adam Smith, as 'a great advance upon the writers who had preceded him'. Narrow it may have been, 'but it was a necessary preliminary to the understanding of economic problems'. Tawney agreed that economic activity had to be placed 'in proper relation to the other elements of human life'. Nevertheless, 'if we forget the economic motive altogether, and overlook the material conditions on which the production of wealth depends, we become mere sentimentalists and dreamers'.[108]

Perhaps it would not be fanciful to suggest that Tawney's brisk comments on Cartwright's essay in early 1908 mark the end of Ruskin's direct influence over the English working class. There are reasons for suggesting that Ruskin's influence was in decline by the end of the first decade of the twentieth century. In the small world of university extension, changes were in process that conspired to end Ruskin's ascendancy. In the late 1880s and 1890s there were always several lecturers offering contributions on Ruskin. After 1900 it was Hudson Shaw who dominated courses on him, however, probably because local centres would not accept anyone less talented as an interpreter of the prophet. But in 1909 Hudson Shaw fell ill, and retired from extension lecturing three years later. In his absence, only occasional courses on Ruskin were given in the years before the Great War, often by inexperienced lecturers. In addition,

---

[108] 'University Extension. Economic History of the 17th Century. Longton Centre. Paper by Ed. S. Cartwright, 17/2/08' in E. S. Cartwright Papers, DES/5/13/7, fo. 3.

after 1908 the creative centre of university extension shifted to the tutorial class, the partnership of Oxford and other universities with the WEA, and the attempt to provide a true higher education of university standard for working people, taught by professional scholars like Tawney. Tawney offered rigorous economic history to his first tutorial classes, not moral uplift. He was a pioneer for a new academic subject, and his teaching was designed to explain to his students where their jobs, communities, and ways of life had come from. Tawney provided his students with the analytical tools to understand and to change their world. The industrial order had to be grappled with as it was, and then reformed, not rejected. Ruskin was associated with an essentially emotional response to capitalism that made younger scholars impatient. In the tough-minded way he dealt with Cartwright (who became his lifelong friend, and whose obituary he wrote), Tawney signalled not only the passing of an intellectual generation which had emerged in the 1880s, but a whole style of education. The platform lecture to hundreds, so well suited to handing down the message of a prophet, gave way to the small class engaged in close analysis of texts and concepts.[109]

Ruskin had offered a point of contact between intellectuals and the working class of a particular generation, in a period when one group had belatedly become aware of the ills of British society, and the other was gradually moving towards a sense of its separate political as well as social identity. Dissenting intellectuals were put in touch with communities which had developed a similar critique of existing economic and social relationships, and the essential similarity of outlook on both sides, and their common reliance on the authority of Ruskin, were sources of mutual confidence. This is why Ruskin proved so popular and useful a subject to the young graduates and dons involved in Oxford university extension. But by 1908, in the era of the Liberal welfare reforms, when concrete social and economic questions called for remedy, Ruskin was of diminished relevance. The tasks had changed to attention to the details and remedies of social deprivation on the one hand, and to the development of a political party to represent the labour interest on the other. As Stephen Yeo has argued, in the process of this transition, the spirit of an ethical and religious crusade against injustice was subordinated to the routine tasks of constructing institutions and winning elections.[110] Those engaged in building the Labour Party outside parliament had

[109] Goldman, *Dons and Workers*, 154–62.
[110] Stephen Yeo, 'A New Life: The Religion of Socialism in Britain, 1883–1896', *History Workshop Journal*, 4(1977), 5–56.

practical and organizational issues to address. Meanwhile, in parliament, those Labour MPs who had mentioned Ruskin in their responses to W. T. Stead in 1906 had now to consider the minutiae of legislation, and if Ruskin gave general moral guidance, he had nothing to contribute to those charged with governing a mass democracy. After all, Ruskin had deprecated democracy, and argued for the outright rejection of competitive capitalism, rather than its reform and regulation. For a Ruskinian, there could be no compromise, on a daily basis, with 'the laws of death' and 'the ethics of the dust'.

If we ask the question, what sort of political party and political response would we have expected to emerge from a movement influenced by Ruskin, then the answer might approximate to the kind of Labour Party which actually did emerge in the years after 1906: one that looked ill-prepared for the political tasks it faced. The party lacked a clear and separate identity, it lacked policy, and until 1914 was pulled along in the wake of Progressive Liberalism. Historians have generally explained this as a consequence of 'labourism': Labour MPs were essentially concerned to establish the case for the separate representation of labour and its interests; in many cases, their social instincts remained narrowly traditional. But it might also be argued that a movement taking Ruskin as an inspiration could be nothing else *but* unfit for parliamentary politics and policy formation. 'Is the Parliamentary Labour Party a Failure?' asked Ben Tillett as early as 1908.[111] In 1914 Beatrice Webb offered 'the cold truth . . . that the Labour Members have utterly failed to impress the House of Commons and the constituencies as a live force'. Among a leadership without direction and purpose, she noted in particular 'that dear, modest, dull but devotedly pious Socialist', Fred Jowett, who, on his own admission, had been so enthralled by Ruskin, and who was evidently out of his depth in parliamentary politics.[112]

Ruskin offered no guidance on social questions, therefore: arguably his political economy was also irrelevant. This is not to say it was wrong, nor that it could not be the origin of creative economic thinking. It is impossible to read *Unto This Last* at the end of the twentieth century without continuing to appreciate its point. And Hobson's luminous example shows just how fertile were Ruskin's distinctive principles and definitions. Rather, it is to recognize, as Hobson did himself, that Ruskin's principles were 'revolutionary' in intent and implications, and hence to

[111] Ben Tillett, *Is the Parliamentary Labour Party a Failure?* (London, 1908).
[112] *Beatrice Webb's Diaries 1912–1924*, ed. Margaret Cole (London, 1952), 23 (22 Apr. 1914).

note how unlike the early Labour Party that made them. A movement keen to establish its moderate credentials and show its respectability could hardly have embraced an ethical structure that, according to Hobson, offered 'no concessions, modifications or alleviations' to the existing economic system, and promised 'nothing short of a complete transformation of its structure'.[113]

But if not Ruskin, then what? As Elizabeth Durbin has argued, Labour had no economic theory nor usable economic policies before the mid-1930s: its tragedy was to take power in the 1920s without a coherent approach to the 'crises of capitalism' then underway, and hence to be 'caught between its long-term goal of overthrowing the system and its belief in the morality of sound finance, whatever the system'.[114] In such circumstances, its failure was almost inevitable. In moments of stress, indeed, Labour was forced back towards Ruskinian denunciation, and, as Skidelsky has argued for the period 1929–31, vacuous utopianism. Because 'there was no practical socialist economic policy, no theory of how to use Parliament for furthering socialist aims', in Skidelsky's words, MacDonald could only tell his party in 1930 as the economic system 'broke down', to 'go back to your socialist faith', and not to confuse that faith 'with pettifogging patching'.[115] Ruskin might have approved. But faith was no solution to mass unemployment, an overvalued currency and unbalanced budgets. As Skidelsky has contended, Labour 'was a parliamentary party with a Utopian ethic. It was not fit for the kind of power it was called upon to exercise.'[116]

The argument is emphatically *not* that Ruskin's influence—or the influence of other prophets of this period—prevented the development of an economic and social approach that was better adapted to the tasks of government: that Ruskin was a false prophet for a movement that had to make something of a flawed economic and social system as it found it. Rather, it is to suggest that Ruskin was influential at a stage when sections of the working class were developing a common consciousness based upon an ethical anticapitalism which was crucial to the emergence

[113] Hobson, 'Ruskin as Political Economist', 97–8.

[114] Elizabeth Durbin, *New Jerusalems: The Labour Party and the Economics of Democratic Socialism* (London, 1985), 53.

[115] Robert Skidelsky, *Politicians and the Slump: The Labour Government of 1929–1931* (London, 1967), 395, 241–2. MacDonald is quoted addressing the party conference at Llandudno on 7 Oct. 1930.

[116] Skidelsky, *Politicians and the Slump*, p. xii. It is not suggested that this is the only, or even the best way of understanding the Labour debacle of 1931. But this interpretation gains in credibility if Ruskin is accorded due influence over the formative Labour movement.

of a separate Labour interest. But after this stage there was no systematic attempt to go beyond Ruskinian critique and moralism, and develop an economic and social policy that could be applied to British society as it was. Ruskin was a prophetic figure whose message captured the imagination of intelligent working people for a generation. That message was spread by a variety of means, among which university extension from Oxford was peculiarly influential. But the succeeding generation had the far more difficult task of harnessing Ruskinian ethics to the practice of governing. In some senses, it has remained the dilemma of the left in Britain to this day.

4

'A Line of Absolute Correctness': Ruskin's Enlargements from Greek Vases and the Drawing Classes at Oxford

DONATA LEVI AND PAUL TUCKER

From 1853, when he gave his first public lectures in Edinburgh, to the 1870s, when Slade Professor of Fine Art at Oxford, Ruskin, like many lecturers prior to the advent of the slide projector, made use of manually enlarged images as visual aids.[1] More than fifty such images survive,[2] some clearly Ruskin's own work and some that of assistants such as George Allen and Arthur Burgess, while in many other cases they cannot be attributed to any specific hand. Further examples are known only from early photographs, taken by E. T. Cook and Alexander Wedderburn in the course of preparing the Library Edition of Ruskin's *Works*.[3]

Though all these enlarged images have traditionally been classified as lecture diagrams, some may well have had other uses, especially in the 1870s at Oxford. In this chapter we shall explore this possibility with regard to a group of ten enlargements of figures from Greek vase-paintings.[4]

---

[1] On the methods used to illustrate lectures in the 19th century, particularly by art-historians, see Trevor Fawcett, 'Visual Facts and the Nineteenth Century Art Lecture', *Art History*, 6 (1983), 442–60. On Ruskin's use of manually enlarged diagrams in particular, see D. Levi and P. Tucker, 'Testimonianze visive nelle conferenze di Ruskin: i *diagrams*', *Ricerche di Storia dell'Arte*, 51 (1993), 85–101, which not only relates it to the general historical context studied by Fawcett, but also examines its distinctive 'rhetoric' (frequently presented in contrasted pairs, Ruskin's diagrams accentuate his customary mode of arguing by binary oppositions).

[2] The majority are in the collections of the Ruskin Foundation at Lancaster and Brantwood, while others are held by the Ruskin Museum at Coniston, the Ruskin Gallery in Sheffield, and the Ashmolean Museum, Oxford.

[3] Also in the Ruskin Foundation (Ruskin Library, Lancaster), recently transferred from Bembridge (RF Photos 901–5, 919–23, 936).

[4] All ten belong to the Ruskin Foundation (Ruskin Library, Lancaster) (RF 0468–72, 3093–7).

These were copied from colour plates in the four-volume *Élite des monuments céramographiques: matériaux pour l'histoire des religions et des mœurs de l'antiquité*, by Charles Lenormant and Jules De Witte (Paris, 1844–61). Ruskin's own copy has survived,[5] and in a state which reveals its importance for his study and use of Greek myth and art at Oxford in the 1870s. Thoroughly underlined and annotated, it also contains two autograph tables in which he has reordered the images (originally grouped alphabetically by divinity) according to chronological and stylistic criteria.[6] In addition, Ruskin removed many of the plates from this copy and inserted them in the collection of examples which he compiled at Oxford for the use of his students. The first catalogue of the collection—the *Catalogue of Examples Arranged for Elementary Study in the University Galleries* (1870)—lists twenty-four plates from Lenormant and De Witte in the Standard Series, intended to illustrate 'standards of methods or school',[7] and seven in the Educational, for use in the teaching of drawing and consisting 'partly of examples to be copied; partly of examples for reference with respect to practical questions'.[8] The function of this particular group of images within the Educational Series was to illustrate the 'Greek treatment of ornamental line' (*Works* 21. 58).

Of the plates in the Standard, all survived into the Reference Series as catalogued in 1872,[9] but after this date three were permanently removed

[5] Ruskin Foundation (Ruskin Library, Lancaster). It may be the copy ordered from the bookseller F. S. Ellis in a letter of 25 Feb. 1870 (*Works* 37. 638). However, a later letter to Ellis, from Geneva, dated 5 May, shows that Ruskin had this copy returned to the publishers as too 'ill-executed' for use in the University 'Art Gallery' (*Works* 37. 638). He may therefore well have owned a copy before this, and was certainly acquainted with the work, since it is cited by Charles Newton, in an Appendix on 'Ancient Representations of Water' which he supplied at Ruskin's request for vol. i of *Stones of Venice* (*Works* 9. 460–9).

[6] The two tables are not easily deciphered, but seem to refer to plates in the second and third volumes only. Each comprises three lists of plate nos., in one case differentiated chronologically ('Early', 'Central', and 'Late'), with subdivisions relating to quality ('Rude', 'Fine', 'Base', 'Pure', 'Transitional', etc.), and in the other on the basis of technique, in particular of the respective colours (black and red) of figure and ground.

[7] *Works* 21. 9 n. The 24 plates were numbered S. 202 (2 pls.), S. 203 (2 pls.), S. 204 (2 pls.), S. 205 (2 pls.), S. 206 (2 pls.), S. 207 (2 pls.), S. 208 (3 pls.), S. 209 (2 pls.), S. 210 (2 pls.), S. 211 (3 pls.), S. 212 (1 pl.), and S. 220 (1 pl.).

[8] *Works* 21. 9 n. The plates were numbered Ed. 23D–23K.

[9] *Catalogue of the Reference Series, including temporarily the First Section of the Standard Series* (London, 1872). In this catalogue the Greek plates bear the same numbers as in the 1870 *Catalogue of Examples*. The Reference Series was subsequently renumbered. Ruskin also published catalogues of the Educational Series in 1871 and 1874 (2nd edn.) and of the Rudimentary in 1872. For the complex bibliographical history of these catalogues, and for the history and scope of the collection in general, see *Works* 21. xvii–lii, 5–7, 55–69, and 161–4; R. Hewison, *The Ruskin Collection at Oxford: The Rudimentary Series* (London, 1984); and id., *Ruskin and Oxford: The Art of Education* (Oxford, 1996), 19–33.

and one (or possibly two) moved to the Educational Series.[10] Of the seven in the 1870 Educational Series four had been permanently removed by 1874 and two of the surviving examples are now missing.[11] By 1874, the Educational Series included fourteen plates from Lenormant and De Witte, divided between Cases II (*Elementary Illustrations of Greek Design*) and VIII (*Elementary Zoology*). Four (or five) of these had been included in the 1870 *Catalogue of Examples*,[12] while the rest were new additions. One of these additional examples is also now missing.[13] As currently available for consultation at the Ashmolean Museum, Oxford, therefore, the Educational and Reference Series number eleven and twenty-one plates respectively. No plates from Lenormant and De Witte were placed in the last of the Series to be prepared, the Rudimentary, intended for practical use by the 'Town' as opposed to 'University' classes.[14]

Of the ten enlargements from Lenormant and De Witte, then, six only are from plates inserted at one period or another in the Standard/Reference and Educational Series.[15]

Everything does indeed suggest that they were prepared as lecture diagrams. Both in size and technique they closely resemble other enlarged images known to have been used by Ruskin as diagrams.[16] Nevertheless, there is no firm evidence that these enlargements were ever shown at lectures. On the other hand, there is some, albeit inconclusive, evidence

---

[10] The plate known to have been moved to the Educational Series is S. 220 ('Aphrodite Driving Poseidon'), which became Ed. 48. Another may have been S. 210 ('Zeus and Hera'), possibly the same as the plate currently numbered Ed. 44 ('Zeus and Hera with Dionysus and Hermes').

[11] The four permanently removed were Ed. 23D, 23E, 23F, and 23K (in the 1870 catalogue). The two now missing are Ed. 23H and 23G (Ed. 41 and 42 respectively in the 1874 catalogue). The latter was already missing in Cook and Wedderburn's time (see *Works* 21.78).

[12] Ed. 23H/41, 23G/42, 23I/46, S. 220/Ed. 48, and possibly S. 210/Ed. 44.

[13] Ed. 39.

[14] This does however include a photograph (Rud. 51) of a white-ground patera in the British Museum showing Aphrodite riding on a swan, of which an enlarged image also survives in the Ruskin Foundation (Ruskin Library, Lancaster) RF Add. A. 75). For the use of this image in lectures at Oxford see J. Clegg and P. Tucker, *Ruskin and Tuscany* (Sheffield, 1993), 141, and cats. 155 and 164.

[15] RF 3093 = S. 202/Ref. 184 (upper plate); RF 3094, 3096 = S. 204/Ref. 186 (upper plate, two images); RF 0472 = S. 205/Ref. 187 (upper plate); RF 0470 = S. 220/Ed. 48; and RF 3095 = Ed. 178.

[16] Executed in pencil, pen, and water-colour on paper laid on canvas, they measure up to 250 × 150 cm. The Ruskin Foundation (Ruskin Library, Lancaster) possesses comparable images certainly used for lectures at Edinburgh in 1853 (RF 0484, 0489), at the Architectural Museum in London the following year (RF 0474, 0475, 0478–82) and at the Royal Institution in 1861 (RF 0464–6, 0485, 0488, 3088).

that they were used in connection with the teaching of drawing at Oxford (which of course does not exclude their use as lecture aids).

Whatever their actual use, as *images* these enlargements from Greek vases are clearly related to an important shift in Ruskin's method of teaching drawing between the 1850s, when he held his first formal classes at the Working Men's College in London, and the 1870s. 'I never doubted or changed my system of teaching except in one comparatively unimportant particular—the use of outline,' he wrote in 1875 to Ebenezer Cooke, who had been his pupil at the Working Men's College and who had gone on to teach drawing there.[17] However, the change to which he offhandedly alludes was considerably more important than he apparently cared to admit in this letter, conflicting as it did with the insistence on mass which had been the basis of the method developed at the College and of the manual, *The Elements of Drawing* (1857).[18] These Greek enlargements allow us to focus on the moment when, following its gradual rehabilitation in the course of the 1860s, outline was established as both a practical and theoretical principle in Ruskin's teaching at Oxford.[19]

As mentioned earlier, there are no explicit references to any of these ten enlarged copies *as such* in the lectures given at Oxford in the 1870s, or in the lecture on Greek mythology given at University College, London, in 1869 and included in *The Queen of the Air*—at least, not in the texts of the lectures as published. Indeed, only five can in any way be matched with passages in these texts. Thus, one of the relevant

---

[17] London, Working Men's College, AF/75. The letter is one of a pair prompted by Cooke's public defence of Ruskin, whose method of teaching drawing had been attacked in the press by William Bell Scott, after portions of *Elements of Drawing* had been reprinted in R. St J. Tyrrwhitt's *Our Sketching Club* (see *Works* 15. 492).

[18] One reason for Ruskin's curiously casual tone may possibly have been his awareness of Cooke's own growing interest in outline as opposed to mass as an 'element' of drawing more suited to the natural interest shown by young children in whole forms, rather than rationally dissected parts of forms. Cooke was to develop this approach in pioneering essays on art-teaching and child psychology published in the 1880s, particularly in a paper entitled *Neglected Elements in Art Teaching* (1888), where in direct challenge to Ruskin's insistence on 'mass as the beginning, not outline', and indeed to the Ruskinian notion of the innocent eye, he writes, 'The child needs outline. Shall we insist that there are no outlines, only masses? and again, that lines have no breadth? Its lines must have breadth. The teacher's safest guide is the child; he must be led by it if he would lead. To assent to this theory is as common as it is to reject and oppose it in practice. It is to begin with the known. To line will soon be added mass or surface, if we allow such materials as colour or chalk. Solidity or thickness comes later' (4–5).

[19] This process is examined in detail in D. Levi and P. Tucker, *Ruskin didatta: il disegno tra disciplina e diletto* (Venice, 1997), ch. 6.

Lenormant and De Witte plates[20] is referred to in the published version of the University College lecture. Yet it is not clear from the text that any images were shown at the lecture itself. The reader is referred to Lenormant and De Witte by volume and plate number, and the images are described verbally (Pls. 1–2).[21] In the lecture on 'Light' from the inaugural series at Oxford (1870) the same plate is discussed, along with its companions in the Standard Series (*Works* 20. 145–7), including one showing Athena accompanied by two nymphs and a fawn, of which an enlarged copy also survives (Pl. 3).[22] From the published text it appears that the plates themselves were shown in the lecture room.[23]

[20] *Élite des monuments*, ii, Pl. CXV: two designs from the same vase, representing Apollo and Athena with Hermes respectively. It was placed by Ruskin in the Standard Series (S. 204/Ref. 186), where it is entitled 'Apollo, as the Solar Power; with Athena and Hermes, as the Morning Breeze and Morning Cloud' (*Works* 21. 49).

[21] *Works* 19. 340: 'In Plate cxv. of vol. ii., Lenormant, are given two sides of a vase, which in rude and childish way, assembles most of the principal thoughts regarding Athena in this relation [conception of Athena as air in its power over the sea]. In the first the sunrise is represented by the ascending chariot of Apollo, foreshortened; the light is supposed to blind the eyes, and no face of the god is seen. (Turner, in the Ulysses and Polyphemus sunrise, loses the form of the god in light, giving the chariot-horses only; rendering in his own manner, after 2,200 years of various fall and revival of the arts, precisely the same thought as the old Greek potter). He ascends out of the sea; but the sea itself has not yet caught the light. In the second design Athena as the morning breeze, and Hermes as the morning cloud, fly over the sea before the sun. Hermes turns back his head; his face is unseen in the cloud, as Apollo's in the light; the grotesque appearance of an animal's face is only the cloud-phantasm modifying a frequent form of the hair of Hermes beneath the back of his cap. Under the morning breeze, the dolphins leap from the rippled sea, and their sides catch the light.'

[22] *Élite des monuments*, i, Pl. LXXXI (S. 205/Ref. 187: 'Athena, as the Morning Breeze on the Hills, with Attendant Nymphs'). The enlarged copy (RF 0472) includes Athena and the fawn, but only one of the two nymphs.

[23] *Works* 20. 145: 'First (S. 204) you have Apollo ascending from the sea; thought of as the physical sunrise: only a circle of light for his head; his chariot horses, seen foreshortened, black against the day-break, their feet not yet risen above the horizon. Underneath is the painting from the opposite side of the same vase: Athena as the morning breeze, and Hermes as the morning cloud, flying across the waves before the sunrise. At the distance I now hold them from you, it is scarcely possible for you to see that they are figures at all, so like are they to the broken fragments of flying mist; and when you look close, you will see that as Apollo's face is invisible in the circle of light, Mercury's is invisible in the broken form of cloud: but I can tell you that it is conceived as reverted, looking back to Athena; the grotesque appearance of feature in the front is the outline of his hair.' In the large lecture theatre of the University Museum, where the inaugural course was given (see *Oxford University Gazette* for 8 Mar. 1870, 7), the enlargements (measuring between 90.9 and 229 cm. in height and between 121.5 and 183 cm. in width) would have been perfectly legible, whereas the plates would certainly not. There is no obvious explanation for the remark relating to the position of Hermes' head, which though indistinct is clearly not reverted, either in the plate or in the enlargement.

1. Apollo, enlarged from C. Lenormant and J. De Witte, *Élite des monuments céramographiques*, ii, Pl. CXV.

2. Athena and Hermes, enlarged from C. Lenormant and J. De Witte, *Élite des monuments céramographiques*, ii, Pl. CXV.

Of the other three enlargements which may in some way be matched with passages in Ruskin's lectures, one represents Scylla,[24] another Triptolemus,[25] and the third the birth of Athena (Pls. 5, 6, 11).[26] Yet though the iconography of Scylla is referred to in *The Queen of the Air* and again in *Val d'Arno*, no reference to a specific image is made in the texts (*Works* 19. 339–40; 23. 103); and while both the figure of Triptolemus and the myth of the birth of Athena are discussed in *Aratra Pentelici*, this instances and reproduces images from other vases.[27]

Again, the lack of specific references in the texts as published hardly proves that Ruskin did *not* use these enlargements to illustrate the lectures themselves. These clearly underwent a process of revision before publication, in the course of which explicit references to images displayed might be excluded or adapted for reference to the plates which substituted the diagrams or other visual aids shown in the lecture-room. Explicit references to *diagrams* in the published texts are rare and indirect. An example is the reference to Arthur Severn's enlarged copy of a photograph of the east door of the Baptistery in Pisa in *Val d'Arno* (Pl. 4).[28] To solve the question of whether these Greek enlargements were made to be shown at lectures would require a thorough comparison of the published texts with the available MSS, proofs, newspaper reports, and other relevant material. Cook and Wedderburn of course had access to much of this material, indeed in their footnotes they occasionally quote references to the showing of diagrams in the MSS.[29] It was probably often on this basis that they assumed that the 'large drawings' found

[24] RF 3095, enlarged from *Élite des monuments*, iii, Pl. XXXVI (Ed. 178 [1874]).

[25] RF 3093, enlarged from *Élite des monuments*, iii, Pl. XLIXA (S. 202/Ref. 184).

[26] RF 3097, enlarged from *Élite des monuments*, i, Pl. LV, not placed in any of the Series.

[27] For Triptolemus see *Works* 20. 243 and Pl. V ('Triptolemus in his Car', engraved by Arthur Burgess after *Élite des monuments*, iii, Pl. LXII, which was not included in any of the Series). For the birth of Athena, see *Works* 20. 245–8, fig. 8 (a woodcut by Burgess after *Élite des monuments*, i, Pl. LVI) and Pl. VI ('The Nativity of Athena', after *Élite des monuments*, i. Pl. LXVA [Ed. 43], originally cut by Burgess, recut by H. S. Ulrich for the Library Edition).

[28] *Works* 23. 87: 'Here is the door of the Baptistery at Pisa,' Ruskin writes, 'again by Mr Severn delightfully enlarged for us from a photograph'; and he adds in a note, 'Plate X is from the photograph itself; the enlarged drawing showed the arrangement of parts more clearly, but necessarily omitted detail which it is better here to retain.' The enlargement is one of those known only from a photograph (RF Photo. 903).

[29] See for example *Works* 12. 127 n., apropos of a pair of images, one from Claude's *Liber Veritatis* and the other from Turner's *Liber Studiorum*, shown at Edinburgh in 1853 and not included in the published text. The image from Turner (RF 0485) is one of the largest of the surviving enlargements (152 × 233.5 cm.).

3. Athena, with nymph and fawn, enlarged from detail of C. Lenormant and J. De Witte, *Élite des monuments céramographiques*, i, Pl. LXXXI.

4. A. Severn, East door of Baptistery, Pisa, enlarged from a photograph.

at Brantwood were used as lecture aids, and employed some of them as sources for additional illustrations to the Library Edition.[30]

In the absence of such a systematic study,[31] we can at least be certain that any references to these images in the published texts are explicitly to the original Lenormant and De Witte plates, and consequently either that references to the enlarged copies were cut when the texts of lectures were revised for publication, or else that Ruskin did not show them at his lectures.

What other uses, then, might these enlargements have had? One possibility is hinted at in the inscription in Ruskin's hand on the enlarged copy of the *Birth of Athena*, now illegible, but in part decipherable in the Cook and Wedderburn photographs: 'Delicious. Begin small A. . . .'[32] (Pl. 5) Could these be Ruskin's instructions for the copying of the image, of the kind to be found on so many drawings made for or by pupils from the 1840s onwards? Were the enlargements used or produced in the Oxford drawing classes?

Some of the original Lenormant and De Witte plates were certainly to be copied by the students. Both the 1870 *Catalogue of Examples* and the *Notes on the Educational Series* appended to the 1874 catalogue include instructions on how to copy figures and details in the plates. Thus, a note

---

[30] For instance, they reproduce an enlargement of a statue of Athena in the Museo Nazionale, Naples (RF 0467), which they found at Brantwood, to illustrate a passage in *The Queen of the Air* (*Works* 19. 306–7), in which Ruskin discusses the goddess's traditional attributes, but without referring to any particular representation of her. *Works* 21, fig. 1, on the other hand, a woodcut of Triptolemus appears to have been engraved directly from the original plate (*Élite des monuments*, iii, Pl. XLIXA), although a photograph of the enlargement (marked B. VI 5), annotated by Cook, has horizontal, vertical, and diagonal lines ruled over the image, apparently to show the area to be engraved (Pl. 6).

[31] Another problem relating to the use of the Greek enlargements as diagrams, is that they are as much as four times as large as the majority of the *surviving* enlarged images known to have been used at lectures given at Oxford, most of which are small enough to fit into the Reference Series cabinet frames, which measure 76.9 × 56.5 cm. (see Hewison, *Ruskin and Oxford*, cats. 64 and 65). For example, an enlargement by Burgess of a panel from the bronze doors of the church of San Zeno, Verona (Ref. 70), made for the *Aratra Pentelici* lectures (see Ruskin's note, *Works* 20. 215), measures 60 × 48 cm. There appear to have been exceptions, however. RF 0463, a diagram of a bird's wing and eight single feathers, a Cook and Wedderburn photograph of which (marked B. IV. 12) is inscribed '181 Rud' (a number in the Rudimentary Series never permanently filled by Ruskin) and 'For Loves Meinie Additional'. The use of such an unusually large diagram for this lecture series is nevertheless puzzling, as it was delivered (March 1873) in the Drawing School in the University Galleries, rather than in the large lecture theatre of the University Museum (*Oxford University Gazette*, 4/114 [4 Mar. 1873], 76). However, it is known that Ruskin also used 'enormously magnified' models of wing feathers at the same lectures. One of these is now at the Ruskin Museum, Coniston (see the catalogue to the 1964 Arts Council exhibition *Ruskin and his Circle*, cat. 203).

[32] RF Photo 932.

to Ed. 23D (1870), 'Apollo before the altar of Delphi', reads 'Outline the head and falling hair with pencil, wash the whole over with red, lay in the black with the brush, and put the ivy leaves on with opaque white' (*Works* 21. 63). Nor does this practice seem to have been limited to the plates in the Educational Series. Cook and Wedderburn state that Ruskin used a detail from a plate in the Standard Series, the wheel of Triptolemus' chariot (S. 202/Ref. 184) as a 'test of drawing' (*Works* 21. 47n.) (Pl. 6). A further indication of the interchangeability of the two series, is that (as we have seen) at least one plate, the 'Aphrodite Driving Poseidon' of which a detail exists as an enlargement,[33] was transferred from the Standard to the Educational Series (Pl. 12).

However, none of the instructions for copying the Lenormant and De Witte plates specifically require the student to enlarge the image. Indeed, there is no mention in any of the catalogues of the collection of the *practice of enlargement* as a drawing exercise, though many enlarged details from engravings and paintings were included among the most elementary exercises in the Educational Series. For example, in the original 1870 arrangement the 'first real exercise' (Ed. 3) was an enlarged (and slightly modified) outline, prepared by Ruskin himself, of the branch of laurel held by Apollo in a fifteenth-century Italian engraving from the series known as the *Tarocchi di Mantegna* (Pls. 7–8).[34] The purpose of copying the enlarged outline of laurel was the lesson 'that refinement in design does not depend on the minuteness or fineness of work, but on its precision and care'.[35]

---

33 RF 0470, enlarged from *Élite des monuments*, iii, Pl. XV (S. 220/Ed. 48).

34 The enlargement was preceded by a photograph of the head of St John the Baptist in a painting by Cima da Conegliano, not to be copied but to be looked at only, 'when you would be put in right temper for work' (*Works* 21. 104); and a drawing by Ruskin of a shoot of Rosa Canina, sketched 'merely that if you have any power of drawing already, you may try how far you can follow simple curves' (*Works* 21. 57). Ruskin owned a complete set of one of the versions of the *Tarocchi*, now thought to have been produced in Ferrara, rather than in Florence, as Ruskin believed. Thirty-two of the set were given to Oxford, and the remaining eighteen were bought by the Ashmolean Museum at one of the Sotheby's sales of the Ruskin estate in the 1930s.

35 *Works* 21. 109. Indeed, to ensure the maximum precision, students were not to copy Ruskin's enlarged outline directly, but a second outline (Ed. 3B.), prepared by Arthur Burgess, which also showed them how they were to 'measure all the rectilinear dimensions accurately' before proceeding to draw the contours, first in pencil and afterwards with the brush (*Works* 21. 58). Another interesting example, in view of the possible use of the Greek enlargements both in the lecture theatre and in the drawing class, is an enlarged sketch of some leaves from the background of Botticelli's *Spring* (Ed. 252 in the 1874 arrangement, measuring 26.67 × 39.37 cm.), known to have been shown in the first of the lectures on landscape, given 26 Jan. 1871 (see *Works* 22. 18–19).

5. The birth of Athena, enlarged from C. Lenormant and J. De Witte,
Élite des monuments céramographiques, i, Pl. LV.

6. Triptolemus, enlarged from C.
Lenormant and J. De Witte, *Élite
des monuments céramographiques*,
iii, Pl. XLIXA.

7. Apollo, engraving from the *Tarocchi di Mantegna*.

8. J. Ruskin, Laurel branch,
enlarged from Fig. 7.

9. A. Burgess, Chariot-race, from vase in British Museum.

Despite the lack of evidence that enlargement was actually practised by students attending Ruskin's drawing classes, we know that Ruskin had earlier contemplated or actually recommended the making of enlarged drawings or copies as a means of ensuring exactly the same qualities of precision and care, as distinct from mere minuteness of work, as he demanded of students at Oxford in copying the enlarged laurel branch. For example, in 1859, in a letter to Ellen Woods, a pupil at Winnington School, where Ruskin acted as drawing master until the mid-1860s, he expressed the wish that 'all Albert Durer's work were as large again as it is—with all the lines twice as thick'. Copying such enlarged lines would oblige the pupil to concentrate on getting 'the lines and gradations right' rather than 'faint or delicate'. For the truth which she was to aim for had nothing to do with size or fineness of work.[36] Two years later, in a letter to George Allen, Ruskin suggested enlarging from Turner etchings and drawing outlines of leaves, each half a foot long, both as practice in the preparation of lecture diagrams and as a corrective to the fine engraving work he was currently engaged in.[37] Again, in 1863 Ruskin advised another pupil, Lady Waterford, to enlarge a detail from a drawing by Holbein, but by squaring, not by guess.[38] Again, the emphasis was on

[36] *The Winnington Letters: John Ruskin's Correspondence with Margaret Alexis Bell and the Children at Winnington Hall*, ed. Van Akin Burd (Cambridge, Mass., 1969), 159. Cf. a slightly earlier letter to the headmistress, Miss Bell, in reply to the comment that the exercises in *Elements of Drawing* had overtired the girls' eyes: 'The remedy for this evil is however simple—I am very wrong not to have stated it more clearly. *Finish* is the statement of all possible truths about the thing:—it has nothing to do with *Scale*. If you magnified a Durer engraving a thousand times—it would be as good as it is now—though each line would be as thick as the bough of a tree' (ibid. 140).

[37] Letter dated Apr. 1861 by Cook and Wedderburn in their transcriptions of Ruskin's correspondence in the Bodleian Library (Bod. MS Eng. lett. c. 34, 302). Ruskin suggests some 'iron work sketches' of his own as models for the kind of large-scale drawing recommended. The phrase probably refers to three diagrams at Lancaster (RF 3090, 3091, 3098), showing details of Italian ironwork balconies, possibly from Verona and Brescia, and a detail of the ornamental trellis enclosing the tomb of Can Signorio in Verona, probably made for the lecture on 'The Work of Iron, in Nature, Art, and Policy', delivered at Tunbridge Wells on 16 Feb. 1858 and later published in *The Two Paths* (1859) (see *Works* 16. 392). They measure between 123.7 and 133.5 cm. in height and between 80.3 and 115.5 cm. in width. The Ruskin Foundation also possesses a large drawing (101 × 193 cm.) of a lilac branch by Allen (RF 0011), prepared for *Modern Painters*, v. Pl. 58. A diagram known to be by Allen is one representing the gable over the south door of St Wulfran, Abbéville, now in the Ruskin Museum, Coniston, and measuring 85 × 54 cm. It was prepared for the lecture on the *Flamboyant Architecture of the Somme*, given at the Royal Institution in 1869, and is included in the catalogue of works exhibited on that occasion (*Works* 19. 277, no. 50 and Pl. XIII).

[38] Cf. Ruskin's remark to another pupil of this period, Anna Blunden, apropos of some lecture diagrams for which she was to prepare drawings: enlargement, he warned, 'must always be done mathematically by squaring' *Sublime & Instructive: Letters from John*

rightness. 'Be sure you are right,' he insisted, 'and finish it in black, so as to leave no blots—no uncertain lines—no careless shadows.'[39]

Once more, it must be admitted that the fact that other enlargements were given by Ruskin to students to copy, or that the practice of making large-scale drawings or enlarged copies was sometimes recommended by him, does not constitute conclusive proof that the Greek enlargements were used or produced in Ruskin's drawing classes.[40] Perhaps the most convincing evidence in favour of this hypothesis is provided by the extremely uneven quality of the enlargements themselves. These have generally been assumed to be the work either of Ruskin himself or of an assistant, such as Arthur Burgess.[41] However, on close inspection, and especially on comparison with the original plates, some prove to be surprisingly inaccurate and clumsily executed, apparently enlarged by guess rather than by measurement (Pls. 10–11). They are generally far less precise than copies of figures from Greek vases made by Ruskin himself or by Burgess. A copy by the latter (Ed. 23/49) of the figure of a charioteer from a black-figure vase in the British Museum (Pl. 9) makes an interesting comparison with the enlargements. This *Chariot-race* headed the sequence of plates from Lenormant and De Witte in the 1870 arrangement, where it was presented as a 'standard to you of good execution in the early vases', but 'a little too difficult, however, for you to copy' (*Works* 21. 120 n). The difficulty had to do with a peculiarity of vases of this style, in which the lines internal to the mass of the figures, painted in black on the red clay, are incised through the paint to reveal the ground. A note in the 1874 catalogue advises less advanced students of a method of copying similar figures which avoids the problems entailed in simulating this procedure in a drawing made on paper. It reads,

Ruskin to Louisa Marchioness of Waterford, Anna Blunden and Ellen Heaton, ed. Virginia Surtees (London, 1975), 133.

[39] Ibid. 57. The use of enlargements prepared as lecture diagrams as aids in the teaching of drawing may have had an early precedent in Ruskin's work at the Architectural Museum, London, in 1854. Enlarged copies of medieval illuminated initials shown at his lecture on outline, given in November of that year, were left at the Museum for 'inspection', with a view to their 'practical' application by ornamentalists and sign-painters etc. (*Works* 12. 499).

[40] Another reason why it is not possible to suppose a strict analogy in function between the Greek enlargements and examples in the Educational Series such as the enlarged outline of laurel is that the former are considerably larger than the latter, far too large in fact to fit into the frames (52.5 × 37.2 cm.) of the cabinets that housed the Series (see *Ruskin and Oxford*, cat. 68), while there is no record of any such images having been hung on the walls of the Drawing School among other 'outsize' works such as Ruskin's copy of Luini's *St Catherine* (see ibid. cat. 19).

[41] See Hewison, *Ruskin and Oxford*, 77.

10. Scylla, colour plate from C. Lenormant and J. De Witte, *Élite des monuments céramographiques*, iii, Pl. XXXVI.

11. Scylla, enlarged from C. Lenormant and J. De Witte, *Élite des monuments céramographiques*, iii, Pl. XXXVI.

A careful drawing by Mr. Burgess, which will show you that all these engravings can be copied by pen and pencil, if you choose. But it is terribly difficult to leave the white lines, as in this drawing, between two delicate black ones, afterwards filling in the field in black. The white lines on Greek vases are incised; and it will be good practice, if you are not skilled enough to leave them clear, to lay the black field first, and draw the white lines with body-white. (*Works* 21. 120)

This is the method adopted in the majority of the enlargements from black-figure vases, in which the fine incised red lines on the vase, represented as such in the Lenormant and De Witte plates (the original lines are 'white' only by contrast with the surrounding black masses), are translated as positively drawn lines in thick white body-colour (Pl. 12). A notable exception, and certainly the finest of the group, represents Athena in a chariot and a fallen giant (Pl. 13),[42] where the lines within the black masses seem to have been produced 'negatively' and are as delicate as those in the drawing by Burgess. However, the fact that the majority of the enlargements follow the alternative method is a strong indication that some, if not all these enlargements may have been produced by pupils attending drawing classes at Oxford, possibly even after Ruskin himself had ceased to supervise them personally.

If it is not at present possible to be more definite about the Greek enlargements' use, more can be said about why these particular images should have made suitable models for Ruskin's students to copy.

Their primary significance was of course as illustrations of Greek myths. Thus, the plates from Lenormant and De Witte in the 1870 Standard Series were placed in pairs or triplets of 'early' and 'late' representations of the same deities, principally, as he explained in the inaugural lectures, deities of light (*Works* 20. 142, 145). This arrangement was intended to illustrate important changes in the Greek conception of deity, entailing the transformation of 'vital embodiments' of physical forces into 'personal intelligences, capable of every phase of human passion' (*Works* 20. 47). Yet Ruskin characteristically stresses the changes in technique accompanying this development, and it is this aspect on which we shall concentrate here. The changes of technique in question regard the matter of outline and the different means used to produce it in the different phases. In the early, 'black-figure' style the figures are outlined by incision, as we saw earlier, then filled with black paint, and the inner lines indicating muscles and drapery are scratched through to the red clay. In the later, 'red-figure' style, the contours of the figures are still

---

[42] RF 0468, enlarged from *Élite des monuments*, i, Pl. XI.

12. Aphrodite, enlarged from C. Lenormant and J. De Witte, *Élite des monuments céramographiques*, iii, Pl. XV.

13. Athena, enlarged from C. Lenormant and J. De Witte, *Élite des monuments céramographiques*, i, Pl. XI.

incised, but then enclosed with a broad black band of paint, subsequently extended over the whole background, and the inner lines are
now painted. According to Ruskin, this new principle opens the way to
less refined and conscientious work. For while it is hard to thicken an incised line, and this guarantees the 'severity and fineness of style in the
drawing', the 'outlining of the figures with a broad band gradually induced carelessness in contour, while also the lines of drapery, etc., being
now painted, became coarse if too quickly laid (the incised line, on the
contrary, might be hasty and wrong, but was always delicate)'. However,
despite this seed of decadence latent in the style, Ruskin finds the 'best
vases . . . those with light [i.e. red] figures on black ground', though he
concludes that 'the best field for general study will be found in vases with
black figures of the most refined epoch'.[43]

This interest in the drawing technique used on Greek vases was
reflected in Ruskin's teaching of drawing at Oxford, where the meticulous distinctions between styles and periods resolved themselves into a
new emphasis on the 'Greek' use of the brush as a drawing instrument.[44]
In a letter to Charles Eliot Norton, written immediately after the close of
his inaugural course of lectures, he writes: 'I have started them [the
Oxford students] on a totally new and defiantly difficult principle—
drawing all with the brush—as on Greek vases,—and I'm choosing a
whole series of the Greek Gods old and young, for them to draw every
detail of with the brush—as the Greeks, did.'[45] The reference is clearly
to the sequence of plates from Lenormant and De Witte in the Standard
and Educational Series. This private remark is matched by statements in
the inaugural lectures themselves, regarding the specific technique which
Ruskin intended the students to adopt at the start of their practical study
of art: 'from the very beginning,' he tells them, 'you shall try to draw a
line of absolute correctness with the point, not of pen or crayon, but of
the brush, as Apelles did, and as all coloured lines are drawn on Greek
vases. A line of absolute correctness, observe . . . the one thing I ask of

43 *Works* 21. 48–9. One of the examples of the latter class given by Ruskin is S.220/Ed.
48 ('Aphrodite Driving Poseidon') (Pl. 12).

44 Much earlier, when about to start teaching at the Working Men's College in 1854,
Ruskin had contemplated the use of the brush and pure outline as an elementary technique, but had rejected the idea in favour of a mixed technique (pen and wash) based on the
mezzotints in the *Liber Studiorum*. See letter to George Richmond, 10 Oct. [1854?] (Bod.
MS. Eng. lett. c. 33, 339): 'Do you think people could learn to draw with the brush from the
beginning? I mean to draw all *lines* with the brush—a quarter of an inch thick? rather than
with chalk or pencil!' Cf. *Works* 36. 181.

45 Letter of 26 Mar. 1870, in *The Correspondence of John Ruskin and Charles Eliot
Norton*, ed. J. L. Bradley and I. Ousby (Cambridge, 1987), 185.

you is, that the line shall be right' (*Works* 20. 132). The brush is in fact systematically used for outlining forms in the most elementary exercises in the Educational Series (such as the enlarged outline of the laurel branch mentioned earlier).

Behind this novel insistence on the use of the brush as a didactic principle is the revaluation of line, of which the remarks to Ellen Woods and the exercises recommended to Allen and Lady Waterford are early symptoms, dating from a period in which Ruskin was beginning to rethink the basic principles of his teaching as laid down in *Elements of Drawing*. The primary emphasis here, as in the classes at the Working Men's College, was on light and shade and delicacy of gradation. This approach was encapsulated in the 'test' required of all new students at the College, who had to draw a white plaster or leather ball suspended by a string. As William Ward later recalled, the instructions were 'to draw exactly' what they saw, 'making no line but merely shading the paper where [they] saw shade' (*Works* 36. lviii–lix). It was practical experiments of this kind which led to the formulation of the famous doctrine of the 'innocence of the eye' in *Elements of Drawing*, and to other statements in the book concerning the absence of outlines in nature and 'mystery' as one of the basic conditions of human sight.[46]

Though *Elements of Drawing* did include preliminary exercises in line drawing as a test of 'accuracy of eye' and discipline of hand (*Works* 15. 15) and though the general optical theory proposed to the students at Oxford in the inaugural lectures remains that first put forward in the manual, line now acquires a new status.[47] For from a more theoretical point of view it is recognized as one (logically and historically the primary) of the three basic elements in the language of art, the others being light and colour. All art begins in line and advances to full representation by following one of these two routes. Thus, in a first phase of development, the 'School of Light' modifies the archaic line in accordance with a peculiar susceptibility to light, while the 'School of Colour' does so in accordance with an antithetical fascination with colour. This historical scheme had precise practical implications, and Ruskin told his students that their study of drawing would follow the historical course:

[46] See for example *Works* 15. 33 n. [Ruskin's note], 74.

[47] The new value put on line is also detected in the unprecedented emphasis on the *shape* of the elementary 'units' of ocular perception: 'all objects appear to the human eye simply as masses of colour of variable, depth, texture, and outline' (*Works* 20. 122). Cf. the original statement of the doctrine in *Elements of Drawing* (*Works* 15. 27): 'Everything that you can see in the world around you, presents itself to your eyes as only an arrangement of patches of different colours variously shaded.'

I wish you to begin by getting command of line, that is to say, by learning to draw a steady line, limiting with absolute correctness the form or space you intend to limit; to proceed by getting command over flat tints, so that you may be able to fill the spaces you have enclosed, evenly, with shade or colour, according to the school you adopt; and finally to obtain the power of adding such fineness of gradation within the masses, as shall express their roundings, and their characters of texture. (*Works* 20. 128–9)

Nor had the revaluation of line yet reached its furthest point of development. Indeed, within this scheme, Greek vase-painting itself is not presented as a product of the archetypal linear schools but of the 'School of Light' (one of the reasons for which this is also called the 'School of Clay'). Ruskin's theoretical and historical scheme of art was later to be revised, and line, light, and colour presented not as variously combined elements in a complex process of development, but as the means of expression chosen by three universal schools of art, defined in the lectures on engraving, given in November and December 1872 and later published as *Ariadne Florentina*, as the Delineators, Chiaroscurists, and Colourists (*Works* 22. 311). Line was thereby freed of any dependence on mass or gradation.

Though less radical from this point of view, the inaugural lectures of 1870 express a substantial shift in emphasis in favour of line with respect to Ruskin's earlier teaching. How had this come about? The attempt to isolate the primary elements of artistic *production* had its origins five years earlier in a series of articles published in the *Art Journal*.[48] These essays represented a new beginning after five years' public silence on the subject of art, determined by a variety of largely personal motives. Ruskin was resolved to find a new basis on which to build, not only privately but collectively, setting out to reform national attitudes to art by inviting professional artists to join him in an attempt to identify and formulate once and for all the principles underlying artistic practice and judgement. It was necessary to provide the public with criteria enabling them to deal with the surfeit of images available to them, especially in the form of engravings. The articles in the *Art Journal* also demonstrate Ruskin's renewed interest in the question of elementary instruction in art (a question explicitly addressed in his contribution to a volume

---

[48] *Works* 19. 49–159. The articles were published at monthly intervals from January to July 1865 and from January to March 1866. The series was then interrupted a second time and never completed. Ruskin reprinted large portions of two of the articles in *The Queen of the Air*. These were excluded from the volume *The Cestus of Aglaia*, published in 1885.

edited by Thomas Acland in 1859 on the proper place of art in a new scheme for regulating middle-class education).⁴⁹

The search for fixed principles thus practically involved the question of where English boys and girls were to begin their study of drawing. Ruskin asserted that most authorities said that this should commence with outline, characteristically glossing over a novelty in his own thinking and passing it off as general consensus (though he could hardly do otherwise given the specific aims in view). In any case, his own mind was by this date probably made up. In 1859 in a lecture at Bradford he had hinted (though with some reservation) at the possibility of basing an elementary course in drawing on 'a truly intelligent practice of conventional drawing, such as that of the Egyptians, Greeks, or thirteenth century French, which consists in the utmost possible rendering of natural form by the fewest possible lines'.⁵⁰ But he had had to admit that the experiment was as yet 'untried'. In 1865 he was evidently ready to try it. Outline was now valued not only because intelligent and economical but also for its moral qualities. The 'black' or pen outline in particular was 'simple and open-hearted'. Still more than the soft chalk or lead outline, it represented the radical cure wanted, a safeguard against error, confusion, and despondency:

> My own idea of an elementary outline is that it should be unvaried; distinctly visible; not thickened towards the shaded sides of the objects; not express any exaggeration of aerial perspective, nor fade at the further side of a cup as if it were the further side of a crater of a volcano; and therefore, in objects of ordinary size, show no gradation at all, unless where the real outline disappears, as in soft contours and folds. Nay, I think it may even be a question whether we ought not to resolve that the line should never gradate itself at all, but terminate quite bluntly! (*Works* 19. 69)

However, if Ruskin was decided on the choice of the black or pen outline as the first step in the elementary teaching of art, he was still uncertain over what outline might be used to draw at this stage, pleading a lack of models: 'For there are no examples whatever of pure outlines by the great masters.'⁵¹

⁴⁹ *Some Account of the Origin and Objects of the New Oxford Examinations for the Title of Associate in Arts and Certificates for the Year 1858* (London, 1858). Ruskin's contribution is reprinted in *Works* 16. 449–54.

⁵⁰ 'Modern Manufacture and Design', later published in *The Two Paths* (*Works* 16. 330).

⁵¹ *Works* 19. 70: 'They are always touched or modified by inner lines, more or less suggestive of solid form, and they are lost or accentuated in certain places, not so much in conformity with any explicable law, as in expression of the master's future purpose, or of what

His study of Greek mythology in the years between the publication of these articles and his appointment as Slade Professor enabled Ruskin to fill this gap with images from Greek vases, if not the early drawings of great masters, nevertheless the noble early efforts of a great tradition. A hint that Ruskin was already moving in this direction in 1865 is given in a passage from one of the *Art Journal* articles in which he imagines his 'discomfiture' in the face of the ingenuously inappropriate demands made by prospective pupils regarding the subjects on which the mandatory black outline was to be exercised: one asks for an outline of a wasp's leg, or if not its leg at least its banded body, another for one of a white snail-shell and a third for one of a horse. These objects are either too minute, too dependent on surface pattern, or too complex to be managed in severe black outline, even by the master himself.[52] So what is to be done for these pupils? What Ruskin would 'like' to do for them, he says, is to

> show them an enlarged black outline, nobly done, of the two sides of a coin of Tarentum, with that fiery rider kneeling, careless, on his horse's neck, and reclined on his surging dolphin, with the curled sea lapping round them; and then to convince my boys that no one . . . could draw a horse like that without learning;—that for poor mortals like us there must be sorrowful preparatory stages; and, having convinced them of this, set them to draw (if I had a good copy to give them) a horse's hoof, or his rib, or a vertebra, or his thunder-clothed neck, or any other constructive piece of him. (*Works* 19. 68–9)

Only a few years later Ruskin would advise the students of the South Lambeth Art School to take coins such as this 'as a first . . . teacher' in their practical study of art. 'Learn to draw carefully from Greek work,'

he wishes immediately to note in the character of the objects. Most of them are irregular memoranda, not systematic elementary work: of those which are systematized, the greater part are carried far beyond the initiative stage; and Holbein's are nearly all washed with colour . . .' Cf. Ruskin's letter to George Richmond of November 1854 (*Works* 36. 181) and *Lectures on Art* (*Works* 20. 131).

[52] This position has been modified in *Lectures on Landscape* (*Works* 22. 23–4): 'The outline of any simple solid form, even though it may have complex parts, represents an actual limit, accurately to be followed. The outline of a cup, of a shell, or of an animal's limb, has a determinable course, which your pen or pencil line either coincides with or does not. You can say of that line, either it is wrong or right . . . But the greater number of objects in a landscape either have outlines so complex that no pencil could follow them (as trees in middle distance), or they have no actual outline at all, but a gradated and softened edge; as, for the most part, clouds, foam, and the like.' By this time, moreover, the Educational Series already included outlines from shells, if in the same passage Ruskin refers to the 'examples of shell outline in your copying series' (Ed. 191 and 193 in the 1874 arrangement), intended to make the students feel 'the exact nature of a pure outline, the difficulty of it, and the value.' Cf. also *Works* 28. 524–5.

he urged. But the specific qualities and lessons stressed ('Learn . . . above all to place forms correctly, and to use light and shade tenderly') (*Works* 19. 419) show the essentially sculptural significance of the work in question and by implication the dominance of chiaroscurist criteria in Ruskin's reading of early Greek art at this date. If our hypothesis is correct, before Ruskin was in a position to apply the novel idea of using an 'enlarged black outline' of a figure from ancient Greek art in the elementary teaching of drawing (suggested in the *Art Journal* largely for rhetorical effect and as a barely practicable ideal), the pen had to be replaced by the brush and the coin by the lines and 'flat' tints of the vase, enhanced through their reproduction in still more purely two-dimensional colour plates.

5

Goddesses of Instruction and Desire: Ruskin and Music

DELIA DA SOUSA CORREA

Throughout his work, Ruskin used musical vocabulary to discuss the visual arts and language, calling colour and form, for instance, 'the musical elements of the arts relating to sight'.[1] In *Elements of English Prosody* (1880), Ruskin revised the definition of poetry at which he had arrived in *Modern Painters* to make it 'the presentiment, *in musical form*, to the imagination . . . of noble grounds for the noble emotions'.[2] Such musical analogies are clearly not without significance in relation to Ruskin's own art. 'Rhythmic' and 'melodious' are terms which readily come to mind when attempting to describe the qualities of his writing. His exploitation of the musical lexicon in his aesthetic and social criticism also makes a specific contribution to the synaesthetic richness of Ruskin's language. His writing was experienced as overwhelmingly 'musical' by at least one of his contemporaries. George Eliot's review of the third volume of *Modern Painters* praised him (in terms closely echoed in the passage from Ruskin's lecture quoted below) for a '*voice* that can thrill the audience and take possession of their souls'.[3]

Ruskin's works are permeated by such assertions of music's paramount aesthetic and moral importance. Despite this, his writing about music has been little considered to date.[4] Ruskin repeatedly alludes to

---

[1] *Works* 20. 209. See also 6. 325, 12. 490, 16. 424, 36. 92–3.

[2] *Works* 31. 351. See also 5. 28.

[3] George Eliot, review of *Modern Painters*, vol. iii, *Westminster Review*, 9 (Apr. 1856) 625–33, 627.

[4] The singer Augusta Mary Wakefield, whom Ruskin heard perform, edited a collection of his writings on music during Ruskin's lifetime, *Ruskin on Music* (London, 1894). W. G. Collingwood's essay on 'Ruskin's Music' in *Good Words* (Oct. 1902), 684–90 describes the part which music played in Ruskin's life. More recently, an article by William J. Gatens, 'John Ruskin and Music', *Victorian Studies*, 30.1 (1986), 77–97, gives a useful survey of some of Ruskin's comments on music throughout his career, but does not extensively discuss these in relation to other areas of Ruskin's thought or to the contemporary context.

music as the most inherently moral of the arts. Indeed, in his 1870 lecture on 'The Relation of Art to Morals', the test of any sentiment lay in whether it could be set to music since 'A maiden may sing of her lost lover, but a miser cannot sing of his lost money':

And with absolute precision, from highest to lowest, *the fineness of the possible art is an index of the moral purity and majesty of the emotion it expresses* . . . Question with yourselves respecting any feeling that has taken strong possession of your mind, 'Could this be sung by a master and sung nobly, with a true melody and art?' Then it is right feeling. Could it not be sung at all, or only sung ludicrously? It is a base one (*Works* 20. 74).

The 'right moral state' which Ruskin famously declared as essential to art at the beginning of this 1870 lecture is directly exemplified, as Harold Bloom has stressed, by the 'pure gladness' of the singing skylark rather than by compliance with conventional ethics.[5] However, as the miser incapable of singing for his lost riches illustrates, human music in this lecture is explicitly the 'expression of joy or grief of noble persons for right causes' (*Works* 20. 73–4). During the decade following, Ruskin's comments on music arise in the context of increasingly active social concerns. Notwithstanding its incorporation into his particular fusion of aesthetic and moral theory, Ruskin's writing about music invokes a more conventionally understood morality than Bloom's account would suggest. Whether his own art exemplifies this morality is of course open to question.

The 1870s is an interesting decade for the exploration of music's role in Ruskin's work, in particular its relevance to his ideas about education. With music, as with other areas of his thought, this was a period when Ruskin increasingly sought to give concrete expression to his theoretical convictions. In addition to writing repeatedly about music education, Ruskin invested considerable time in his own musical training.[6] Music continued to provide an important source of analogy for the other arts in his writing, as is affirmed in his redefinition quoted above of poetry in musical terms. This chapter investigates the importance of music within Ruskin's educational projects of the 1870s. It compares his views on the art with those of some of his contemporaries and briefly considers the significance of music for Ruskin's ideas about language and for his own poetic practice.

---

[5] *Works* 20. 73. See *The Literary Criticism of John Ruskin*, ed. Harold Bloom (New York, 1987), p. xvii.
[6] See Collingwood, 'Ruskin's Music', 685.

In his 1877 *Fors Clavigera* letter 'Heavenly Choirs' (82) Ruskin comments that:

the action of the devilish or deceiving power is in nothing shown quite so distinctly among us at this day, not even in our commercial dishonesties, or social cruelties, as in its having been able to take away music as an instrument of education altogether, and to enlist it almost wholly in the service of superstition on the one hand, and of sensuality on the other. (*Works* 29. 244)

Ruskin refers his readers back to an almost identical passage in *Time and Tide* and announces that he is finally embarking on the project which he had promised to undertake in that work (*Works* 17. 368–9). His mission is no less than to reclaim music 'as an instrument of education'. *Fors* 95 shows Ruskin still adamant that 'No greater benefit could be conferred on the upper as well as the lower classes of society than the arrangement of a grammar of simple and pure music, of which the code should be alike taught in every school in the land' (*Works* 29. 500). In *Rock Honeycomb*, published in the same year as the 'Heavenly Choirs' letter, Ruskin affirms music's primary role in education, proclaiming that:

not to be able to sing should be more disgraceful than not being able to read or write. For it is quite possible to lead a virtuous and happy life without books, or ink; but not without wishing to sing, when we are happy; nor without meeting with continual occasions when our song, if right, would be a kind service to others. (*Works* 31. 108)

To sing may be of more fundamental importance than to write, but this does not mean that Ruskin consistently argues for the superiority of music over verbal language. Also in *Rock Honeycomb*, Ruskin conducts a lengthy footnote debate with a correspondent who has written to him insisting on the independent power of music, unassociated with words. To the assertion that 'to a musician, no words could express so much as [Bach's] music does', Ruskin retorts:

In the instance given by my friend, the music of Bach would assuredly put any disagreeable piece of business out of his head, and prepare him to listen with edification to the sermon, better than the mere *repetition* of the words 'Dona nobis pacem.' But if he ever had needed peace, and had gone into church really to ask for it, the plain voices of the congregation, uttering the prayer but once, and meaning it, would have been more precious to him than all the quills and trills that ever musician touched or music trembled in. (Works 31. 111–12 n.)

Ruskin himself was a keen attender of the opera and concerts and his diaries for the 1870s also mention visits to Oxford chapels to hear liturgical music.[7] Nonetheless, he undeniably responded more intensely to visual and verbal forms of expression. Granted this verbal primacy, it is particularly interesting to consider the ways in which music took on so much more than metaphorical or conceptual significance in his work.

During the 1870s, Ruskin provides increasingly exact directions for how music is to be utilized. Much of this instruction emerges in the context of his educational programme for the proposed Guild of St George. Music features prominently in his vision of the form of life and education he wishes to support under the Guild. He introduces this in *Fors* 5 as a state of peaceful self-sufficiency in which 'We will have some music and poetry; the children shall learn to dance to it and sing it;—perhaps some of the old people, in time, may also' (*Works* 27. 96).

In issuing his prescriptions for proper musical training, Ruskin draws on ideas established in his previous works, particularly the distinction between 'exalting' and 'corrupting' music. In his 1867 lecture on *The Relation of National Ethics to National Arts*, this is 'expressed by the contest between Apollo and Marsyas, and between the Muses and the Sirens' (*Works* 19. 177; 17. 212–15). The Muses are the 'Goddesses of Instruction', as opposed to the Sirens, who are 'Goddesses of Desire' (*Works* 19. 178; 17. 211–12). Music, 'the most effective of all instruments of moral instruction' becomes 'in the failure and betrayal of its functions . . . the subtlest aid of moral degradation' (*Works* 19. 176). Ruskin also discusses the opposition of 'music in her two powers' in *The Queen of the Air* (1869) defining 'Music . . . in her health' as 'the teacher of perfect order' and 'the voice of the obedience of angels' whilst 'in her depravity she is also the teacher of perfect disorder and disobedience' (*Works* 19. 344; 19. 78–81). Education (instruction) is thus inherent to true music.

In *Fors* 82 and 83, Ruskin develops an extended discussion of Plato's teaching as his major authority on the subject of music, quoting Plato's prescription that 'the first education must be by the Muses and Apollo'.[8] Ruskin explains how he has derived the terminology for his distinction between Apollonian and Sirenic musical powers from the Greek opposition of the Muses and Amusia, insisting that 'sirenic' is the adjective which properly emerges from 'Amusia':

[7] See for example *The Diaries of John Ruskin*, 3 vols., ed. Joan Evans and John Howard Whitehouse (Oxford, 1956–9), ii. 769.

[8] *Works* 29. 238. See also Ruskin's diary entry for 27 May, written as he was planning these letters, in which he expresses the hope that he will successfully develop his earlier comments on music in *Time and Tide* in the light of his further study of Plato, *Diaries*, iii. 955.

the Greeks only called 'Music' the kind of sound which induced right moral feeling . . . and any other kind of sound than that, however beautiful to the ear or scientific in composition, they did not call 'Music' (exercise under the Muses), but 'Amusia,'—the denial, or desolation for want, of the Muses . . . The Greek himself, however, did not express his idea fully in language, but only in myth. His 'amusia' does not mean properly the opposing delightfulness, but only the interruption, and violation, of musical art. The proper word for the opposed delightful art would have been 'sirenic'. (*Works* 29. 261–2)

Ruskin's writing about music during the 1870s participates in what Dinah Birch calls 'the complex association between education, religion, and myth in Ruskin's mature work'.[9] In *Fors Clavigera*, his advocacy of music education combines allusions to myth and classical theory with invocations of biblical authority. *Fors 82* reminds his readers that in *Time and Tide* he had promised:

that, after explaining, as far as I know it, the significance of the parable of the Prodigal Son . . . I should 'take the three means of human joy therein stated, fine dress, rich food, and music, and show you how these are meant all alike to be sources of life and means of moral discipline, to all men, and how they have all three been made by the devil the means of guilt, dissoluteness, and death'. (*Works* 29. 244)

'This promise', Ruskin confesses, 'I have never fulfilled, and after seven years am only just coming to the point of it':

Which is, in few words, that to distribute good food, beautiful dress, and the practical habit of delicate art, is the proper work of the fathers and mothers of every people . . . and that only by *direct* doing of these three things can they now act beneficently or helpfully to any soul capable of reformation. (*Works* 29. 244–5)

This is clearly directed at underpinning the general tenets declared in *Fors 67*, that 'The first duty of government is to see that the people have food, fuel, and clothes' and 'The second, that they have means of moral and intellectual education' (*Works* 28. 651). After exhorting his audience to take responsibility for a fairer distribution of food and clothing, Ruskin continues: 'and you who can sing and play on instruments, hang your harps on the pollards above the rivers you have poisoned, or else go down among the mad and vile and deaf things whom you have made, and put melody into the soul of them,—else you are no Christians' (*Works* 29. 245).

9 Dinah Birch, *Ruskin's Myths* (Oxford, 1988), 4.

Ruskin particularly objects to the appropriation of music as a commodity for the rich when they should be using it as a tool of education to illuminate the lives of the poor. In *Fors* 83, Ruskin therefore classes oratorio and opera amongst the music of the sirens:

this cry of the wild beasts of the islands, or sirenic blasphemy, has in modern days become twofold; consisting first in the mimicry of *devotion* for pleasure, in the oratorio, withering the life of religion into dead bones on the siren-sands; and secondly, the mimicry of *compassion*, for pleasure, in the opera, wasting the pity and love which should overflow in active life, on the ghastliest visions of fictitious grief and horriblest decoration of simulated death.[10]

Examples of music-inspired depravity amongst the poor are characterized as relatively innocent besides that of their social superiors. They may occasionally be found: 'Waltzing, drunk, in the country roads by our villages' yet they are 'innocently drunk, and sleepy at sunset; not like their born masters and teachers, dancing, wilfully, the cancan of hell, with harlots, at seven in the morning'.[11] This outburst, in *Fors* 57, characteristically concludes with Ruskin stressing music's crucial educational function, debased (like the harlot) once it becomes a commodity for the socially privileged: 'At present, you keep the dancing to yourselves, and graciously teach *them* the catechism. Suppose you were to try for a little while learning the catechism yourselves; and teaching *them*— to dance?' (*Works* 28. 406).

Whether popular revelry was relatively innocent or not, Ruskin's prescriptions for musical education endorse the principles which he emphasized as fundamental to education in general. 'Moral education begins in making the creature to be educated, clean, and obedient', he asserted in *Fors* 67 (*Works* 28. 655). Ruskin's accounts of popular music and his proposals for musical education may stress that music and poetry are the 'necessary and natural expression of pure and virtuous human joy, or sorrow', but there is overriding emphasis in his writing on musical

---

[10]   *Works* 29. 269–70. Collingwood describes Ruskin's own enjoyment of opera and 'more popular entertainment such as the Christy Minstrels' and draws an analogy with the discrepancy between his published condemnation of railway travel and his own constant train travel, 'Ruskin's Music', 686. Outrage against railways and modern 'music' coincide in Ruskin's swipe at the anti-musical influence of excursion trains in *Fors* 57 (quoted below) and in his injunction to 'stand in the midst of the main railroad station at Birmingham; and think—what music, or dancing, or other entertainment fit for prodigal sons could be possible in that pious and little prodigal locality' (*Works* 28. 404–5).

[11]   *Works* 28. 405. The title 'Michal's Scorn' refers to Saul's daughter 'leaping and dancing before the Lord'; a rejected title for the letter had been 'Music and Dancing', see *Works* 28. 402 n.

training as 'discipline' (*Works* 31. 107). In *Fors* 9, Ruskin paradoxically proposes 'regulations' for spontaneous musical expression:

in their first learning of notes they shall be taught the great purpose of music, which is to say a thing that you mean deeply, in the strongest and clearest possible way; and they shall never be taught to sing what they don't mean. They shall be able to sing merrily when they are happy, and earnestly when they are sad; but they shall find no mirth in mockery, nor in obscenity; neither shall they waste and profane their hearts with artificial and lascivious sorrow. (*Works* 27. 157)

'Regulations' continues Ruskin with wry satisfaction, 'which will bring about some curious changes in piano-playing, and several other things' (*Works* 27. 157). The letter, entitled 'Honour to Whom Honour', specifies that music is to be employed in the education of a suitably deferential citizenry. It emphasizes that a vital component in the education of future citizens will be their learning to sing the praises of appropriate national heroes (*Works* 27. 157). Musical training is evidently to play a part also in the intellectual education which Ruskin stipulates in *Fors* 67 as essential to the completion of moral education, for, 'Intellectual education consists in giving the creature the faculties of admiration, hope and love' which are to be taught, amongst other things, by 'the sight and history of noble persons' (*Works* 28. 656).

Ruskin's summary of his principles of education in *Fors* 67 emphasizes the absolute authority of the educator. Moral education is to be achieved 'at any cost, and with any kind of compulsion rendered necessary' (*Works* 28. 655). The Latin etymology of Ruskin's *Fors Clavigera* title is emphasized in his declared purpose to 'enforce' the practice of his previous teaching (*Works* 28. 656). Talk of 'compelling the affections' within an educative context suspends distinctions between promoting the affective power of art and exerting social control. Music is by no means exempt from this process. In *Fors* 8, Ruskin had moved directly from proposing compulsory practical education for children: agricultural or naval schools for boys, a training in spinning, weaving, sewing, and cooking for girls, to stipulating that 'the youth of both sexes' are: 'to be disciplined daily in the strictest practice of vocal music; and for morality, to be taught gentleness to all brute creatures,—finished courtesy to each other,—to speak truth with rigid care, and to obey orders with the precision of slaves' (*Works* 27. 143).

This implicitly makes music an instrument of indoctrination and social control. A dream which Ruskin records in his diary for 4 September

1872 provides a contrasting vision of musical insubordination amongst a group of workers resistant to his educative efforts:

> Most vivid dream of a party at working men's college, where the people were well meaning, but ill behaved and radical. A man tried an alliterative sentence about 'church' and 'cheat', and I told him we must mind our own business and let that old quarrel alone. Then a man in a quaint dress began to play on the violin; I asked who he was, and was told he was a renowned player. Presently he broke a string, and began to play on his violin as if it were a guitar, and then he struck such a wrong note that I woke. I had been much offended just before by a girl's leaning her head on her lover's shoulder.[12]

An Apollonian music of *order* is pre-eminent in Ruskin's prescriptions for music as the first principle of education. His situating of musical authenticity and authority in classical mythology and in Plato later found tangible expression. In *Fors* 95, Ruskin records an ill-fated attempt to reintroduce the lyre of Apollo as the basis for elementary musical training:

> During the last year, . . . I have been making experiments with a view to the construction of an instrument by which very young children could be securely taught the relations of sound in the octave; unsuccessful only in that the form of lyre which was produced for me, after months of labour, by the British manufacturer, was as curious a creation of visible deformity as a Greek lyre was of grace, besides being nearly as expensive as a piano! (*Works* 29. 500)

This project in 1884 to manufacture a modern equivalent to the ancient Greek lyre for popular use saw Ruskin making a material attempt to restrain music within an Apollonian frame. It marks a concrete realization of his discovery in *The Queen of the Air* (1869) of Athena, as the Goddess of the air whose passionate music requires the ordering and measuring discipline of Apollo's lyre (*Works* 19. 342–5).

Music is also invoked to describe the state of individual and social harmony which Ruskin envisaged as resulting from his educational principles. In *Fors* 82 and 83, he endorses 'Plato's distinct assertion that, as gymnastic exercise is necessary to keep the body healthy, musical exercise is necessary to keep the soul healthy; and that the proper nourishment of the intellect and passions can no more take place without music, than the proper functions of the stomach and the blood without

---

[12] *Diaries*, ii. 731. Ruskin had numerous 'musical' dreams during the 1870s including a combined painting and music dream where he is teaching someone 'how angels should be represented as flying to music', a 'wonderful' recurrent dream of an '*opera* imitating hell', dreams of enchanting singing, and a frightening dream about an old woman with a wooden leg dancing a wild minuet, see *Diaries*, ii. 734, iii. 783, iii. 830, iii. 989, iii. 867.

exercise' (*Works* 29. 239). He adopts Plato's musical terminology in describing the desired outcome of education as 'the symphony of acquired reason with rightly compelled affection' (*Works* 29. 260). In his 'Heavenly Choirs' letter, Ruskin advocates the literal importance of Plato's 'choral discipline' and stresses that participation in 'choral association' rather than passive listening to professional singers, is crucial to promoting music's beneficial power to 'modify existing civilized life' (*Works* 29. 239). (In *Munera Pulveris*, Ruskin had elaborated this idea by evolving an etymological relationship between 'choral' and 'Charitas' (*Works* 17. 225–7).) Ruskin also emulates Plato's ranking of different age-groups by appointing them to membership of the respective 'choirs' of the Muses, Apollo, and Dionysus (*Works* 29. 24). Pausing to reflect on the status of his own project, Ruskin imagines his reader's astonishment at the impracticality of 'Belief in Gods! belief in divine tradition of Myths! Old men, as a class, to become mythologists, instead of misers! and music, throughout life, to be the safeguard of morality!—What futility is it to talk of such things *now*' (*Works* 29. 242). Plato's scheme, he acknowledges, 'was impossible even in his own day' but the contributions of visionary reformers (Ruskin, by implication, included) 'in ministry to the continuous soul of this race, may yet be known in the day when the wheat shall be gathered into the garner' (*Works* 29. 242).

Ruskin finds in Greek myth authority for his own consistent conflation of musical and social theory 'there being scarcely a word in Greek social philosophy which has not reference to musical law; and scarcely a word in Greek musical science which has not understood reference to social law' (*Works* 29. 261). Musical images of an ideal civic order, endorsed by Plato's use of musical terminology, are repeatedly contrasted in *Fors Clavigera* with the discordant 'modern music' of industrialization. The harmony governing the early city of Thebes, described by Ruskin in 'The Story of Arachne', may be contrasted with these fulminations against the discord of modern life. 'The walls of Thebes' writes Ruskin, 'were of stones, which Amphion, the son of Jupiter, made join each other by music; and the first queen of the city was Harmonia—Harmony' (*Works* 20. 379). Harmony is thus literally and metaphorically established as the basis for successful social organization:

the strength of states, for defence against foreign war, consists in harmony; or musical and joyful concord among all the orders of the people . . . observe chiefly; your walls must be built by music. All your defences of iron and reserves of cold shot are useless, unless Englishmen learn to love and trust each other, in all classes.[13]

In contrast, Ruskin describes modern Britain in *Fors 5* as a degenerate Arcadia in which a steam plough substitutes for the whistling which ploughboys would once have provided for themselves. Ruskin describes 'a country festival':

such as the old heathens, who had no iron servants, used to keep with piping and dancing. So I thought, from the liberated country people—their work all done for them by goblins—we should have some extraordinary piping and dancing. But there was no dancing at all, and they could not even provide their own piping. They had their goblin to pipe for them. They walked in procession after their steam-plough, and their steam-plough whistled to them occasionally in the most melodious manner it could. Which seemed to me, indeed, a return to more than Arcadian simplicity; for in old Arcadia, ploughboys truly whistled as they went, for want of thought; whereas, here was verily a large company walking without thought, but not having any more even the capacity of doing their own whistling. (*Works* 27.89)

Outrage at steam whistles is recurrent in *Fors Clavigera*. Whilst visiting Italy, Ruskin complains vociferously about their noise on the Venice lagoon. *Fors 19* complains of the 'devilish noise' of steamers summoning the 'miserable mob' of bathers near the Ducal Palace 'which has not brains enough to know so much as what o'clock it is, nor sense enough so much as to go aboard a boat without being whistled for, like dogs' (*Works* 27. 329). In *Fors 20*, Ruskin interposes fragments of the biblical text which he is trying to elucidate, with accounts of the persistent interruptions from outside his window. The musical allusions of Ruskin's chosen text contribute to a dramatization of the conflict between authentic biblical music and 'devilish' modern noise: 'Do you suppose that when it is promised that "the lame man shall leap as an hart, and the tongue of the dumb sing" . . . Steam-whistle interrupts me from the *Capo d'Istria*' (*Works* 27. 341). Ruskin continues in similar vein to describe the intrusions of several steamers:

the biggest,—English and half a quarter of a mile long,—blowing steam from all manner of pipers in her sides, and with such a roar through her funnel—whistle number two from *Capo d'Istria*—that I could not make any one hear me speak in this room without an effort . . . whistle number three from *Capo d'Istria*; I am writing on, steadily, so that you will be able to form an accurate idea, from this

---

[13] *Works* 20. 379. Compare Tennyson's 'cities built to music': 'Oenone' 39–40, 'Tiresias' 96, 'Gareth & Lynette' 276.

page, of the intervals of time in modern music. The roaring from the English boat goes on all the while, for bass to the *Capo d'Istria's* treble, and a tenth steamer comes in sight . . . a particular kind of activity is meant, I repeat, in both cases. The lame man is to leap, (whistle fourth from *Capo d'Istria*, this time at high pressure, going through my head like a knife) as an innocent and joyful creature leaps, and the lips of the dumb to move melodiously . . . Fifth whistle, a double one, from *Capo d'Istria*, and it is seven o'clock, nearly; and here's my coffee, and I must stop writing. Sixth whistle—the *Capo d'Istria* is off, with her crew of morning bathers. Seventh,—from I don't know which of the boats outside—and I count no more. (*Works* 27. 341–2)

Further complaints about the 'steam music' of Venice, which Ruskin terms 'the modern Tasso's echoes, practised on her principal lagoon' appear in *Fors* 42 ('Misericordia') (*Works* 28. 93). *Fors* 57 recounts how, on a visit to Wakefield, the 'hideous sound' produced by 'the long malignant yell' of a foundry whistle obliterated the chiming of church bells:

I woke with an expectant heart. It was a bright May day, such as I remembered twenty years before. The big church bell tolled nine: then came a pause, and my thirsty ears were strained to catch the first sounds of the dear old chimes. 'Ding' went a treble bell high in the air, the first note of 'Tara's Halls,' and then!—a hideous sound I cannot describe, a prolonged malignant yell, broke from the sky and seemed to fill the earth. I stopped my ears and ran indoors, but the sound followed to the innermost chambers. It gathered strength and malignancy every moment, and seemed to blast all within its reach. It lasted near two minutes, and ended with a kind of spasm and howl that made every nerve shudder. I do not exaggerate. I cannot adequately describe the hideous sound. (*Works* 28. 412)

These letters constitute a commentary on 'modern music'. The Venetian steam whistles are satirized in *Fors* 57 as 'our modern pastoral music' and a 'modern Venetian "Barcarolle" '; the factory whistles in Wakefield become 'our modern Campanile, and Muezzin call to prayer'.[14] Ruskin provides this summary of his response to the 'music' of modern life in reply to a correspondent who complains of debased popular musical taste where music is of 'little attraction, except in the form of *dance*' (*Works* 28. 395). He insists that she might none the less be grateful that even this much of musicality remains in popular culture:

Yes; my correspondent may be thankful that still some feeble lust for dancing on the green,—still some dim acknowledgment, by besotted and stupefied brains, of the laws of tune and time known to their fathers and mothers—remains

[14] *Works* 28. 405. See also Ruskin's preface to *Rock Honeycomb*, where train whistles are a 'musical entertainment and psalm of modern life' interrupting his meditations on Sir Philip Sidney's Psalter, *Works*, 31. 124.

possible to the poor wretches discharged by the excursion trains for a gasp of breath, and a gleam of light, amidst what is left to them, and us, of English earth and heaven. (*Works* 28. 405)

Ruskin's fulminations against 'modern music' and his educative zeal invite comparison of his views with those of his contemporaries. His thoughts on music emerge as idiosyncratic, yet also more representative than they might at first seem. In the only recent article to consider Ruskin's ideas about music, William Gatens regards them as chiefly of interest because Ruskin is too important a figure for any of his work to be overlooked.[15] Whilst clearly eccentric in many respects, Ruskin's views on music are important not just because Ruskin wrote them, but in relation to the rest of his work and to the context in which they were read. Music featured importantly in educational and social debates of the time where it enjoyed an ambivalent status as both a powerful educative tool and an emotive force requiring containment.

Those amongst Ruskin's contemporaries most actively concerned with promoting improvements in popular music education also advocated the proper employment of music's affective power to aid social reform. Since the 1840s, there had been efforts throughout the nation to mobilize popular musical education to induce good citizenship. Ideas about music's power to transform society were finding direct application in English musical reforms through, for example, the national singing movement instigated by John Hullah and other musical campaigners.[16] Hullah, who obtained an appointment as inspector of music in training colleges, was a friend of Ruskin's. Collingwood records that Ruskin's 'copy of Hullah's "Manual" is scribbled with devices for simplifying the teaching of the keyboard'—an example of real connection therefore between Ruskin and contemporary campaigns for transforming musical education.[17] Amongst other musical educators, John Curwen pioneered the sol-fa method of teaching sight-singing, an enterprise which might have met Ruskin's criteria for 'a grammar of simple and pure music, of which the code should be alike taught in every school in the land'.[18] Joseph Mainzer, another leading figure in the mass-singing movement,

---

[15] Gatens, 'John Ruskin and Music', 77–8.
[16] Hullah's national singing movement began in 1841 at Exeter Hall. For details of this movement see Bernarr Rainbow, *The Choral Revival in the Anglican Church: 1839–1872* (Oxford, 1970), 42, 47, 97, 128, 234.
[17] Collingwood, 'Ruskin's Music', 688.
[18] *Works* 29. 500. A history of Curwen's life as a musical educator can be found in Herbert A. Simon, *Songs and Words: A History of the Curwen Press* (London, 1973).

campaigned for music to form a major part of a properly balanced education, insisting, like Ruskin, that there was a direct relationship between states of art and of morality, since, 'The music of a people depends upon their mental and moral development'.[19] Mainzer's drive for music education also had the reformation of society as its ultimate goal; 'what better, what surer foundation', he asks in his highly popular *Singing for the Million*, 'could be laid to prepare . . . children for being in their after-life good men, good citizens, and elevated moral beings?'[20] Whilst citing Plato and the Bible as his only authorities and displaying no explicit acknowledgement of the fervent campaigns for music education in which his contemporaries were engaged, Ruskin's concerns connect significantly with theirs. They promoted the civic benefits of choral music as diligently as Ruskin advocated the discipline of Plato's choirs. Ruskin's view of music as requiring the expression of noble emotions was matched by the preference of practical musical reformers for morally appropriate texts. Mistrust of music's unbridled power and mistrust of an uncontrolled citizenry were also implicit to their concerns. Ruskin is entirely representative of his time in finding in music both a potent instrument for civic virtue and a potentially perilous influence.

Ruskin's emphasis on myth and Platonic theory in his writing on music is distinctively his own, yet the terms of his attacks on modern musical practice, are in other respects not unlike those employed by a variety of commentators on music's social function. His invocations of biblical authority have strong affinities with discussions commonly pursued in evangelically inclined advice books and journals, where concern about the proper role of music would, for example, frequently prompt the same sort of comparison between dancing in the biblical and present ages which Ruskin exploits in his attack on Mill's social philosophy quoted below.[21] Ruskin's views on music certainly might be accounted

---

[19] Joseph Mainzer, *Music and Education* (London, 1848), 7, 15. See *Works* 20. 39.

[20] Mainzer, *Singing for the Million: A Practical Course of Musical Instruction, Adapted from its Pleasing Simplicity and Rapid Effect to Render Musical Reading and Singing Familiar to all Ages, Capacities and Conditions*, [1841] repr. in *Classic Texts in Music Education*, vol. ix (Kilkenny, 1984), p. xxi. For accounts of musical education in nineteenth-century Britain see Nicholas Temperley (ed.), *The Romantic Age: 1800–1914* (London, 1981); Bernarr Rainbow, *A Land without Music: Musical Education in England 1800–1860 and its Continental Antecedents* (London, 1967), 'The Rise of Popular Music Education in Nineteenth-Century England', *Victorian Studies*, 30 (1986), 25–50; Percy Alfred Scholes, *The Mirror of Music, 1844–1944: Musical Life in Britain as Reflected in the Pages of the Musical Times*, 2 vols. (London, 1947).

[21] See for example David Gunton, 'Ancient and Modern Dancing', *British Mothers' Magazine*, 9 (1853), 251.

as evangelical in more respects than one: music was at least a mode of conversion, if not of coercion. Ruskin combined an evangelical mistrust of music's uncontrolled sensual and affective power on one hand, with on the other, an appreciation of music as a potent evangelizing force on behalf of his educational and social beliefs.

Ruskin's views on music in relation to women also parallel ideas commonly expressed in advice literature. There was widespread consensus that women should direct their musical skills towards fostering domestic piety and harmony rather than toward 'self display'. Sarah Ellis expressed the common opinion that female attainments, including a training in instrumental music, 'which in the crowded drawing-room were worse than useless in their display', might 'sometimes be accounted as actual wealth, to her who has the good feeling to render them conducive to the amusement or the happiness of her own fireside'.[22] In *The Cestus of Aglaia*, Ruskin had commented, with approbation, on how he had observed a group of schoolgirls, listening to Charles Hallé, change from polite to rapt attention when he transferred from Bach to the simple and familiar strains of 'Home Sweet Home' (*Works* 19. 78–9). This contrast would have followed a pattern recognizable to many of his readers. Ruskin's complaint about fashions of piano playing in *Fors* 9, quoted above, was also very familiar territory. It would have been read in relation to long-standing criticism of fashions of female piano playing in particular. Women were firmly counselled not to 'attempt in a drawing room to perform some impossibility of Liszt'.[23] A judicious awareness of limits was widely advocated and these very limitations were desirable, 'for who would wish a wife or daughter, moving in private society, to have attained such excellence in music as involves a life's devotion to it'.[24] The *British Mothers' Magazine* suggested that 'In cases where true musical talent exists, a moderate degree of skill, such as is necessary to accompany a simple song or ballad for the recreation of the domestic circle, may be easily attained, without involving a sacrifice of the time required for other pursuits'.[25]

A contemporary whom Ruskin does mention by name and whose views on educational freedom particularly aroused his ire, was J. S. Mill with whom, in the course of outlining his rules for proper musical training,

---

[22] Sarah Ellis, *The Wives of England: Their Relative Duties, Domestic Influence, and Social Obligations* (London, 1843), 97; see also 99.

[23] Mrs [Matilda Marian] Pullan, *Maternal Counsels* (London, 1855), 81.

[24] Ibid. 81.

[25] T. Herbert Baker, 'Early Education', *British Mothers' Magazine*, 7 (1851), 245.

Ruskin expressed his violent disagreement. In *Fors* 12, he quotes from *Principles of Political Economy* where Mill speculates that better education would result in more intelligent and thus less biddable lower classes (*Works* 27. 211). Mill's comment is not specifically about music and it is interesting that Ruskin decides to deploy his musical ideas in an attack on Mill's political thought. His incorporation of such an attack into a discussion of music and dance in *Fors* 57 confirms the impression that he wishes to appropriate music as a mode of exerting social control:

Music and dancing! They are quite the two primal instruments of education. Make them licentious; let Mr. John Stuart Mill have the dis-ordering of them, so that . . . 'no one shall be guided, or governed, or directed in the way they should go,'—and they sink to lower and lower depth—till the dance becomes Death's; and the music—a shriek of death by strychnine. But let Miriam and David, and the Virgins of Israel, have the ordering of them, and the music becomes at last the Eternal choir; and the Dance, the Karol-dance of Christmas, evermore. (*Works* 28. 405–6)

Mill is also anathema when it comes to the relationship of music and woman. In *Fors* 24, 'Cradle Song', Ruskin derides the 'enlightened notion among English young women, derived from Mr. J. Stuart Mill,— that the "career" of the Madonna is too limited a one, and that modern political economy can provide them . . . with "much more lucrative occupations than that of nursing the baby" ' (*Works* 27. 43). He quotes newspaper reports of maternal neglect, including opium poisoning, contrasting this with the wholesome influence of cradle songs:

'Hush-a-bye, baby, upon the tree top,' my mother used to sing to me: and I remember the dawn of intelligence in which I began to object to the bad rhyme which followed:—'when the wind blows, the cradle will rock.' But the Christmas winds must blow rudely, and warp the waters askance indeed, which rock our English cradles now. (*Works* 27. 432–3)

His counter example is that of the woman 'karolling' in Chaucer's *Romaunt of the Rose*:

> She was not rude, nor unmeet,
> But couth enough for such doing,
> As longeth unto karolling;
> For she was wont, in every place,
> To singen first, men to solace.
> For singing most she gave her to,
> No craft had she so lefe to do.
>
> (*Works* 27. 433)

'Mr John Stuart Mill', continues Ruskin:

would have set her to another craft, I fancy (not but that singing is a lucrative one, nowadays, if it be shrill enough); but you will not get your wives to sing thus for nothing, if you send them out to earn their dinners (instead of earning them yourselves for them), and put their babies summarily to sleep. (*Works* 27. 434)

This sense of woman's domestic role as essentially 'musical' (combined with a horror of professional female musicianship) is something which Ruskin shared with numerous authors of advice literature. Under Ruskin's scheme both sexes are to be educated in musical discipline, but it is scarcely surprising to find him as concerned to define and regulate the musical role of actual women as to mediate the contest of the Muses and Sirens.

A comparable figurative affinity between music and woman also existed in other texts which debated the role of music in women's lives. It was woman's role to be 'the moral regenerator of society' and music, when correctly practised, was deemed 'an instrument of important moral improvement and civilization'.[26] Music's sympathetic qualities moreover, like woman's, made its first purpose self-evidently domestic:

music is the very art, which by its mastery over the feelings and affections, calls forth more tenderness than any other. . . . Surely it ought not to be cultivated as the medium of display, so much as the means of home enjoyment; not so much as a spell to charm the stranger, or one who has no other link of sympathy with us, as a solace to those we love, and a tribute of gratitude and affection to those who love us.[27]

If the roles of music and woman in fostering domestic sympathy and morality were parallel, so was the need to contain their potential to disrupt social harmony. The latter arose particularly from distrust of the dangerous sensual potential of both music and woman. Music, 'the hand-maid of devotion' could 'easily become, and unawares, the most sensuous of accomplishments'.[28] The way in which music and woman mirrored one another in such texts and the existing ambivalence in their representation must have informed the reception of Ruskin's Muse/Siren distinction—here in the form of the woman karolling, and the shrill professional singer neglecting her true familial duties.

---

[26] 'E. E.', 'On the Progress of Female Education', *British Mothers' Magazine*, 9 (1853), 173. Mrs William [Margaret] Fison, *Hints for the Earnest Student: Or, A Yearbook for the Young* (London, 1850), 279.

[27] Ellis, *Daughters of England* (London, 1842), 106–7.

[28] Revd W. R. Williams, 'The Social Position and Culture Due to Women', *British Mothers' Magazine*, 6 (1850), 233.

By the 1870s therefore, Ruskin's writing on music would have been read in relation to a number of already familiar debates. Moreover, it follows in the wake of two decades of heated debate amongst contemporary scientists over music's origins and current purpose. An article in on 'The Origin and Function of Music' by Herbert Spencer (1857) sparked off discussion in which Darwin, amongst others, took part.[29] Most commentators agreed in seeing music as of enormous social value. Like Ruskin, Spencer was concerned with music's relation to spoken language and valued its moral powers. He however saw these as vital agents of evolutionary progress. Ruskin's renowned hostility to biological science must have meant that he was anything but favourably disposed to music's assimilation within an evolutionary agenda.[30]

One important contrast between Ruskin and other contemporary commentators on music is obvious in that he does not see the history of music itself as one of progressive development. His degenerative view of musical history leads Ruskin to adopt some very different assessments of various musical styles from others with similar ethical and educational concerns. Unlike many of his contemporaries who valorized serious German music in contrast to the frivolities of Italian opera, or French virtuoso piano playing, Ruskin expresses his disparagement of 'Scientific German music—full of conceit and effort'.[31] His view of music's historical decline also influences his assessment of musical practitioners. Whilst Herbert Spencer saw the musician as a uniquely advanced representative of the rest of human kind's potential for development, Ruskin saw himself as pitted against the generally corrupting influence of musicians upon music since, 'Musicians, like painters, are almost virulently determined in their efforts to abolish the laws of sincerity and purity; and to invent, each for his own glory, new modes of dissolute and lascivious sound' (*Works* 29. 500). Despite obvious parallels with the concerns voiced by many of his contemporaries, there would appear to be a conscious disregard on Ruskin's part of existing musical reforms and theories in the interests of promoting an authentic aesthetic and social integrity.

Characteristically, Ruskin's view of musical development (or rather degeneration), like his views on music education, become woven into the

[29] Herbert Spencer, 'The Origin and Function of Music' (*Fraser's Magazine*, 56 (1857), 396–408) repr. in *Essays: Scientific, Political, and Speculative*, i (London, 1858), 359–84.

[30] Ruskin certainly detested Spencer in particular as well as Scientific Positivism in general, see for example his letter to Frederic Harrison of 26 Mar. 1884, *Works* 37. 479–80.

[31] Ruskin, *Praeterita* (1886–7) (deleted passage) *Works* 35. 619. See also Collingwood, 'Ruskin's Music', 687.

mythopoeic structures of his work. The threat to the hegemony of plucked string and voice by the lascivious pleasing of a flute, as recounted in the myth of the contest between Apollo and Marsyas, represents an original scene of corruption. This is echoed in the history of Western music, by the move away from predominantly vocal music to pure instrumental sound. In *Fors* 83, Ruskin proclaims that 'the essential work of Stradivarius, in substituting the violin for the lyre and harp, was twofold':

> Thenceforward, (A) instrumental music became the captain instead of the servant of the voice; and (B) skill of instrumental music, as so developed, became impossible in the ordinary education of a gentleman. So that, since his time, old King Cole has called for his fiddlers three, and Squire Western sent Sophia to the harpsichord when he was drunk: but of souls won by Orpheus, or cities built by Amphion, we hear no more. (*Works* 29. 259)

His view that the historical development away from the hegemony of vocal music represents a decline, positions Ruskin as virulently antithetical to the Romantic ideal of instrumental as the purest, because least referential, music. Ruskin stresses that at the heart of music's corruption lies the inversion of the proper relation of music and verbal language. In *Fors* 24, Ruskin's discussion of feminine musicality includes comments on how Mendelssohn's Songs without Words are currently enjoying a vogue whilst worded domestic music, including lullabies, suffers neglect (*Works* 27. 433). Whilst for many of his English contemporaries, Mendelssohn represented an ideal combination of musical and moral virtue, for Ruskin, Mendelssohn's music falls into the category of degenerative music which, in addition to being German, has grown away from the the controlling structure of words.[32] The 'ordered' music of Apollo is emphatically 'worded' sound, for: 'in the change from stringed to wind instrument lies essentially the abdication of its authority by the word and the assumption of it by the note' (*Works* 19. 176–7). The steam whistles about which Ruskin so frequently complained, doubtless represent a nightmarish extension of the original insult to Apollo's lyre by the pipes of Marsyas (*Works* 19. 176–7; 19. 342–5).

Ruskin's long-held conviction that music requires the ordering structure of words to guarantee its expression of only noble sentiments seems manifest in *Rock Honeycomb*, where the preface to his 'edition of Sir

---

[32] See also *Works* 22. 497, Ruskin's dislike of Mendelssohn does not seem to have been absolute in practice. He paid a visit to Christ Church cathedral in November 1884 specifically to hear an anthem by Mendelssohn; see *Diaries* 2. 1086.

Philip Sidney's Psalter prepared for school service' stipulates the proper requirements for musical settings of text (*Works* 31. 107). This is affirmed also in his debate with a correspondent, from which I quoted at the outset of this chapter where Ruskin asserts the ultimate superiority of the spoken word over the musical note (*Works* 31. 111–2 n.). However, Ruskin also draws analogies in this preface between the arts of music and poetry which suggest that his thinking about practical musical education during the 1870s had fostered a sense of precise correspondence between music and verbal language: 'The law of nobleness in music and poetry is essentially one. Both are the necessary and natural expression of pure and virtuous human joy, or sorrow, by the lips and fingers of persons trained in right schools to manage their bodies and souls' (*Works* 31. 107). 'All perfectly rhythmic poetry is meant to be sung to music, and all entirely noble music is the illustration of noble words', he declares: a synergistic coexistence essential to the fulfilment of either musical or poetic art, for, 'The arts of word and of note, separate from each other, become degraded and the muse-less sayings, or senseless melodies, harden the intellect, or demoralize the ear' (*Works* 31. 107).

Ruskin describes his essay on *Elements of English Prosody* as an exercise aimed at 'obtaining more direct correspondence between verbal and harmonic intention' (*Works* 31. 325). By 1880, Ruskin was composing song-settings himself in what would seem a concrete attempt to give form to his assertion that language depends on the structures of music as much as music upon language.[33] The peculiar results of his imposition of musical notation on verbal metre in *Elements of English Prosody*, where unstressed syllables frequently appear at the first beat of the bar, is perhaps less significant than the extent to which Ruskin identified the arts of music and poetry. Whether read as referring to actual or to metaphorical music, his revised definition of poetry as 'the presentiment, *in musical form*, to the imagination . . . of noble grounds for the noble emotions' confirms our apprehension that Ruskin's concern to contain the affective power of music is ultimately as much about the control of language (*Works* 31. 351). Is language therefore any more amenable than wordless music to recruitment by Apollo rather than by the sirens?

33 See *Works* 31. 511–21 for specimens of Ruskin's music, including his setting of 'Come unto these yellow sands', a text which he discusses in *Rock Honeycomb*, *Works* 31. 109. Collingwood records his music teacher's attempts to uphold the laws of harmony in terms amenable to Ruskin by pleading 'But you wouldn't be ungrammatical, Dr Ruskin?' 'Ruskin's Music', 685.

In *The Queen of the Air*, Athena's passionate 'strength of voice' is to be subject to the 'limiting or restraining modes of music [which] belong to the Muses' (*Works* 19. 342). In his lecture on *The Relation of National Ethics to National Arts*, Ruskin had specified that 'In good music the pleasure received by the ear is wholly subordinate to the purpose of expression' (*Works* 19. 177). It is ironic then, that Ruskin's voice, as described by George Eliot, emerges as both musical and, to some degree, 'sirenic'. Her account of *Modern Painters* portrays Ruskin's 'voice' as having the power 'to compel . . . attention and sympathy' almost independently of what he has to say: 'Now, Mr Ruskin has a voice, and one of such power, that whatever error he may mix with his truth, he will make more converts to that truth than less erring advocates who are hoarse and feeble'.34 Ruskin's voice converts us, Eliot is assured, to 'the truth', but its melodious allurements in 'this very seductive book' would seem a more decisive attraction than 'the teacher of perfect order'.35

34 George Eliot, review of *Modern Painters*, 627.
35 Ibid. 633. *Works* 19. 344.

6

Ruskin and the Aesthetes

Nicholas Shrimpton

Writers on Ruskin sometimes promise that their work will be 'Ruskinian', not merely in topic but also in form. It is a claim which can be very variously interpreted. According to one estimate of Ruskin's literary manner, it means that the argument will be original and imaginative. According to another, it suggests eccentricity, digressiveness, and internal self-contradiction. My approach to the problem of Ruskin's relationship to Aestheticism will not seek to be (for good or ill) Ruskinian. But it will share a characteristic with the work of another Victorian writer, Robert Browning. Browning's poem *The Ring and the Book* was issued in monthly parts between November 1868 and February 1869, and revised for book publication in 1872. The most salient formal feature of Browning's poem is, of course, that it tells the same story eleven times.

This will be a Browningesque enquiry. I do not propose to tell the story of Ruskin and the Aesthetes eleven times. But I am going to tell it four times, on each occasion from a different perspective. I am going to do this because I think it is a mistake to give too single-minded an account of this complex and elusive intellectual relationship.

My starting point, at least, is obvious. Ruskin, the 1870s, and the English Aesthetic Movement come into unmistakable conjunction on 25 and 26 November 1878, when the case of *Whistler v. Ruskin* was heard in the Court of Exchequer before Baron Huddleston and a Special Jury.[1]

Ruskin had belatedly reviewed the inaugural exhibition of the Grosvenor Gallery in Letter 79 of *Fors Clavigera*. He praised the paintings of Edward Burne-Jones as 'the only art-work at present produced in England which will be received by the future as "classic" in its kind,—the

---

[1] The best-known account of the trial, in Whistler's *The Gentle Art of Making Enemies* (London, 1890), 2–19, is enjoyable but untrustworthy. Appendix 20(a) of *Works* 29 reprints the *Times* law report. See also G. H. Fleming, *James Abbott McNeill Whistler: A Life* (Moreton-in-Marsh, 1991), chs. 27–32.

best that has been or could be', while acknowledging the sketchy quality of one particular group of paintings: the six panels in the *Days of Creation* series. But, he argued, Burne-Jones's incompleteness here was like that of 'Giotto, Masaccio, Luini, Tintoret, and Turner',

> . . . the mannerisms and errors of these pictures, whatever may be their extent, are never affected or indolent. The work is natural to the painter, however strange to us; and it is wrought with utmost conscience of care, however far, to his own or our desire, the result may yet be incomplete. Scarcely so much can be said for any other pictures of the modern schools: their eccentricities are almost always in some degree forced; and their imperfections gratuitously, if not impertinently, indulged. For Mr. Whistler's own sake, no less than for the protection of the purchaser, Sir Coutts Lindsay ought not to have admitted works into the gallery in which the ill-educated conceit of the artist so nearly approached the aspect of wilful imposture. I have seen, and heard, much of Cockney impudence before now; but never expected to hear a coxcomb ask two hundred guineas for flinging a pot of paint in the public's face. (*Works* 29. 160)

Whistler was not a reader of *Fors Clavigera*. But he saw the paragraph when it was quoted in the *Spectator* and sued for libel. The jury retired on 26 November, came back to ask the judge for legal guidance on the words 'wilful imposture', and returned to deliver a verdict for the plaintiff (Whistler) with damages at one farthing. The judge then gave judgement for the plaintiff, without costs. Ruskin's costs of £400 were raised for him by public subscription. Whistler was declared bankrupt in June 1879.

The trial was a major event in the cultural life of the 1870s—one of those rare occasions when a technical quarrel within the world of the arts is articulated in a way which makes it of immediate interest to the general public. It was also a significant event in the career of John Ruskin. He dismissed the trial itself, in a letter to Charles Eliot Norton on 26 November 1878, as comic ('Today, I believe the comic Whistler law suit is to be decided').[2] But he gave the verdict as the chief reason for his first resignation from the Slade professorship,[3] and the strain involved almost certainly contributed to his mental ill-health. The trial was also a landmark in the history of English Aestheticism. Lionel Lambourne, for example, describes it as the 'watershed' of the Aesthetic Movement.[4]

---

[2] *The Correspondence of John Ruskin and Charles Eliot Norton*, ed. J. L. Bradley and I. Ousby (Cambridge, 1987), 417.

[3] See Ruskin's letter to Liddell, 28 Nov. 1878, 'I hesitated in giving in my resignation . . . the result of the Whistler trial leaves me no further option' (*Works* 29. xxv).

[4] L. Lambourne, *The Aesthetic Movement* (London, 1996), 91.

The outstanding established art critic and the chief representative of a new artistic creed had fought a public battle. Here, more obviously than anywhere else, Ruskin and the Aesthetes come into significant contact.

The story which the *Whistler* v. *Ruskin* trial points us to is an antagonistic one. In this narrative (the first of my four stories) Ruskin is the enemy of the Aesthetes, a thinker who helps to define Aestheticism precisely by his persistent opposition to it.

Whistler certainly saw the relationship between Ruskin and the Aesthetes in these oppositional terms. In his pamphlet *Whistler v. Ruskin: Art and Art Critics*, published in December 1878, Whistler spends most of his time arguing that critics who are not themselves professional painters are not equipped to understand paintings. But his conclusion is a suggestion that Ruskin should move from the Professorship of Fine Art to the Chair of Ethics, thus deliberately stressing the gulf between, on the one hand, the amoral stance of art for art's sake (with its Baudelairian hostility to 'l'hérésie de l'enseignement') and, on the other, the moralism on which Ruskinian criticism is based.[5]

Ruskin's writing, from the 1840s to the 1880s, provides plenty of evidence, not just for a strongly moralized theory of art (that goes without saying), but also for a specific antagonism to the body of ideas which we now group under the heading of Aestheticism. In 1843, in the first volume of *Modern Painters*, he comes very quickly to the topic of beauty: chapter 6 is entitled 'Of Ideas of Beauty'. At first glance Ruskin's theory of beauty here, at the very inception of his critical career, can seem Aesthetic, since he begins by defining beauty as a pleasure wholly distinct from any activity of the intellect:

> Any material object which can give us pleasure in the simple contemplation of its outward qualities without any direct and definite exertion of the intellect, I call in some way, or in some degree, beautiful. (*Works* 3. 109)

And Ruskin immediately expands this point to make it clear that what he will call, three years later, in the second volume of *Modern Painters*, 'Typical Beauty' (that is, the belief that physical beauty is a type, or symbol, of God) is a merely secondary quality of the experience of the beautiful:

---

5 Whistler's pamphlet is reprinted in *The Gentle Art of Making Enemies* (London, 1890), 25–34. Baudelaire's famous phrase first occurs in 'Notes nouvelles sur Edgar Poe', the preface to *Nouvelles histoires extraordinaires* (Paris, 1857); it is a translation of Poe's phrase, 'the heresy of *the Didactic*', from his lecture 'The Poetic Principle', first published in the *Home Journal*, 31 Aug. 1850.

We may indeed perceive, as far as we are acquainted with His [God's] nature, that we have been so constructed as . . . to derive pleasure from whatever things are illustrative of that nature; but we do not receive pleasure from them *because* they are illustrative of it, nor from any perception that they are illustrative of it, but instinctively and necessarily, as we derive sensual pleasure from the scent of a rose. (*Works* 3. 109)

This instinctual and sensual *jouissance* sounds very Aesthetic.

But Ruskin is distinguishing the beautiful from the intellectual, not from the moral, and he makes this clear in his second paragraph:

Perfect taste is the faculty of receiving the greatest possible pleasure from those material sources which are attractive to our moral nature in its purity and perfection. (*Works* 3. 110)

What this sudden, and surprising, insertion of the moral suggests is that Ruskin, as an ethical thinker, is at root an intuitionist. Our sense of the beautiful and our sense of the moral are, for him, alike in their instinctual quality. As such, both stand opposed to the modes of judgement which fall within the realm of the intellect: 'Ideas of beauty', the chapter concludes, 'are the subjects of moral, but not of intellectual perception' (*Works* 3. 111). As such Ruskin is able to elide them, the 'sensual', that is, and the 'moral', into a single category.

Coleridge in 1817 had pointed to the primacy of pleasure in our experience of art: 'A poem is that species of composition, which is opposed to works of science, by proposing for its *immediate* object pleasure, not truth . . .'[6] Leigh Hunt reviewed Keats's *Poems* as 'poetry for its own sake' in the same year.[7] Victor Hugo and Théophile Gautier had, in the early 1830s, enlarged the claim for the hedonic as the definitive characteristic of artistic experience, and for the amoral and autonomous status of beauty. Ruskin, in 1843, is attempting to keep this new stress on artistic pleasure within the boundaries of the moral. By the second volume of *Modern Painters*, in 1846, he has moved on from his discreet attempt to *contain* the implications of the new Aestheticism to a direct assault upon it,

. . . the Theoretic faculty, is concerned with the moral perception and appreciation of ideas of beauty. And the error respecting it is, the considering and calling it Aesthetic, degrading it to a mere operation of sense, or perhaps worse, of custom; so that the arts which appeal to it sink into a mere amusement, ministers to morbid sensibilities, ticklers and fanners of the soul's sleep. (*Works* 4. 35–6)

---

[6] *Biographia Literaria*, ed. J. Engell and W. Jackson Bate, 2.13, in *Collected Works of Samuel Taylor Coleridge*, vol. vii. 2 (London and Princeton), 1983.

[7] *Examiner*, 492 (1 June 1817), 345.

Thirty-seven years later, in the footnotes added to the 1883 edition of *Modern Painters*, volume ii, Ruskin would apologize for having introduced the Greek word 'Theoria' (the Theoretic, or contemplative, faculty) so abruptly (*Works* 4. 33). The reason he had needed to do so in 1846 was, I believe, that he then urgently required a term which would clearly distinguish his position, sketched out in 1843, from Aestheticism. The word 'Aesthetic' (originally, of course, an inoffensively neutral philosophical category) has by 1846 been appropriated by thinkers with whom Ruskin is already anxious not to be confused.

This distinction is spelt out in the second chapter of *Modern Painters*, volume ii, where we find Ruskin in rapid retreat from his use of the word 'sensual' five years before:

I proceed, therefore, first to examine the nature of what I have called the Theoretic faculty, and to justify my substitution of the term 'Theoretic' for 'Aesthetic,' which is the one commonly employed with reference to it.

Now the term 'aesthesis' properly signifies mere sensual perception of the outward qualities and necessary effects of bodies; in which sense only, if we would arrive at any accurate conclusions on this difficult subject, it should always be used. But I wholly deny that the impressions of beauty are in any way sensual; they are neither sensual nor intellectual, but moral: and for the faculty receiving them, whose difference from mere perception I shall immediately endeavour to explain, no term can be more accurate or convenient than that employed by the Greeks, 'Theoretic' . . . (*Works* 4. 42)

Ruskin retains the term 'Aesthetic', but only in a negative signification,

. . . the mere animal consciousness of the pleasantness I call Aesthesis; but the exulting, reverent, and grateful perception of it I call Theoria. For this, and this only, is the full comprehension and contemplation of the Beautiful as a gift of God . . . (*Works* 4. 47)

'It will now be understood,' Ruskin (perhaps a little optimistically) declares,

. . . why it was formerly said in the chapter respecting ideas of beauty, that those ideas were the subject of moral, and not of intellectual, nor altogether of sensual perception . . . For, as it is necessary to the existence of an idea of beauty, that the sensual pleasure which may be its basis should be accompanied first with joy, then with love of the object, then with the perception of kindness in a superior intelligence, finally, with thankfulness and veneration towards that intelligence itself; and as no idea can be at all considered as in any way an idea of beauty, until it be made up of these emotions . . . it is evident that the sensation of beauty is not sensual on the one hand, nor is it intellectual on the other, but is dependent on a pure, right, and open state of the heart. (*Works* 4. 48–9)

With this hostility to Aestheticism, and with this alternative construction of the beautiful, Ruskin embarks on his career as an art critic, leading what one might suggest to be a Theoretic Movement in opposition to the growing power and prominence of the Aesthetic Movement which he deplores.

In 1858, for example, we find him glancing at the growing currency of the phrase 'art for art's sake' (or, as it is more commonly used in England, 'art for its own sake'):

Wherever art is practised for its own sake, and the delight of the workman is in what he *does* and *produces*, instead of in what he *interprets* or *exhibits*,—there art has an influence of the most fatal kind on brain and heart, and it issues, if long so pursued, in the *destruction both of intellectual power* and *moral principle . . .* (*Works* 16. 268)

In November 1870, in the first of his *Aratra Pentelici* series of Oxford lectures, he argues that

. . . all aesthetics depend on the health of soul and body, and the proper exercise of both, not only through years, but generations. Only by harmony of both collateral and successive lives can the great doctrine of the Muses be received which enables men "*Χαῖρειν ὀρθῶς*,"—'to have pleasure rightly;' and there is no other definition of the beautiful, nor of any subject of delight to the aesthetic faculty, than that it is what one noble spirit has created, seen and felt by another of similar or equal nobility. So much as there is in you of ox, or of swine, perceives no beauty, and creates none: what is human in you, in exact proportion to the perfectness of its humanity, can create it, and receive. (*Works* 20. 208–9)

When Ruskin published these lectures, in January 1872, he prefaced them with a fierce attack on the Royal Academy Exhibition of 1871:

The Exhibition of 1871 was very notable in this important particular, that it embraced some representation of the modern schools of nearly every country in Europe: and I am well assured that, looking back upon it after the excitement of that singular interest has passed away, every thoughtful judge of Art will confirm my assertion that it contained not a single picture of accomplished merit; while it contained many that were disgraceful to Art, and some that were disgraceful to humanity. (*Works* 20. 195)

Whistler did not exhibit in the RA of 1871. But in other respects it was an exhibition unusually hospitable to Aesthetic Movement work. Frederick Leighton, for example, exhibited both his great *Hercules Wrestling with Death for the Body of Alcestis* and (more significantly in this context) *Greek Girls Picking up Pebbles by the Sea*—a painting which Christopher Newall describes as 'a seminal work of the Aesthetic

Movement'.⁸ Albert Moore showed *Battledore* and *Shuttlecock*, Thomas Armstrong *A Music-Piece*. The critic of the *Art Journal* remarked that 'a large part of the pictures in Gallery VII would have been simply excluded from any exhibition in London ten or twenty years ago'. But this 'new and abnormal' school of painting is not Pre-Raphaelite:

In fact, since Pre-Raphaelitism has gone out of fashion a new, select, and also small school has been formed by a few choice spirits . . . The brotherhood cherish in common, reverence of the antique, affection for modern Italy; they affect southern climes, costumes, sunshine, also a certain *dolce far niente* style, with a general Sybarite state of mind which rests in Art and aestheticism as the be-all and end-all of existence.⁹

Two years later, in the winter of 1872–3, Ruskin was rash enough to attend an exhibition at the first recognized showcase of Aesthetic Movement painting, the Dudley Gallery. Whistler was showing three paintings: a *Symphony in Grey and Green: The Ocean*, a *Nocturne in Blue and Silver*, and a *Nocturne in Grey and Gold*.¹⁰ On 27 October 1873, in his *Val d'Arno* series of Oxford lectures, Ruskin made his first explicit attack on Whistler (published in book form in 1874):

I never saw anything so impudent on the walls of any exhibition, in any country, as last year in London. It was a daub professing to be a 'harmony in pink and white' (or some such nonsense); absolute rubbish, and which had taken about a quarter of an hour to scrawl or daub—it had no pretence to be called painting. The price asked for it was two hundred and fifty guineas. (*Works* 23. 49)

Eight years later, in 1881, having again insulted Whistler and been sued for it, Ruskin delivered the fiercest of all his attacks on the Aesthetic Movement, in the 'Dabchicks' chapter, added to the *Love's Meinie* Oxford lectures of 1873 when they were finally published as a book:

⁸ Christopher Newall, *The Art of Lord Leighton* (London, 1990), 74.
⁹ *Art Journal*, 10 (1 July 1871), 176; quoted in part in Lambourne, *The Aesthetic Movement*, 95.
¹⁰ I follow Cook and Wedderburn here, in linking Ruskin's attack to the 1872/3 exhibition. There are strong reasons to believe, however, that Ruskin was thinking of the 1871/2 Dudley Gallery exhibition, at which Whistler exhibited a 'harmony': the *Harmony in Blue-Green: Moonlight* (Dudley Gallery, 4th Winter Exhibition, Exhibit 265), which prompted Tom Taylor, in *The Times*, to praise this new use of musical titles. Ruskin was in London throughout the Winter of 1871–2. He gave up his Denmark Hill house in March 1872 and seems to have spent only a week in London the following Winter. In October 1873, 'last year' could refer to either exhibition. Ruskin had previously dismissed 'aesthetics' as the branch of art-philosophy concerned with the merely 'musical or harmonic element in every art' in the *Aratra Pentelici* lecture of November 1870 (*Works* 20. 207). Whistler's first use of a musical title was *Symphony in White, No. 3* (RA, 1867); he exhibited *Variations in Flesh Colour and Green: The Balcony* at the RA in 1870.

I intended never to have reprinted the second volume of *Modern Painters* . . . But I find now that the 'general student' has plunged himself into such abysses, not of analytic, but of dissolytic,—dialytic—or even diarrhoeic—lies, belonging to the sooty and sensual elements of his London and Paris life, that, however imperfectly or dimly done, the higher analysis of that early work of mine ought at least to be put within his reach; and the fact, somehow, enforced upon him, that there were people before *he* lived, who knew what 'aesthesis' meant, though they did not think that pigs' flavouring of pigs'-wash was ennobled by giving it that Greek name: and that there were also people before his time who knew what vital beauty meant, though they did not seek it either in the model-room, or the Parc aux Cerfs . . . The reader should know . . . that for what is now called 'aesthesis,' *I* always used, and still use, the English word 'sensation'—as, for instance, the sensation of cold or heat, and of their differences;—of the flavour of mutton and beef, and their differences . . . (*Works* 25. 122–3)

As Ruskin proceeds here with his examples, the contrasts point us more and more to Whistlerian Aestheticism,

. . . of a peacock's and a lark's cry, and their differences;—of the redness in a blush, and in rouge, and their differences;—of the whiteness in snow, and in almond-paste, and their differences;—of the blackness and brightness of night and day, or of smoke and gaslight, and their differences, etc., etc. But for the Perception of Beauty, I always used Plato's word, which is the proper word in Greek, and the only possible *single* word that can be used in any other language by any man who understands the subject,—'Theoria' . . . (*Works* 25. 123)

This is the voice, in 1881, of a dedicated enemy of the Aesthetic Movement.

At which point I must pause to raise the question of what that movement actually was. There is a lingering scepticism as to whether it ever existed in coherent form in Britain. Even among non-sceptics there is a persistent debate about its chronological boundaries, especially its *terminus ab quo*. Du Maurier's *Punch* cartoons of Aesthetes began to appear in the 1870s. The 'Aesthetic Eighties' is the decade conventionally associated with the enthusiasm. Have I not, perhaps, been over-reading Ruskin's publications of the 1840s and 1850s, to construct a fictitious 'Aesthetic Movement' to which he stands opposed? In this context it is, I think, useful to note that Ruskin himself explicitly stated that he had been attacking Aestheticism as early as 1846. Annotating his distinction between the Theoretic and the Aesthetic, in one of the 1883 footnotes to *Modern Painters* ii, Ruskin writes:

It is one of the principal reasons for my reprinting this book, that it contains so early and so decisive warning against the then incipient folly, which in recent days has made art at once the corruption, and the jest, of the vulgar world. (*Works* 4. 35)

Ruskin, in 1883, sees his own career, in retrospect, as a sustained opposition to Aestheticism.

But what were the symptoms of the 'incipient folly' which Ruskin here claims to have denounced in 1846—twelve years before Morris's *Defence of Guenevere* volume, fifteen years before Rossetti's *Fair Rosamund*, sixteen years before Swinburne's review of Baudelaire and Whistler's *The White Girl*, twenty-two years before Swinburne's *William Blake*, and more than a quarter of a century before Pater's *The Renaissance*?

A good specimen of the English Aestheticism of the mid-century might be this—a piece of writing published by a young Englishman in 1851:

You were made for enjoyment, and the world was filled with things which you will enjoy, unless you are too proud to be pleased by them, or too grasping to care for what you cannot turn to other account than mere delight. Remember that the most beautiful things in the world are the most useless; peacocks and lilies for instance . . .

This is a strikingly Aesthetic statement in two ways. The first is its argument, its theoretical content. Published in the same year as Baudelaire's essay 'Of Virtuous Plays and Novels', and a year before Gautier's *Émaux et camées*, it directly parallels both Gautier's disjunction of the beautiful from the useful ('dès qu'une chose devient utile, elle cesse d'être belle', Gautier had written in the preface to *Albertus* in 1832) and his uninhibited stress on the hedonic quality of beauty. But the passage is also remarkable for its imagery, its anticipation of two key icons of the High Aestheticism of the 1870s: 'peacocks and lilies for instance'. Here are the lilies which a satirist of the 1880s, like W. S. Gilbert, would associate with Aestheticism ('Though the Philistines may jostle, you will rank as an apostle in the high aesthetic band, | If you walk down Piccadilly with a poppy or a lily in your medieval hand', as we are told in *Patience* in 1881).[11] And here, too, are the peacocks, whose feathers would feature in the Aesthetic interiors depicted in Du Maurier's cartoons in the 1870s, and whose cry Ruskin would distinguish so sharply from the song of the lark (an irreproachably Theoretic bird) in his attack on Aestheticism in *Love's Meinie*.

Who, then, was this young English Aesthete of 1851? The answer becomes immediately obvious if one reads the sentence to its conclusion:

[11] *Original Plays by W. S. Gilbert*, 3 vols. (London, 1910), iii. 103.

Remember that the most beautiful things in the world are the most useless; pea-cocks and lilies for instance; at least I suppose the quill I hold in my hand writes better than a peacock's would, and the peasants of Vevay, whose fields in spring time are as white with lilies as the Dent du Midi is with its snow, told me the hay was none the better for them. (*Works* 9. 72)

The intimate tone of voice, the distinctive cadence, the characteristic de-tail of locality, all tell one that this is, of course, John Ruskin, writing here in the second chapter of the first volume of *The Stones of Venice* (and who had been at Vevay in 1849).

I do not wish to claim that the whole of *The Stones of Venice* rests upon the attitude articulated in this particular passage. But, equally, I have not omitted any words from it, nor have I torn it misleadingly from its im-mediate context. This is an opinion which Ruskin published in 1851.

As such, it forms a convenient introduction to my second story, a story which wholly contradicts the one which I have been telling hitherto. In this narrative Ruskin is not the enemy of the Aesthetic Movement. On the contrary, he is a key contributor to it: in part its founder, and a con-tinuing inspiration for its activity. The classic statement of this view is given by Amy Cruse in the chapter on 'The Aesthetes' in her *The Victorians and Their Books* (1935), a pioneering study of the English Aesthetic Movement. Cruse's chapter opens with a description of a 'campaign . . . directed against the dullness of spirit that made man in-sensitive to the loveliness, both in nature and in art, that he might enjoy, and made him, of choice, surround himself with things drab and ugly and uninspiring':

The watchword of the campaign was Beauty . . . The advance was made on many and various lines, and one of them lay through books. When twenty-five-year-old John Ruskin opened the campaign by way of the first volume of *Modern Painters*, the immediate result was to bring many who were already lovers of Beauty to his side. The second and third volumes . . . brought many more, and the forces gathered.[12]

Cruse goes on to survey literary Aestheticism, from *Modern Painters* in 1843 to *Marius the Epicurean* in 1885, concluding that Ruskin was, 'the writer to whom beyond all others the Aesthetic Movement owed its in-spiration'.[13]

She is not, of course, unaware that Aesthetes did not always speak en-thusiastically about Ruskin, and deals with this problem by borrowing a

[12] Amy Cruse, *The Victorians and Their Books* (London, 1935), 364.
[13] Ibid. 389.

four-stage description of his career from William de Morgan's novel, *The Old Man's Youth*. In the 1840s, Ruskin, the young rebel, was 'an object of literary ferocity to the standard art critics'. By 1857 he was 'the Apostle whose sayings it was blasphemy to contradict'. By the 1870s, however, he had become 'a fogey with a niche in the Temple of Orthodoxy'. Finally, in the 1890s, he was 'a successful candidate for a niche in the temple of Oblivion'.[14] Ruskin stays the same, while perceptions alter. Though sometimes misunderstood, in other words, he is consistently the friend of Aestheticism.

It might seem easy to dismiss Amy Cruse's analysis. Published in 1935, too early to enjoy the benefits of a more rigorous modern scholarship, yet too late to claim the authority of contemporary witness, perhaps it is irrelevant? In fact there is a good deal of contemporary witness to support her view. In July 1877, for example, Oscar Wilde reviewed the inaugural exhibition of the Grosvenor Gallery, the very event which provoked Ruskin's key attack on Whistler. 'Sir Coutts Lindsay', Wilde writes,

. . . in showing us great works of art, will be most materially aiding that revival of culture and love of beauty which in great part owes its birth to Mr. Ruskin, and which Mr. Swinburne, and Mr. Pater, and Mr. Symonds, and Mr. Morris, and many others are fostering and keeping alive, each in his own peculiar fashion.[15]

Lewis Carroll's 1857 parody of the Aesthete, the 'stunning Cantab' of 'Hiawatha's Photographing' had, Carroll suggested, 'learnt it all from Ruskin'.[16] Richard D'Oyly Carte's circular explaining the satirical point of *Patience* to benighted provincial audiences carefully pointed out that it was designed to mock a ' "movement" in the direction of a more artistic feeling, which had its commencement some time since in the works of Mr Ruskin and his supporters'.[17] Walter Crane, in his article on 'The English Revival in Decorative Art', praised 'aestheticism' as 'a sincere search after more beauty in daily life' and observed that:

---

[14] Ibid. 367, 369, 384, and 389 (slightly adapting the phrasing of William de Morgan, *The Old Man's Youth* (London, 1921), 243).

[15] 'The Grosvenor Gallery', *Dublin University Magazine*, 90 (July 1877), 126.

[16] *The Complete Works of Lewis Carroll*, ed. A. Woollcott (London, 1939), 770. The poem was first published in *The Train*, 4 (July–Dec. 1857), 332–5. It was reprinted in Carroll's *Phantasmagoria* (1869), and again, with illustrations by A. B. Frost satirizing contemporary Aestheticism, in *Rhyme? And Reason?* (1883). Dodgson met Ruskin, at Christ Church, in October 1857.

[17] Quoted in Lambourne, *The Aesthetic Movement*, 123.

Above all influences from the literary side . . . must be placed the work of John Ruskin, an enormously vitalizing and still living force, powerful to awaken thought, and by its kindling enthusiasm to stir the dormant sense of beauty in the minds that come under the spell of his eloquence . . .[18]

Ruskin was, in practice, a close friend of many Aesthetes: of Burne-Jones from the late 1850s until the end of his life; of Dante Gabriel Rossetti from 1854 until their falling-out in 1866 (after which he could still send an encouraging letter on the publication of Rossetti's *Poems* in 1870, and praise his paintings in *The Art of England* lectures of 1883).[19] Without Ruskin's financial support in the 1850s, indeed, it is possible to wonder whether Rossetti would have been able to play his key role in stimulating the flowering of English Aestheticism in the next decade. Ruskin actually owned Rossetti's *Golden Water* of 1858, a crucial transitional painting in the shift from Pre-Raphaelitism to Aestheticism.[20]

William Morris, who in the 1860s at least was an Aesthete (as the utterance of 'The idle singer of an empty day',[21] *The Earthly Paradise* is very much a purposeless, self-sufficient work of art), regarded himself as a disciple of Ruskin. And Ruskin's friendship with Swinburne, in the 1860s, provides the most remarkable instance of Ruskinian involvement in Aestheticism.

In 1864 Whistler painted *The Little White Girl* (later to be retitled *Symphony in White, No. 2*). In 1865, shortly before it was sent to the Royal Academy Exhibition, Swinburne composed 'Before the Mirror' in homage to it. On 2 April he wrote to Whistler enclosing the manuscript of the poem. Whistler responded enthusiastically: two stanzas were printed in the RA catalogue, and the whole text was inscribed on the painting's original frame. What is surprising is the fact that four months

---

[18] Walter Crane, *William Morris to Whistler* (London, 1911), 50 (originally published in the *Fortnightly*, Dec. 1892).

[19] On this relationship see *Works* 36. xliii–li. In 1865 Ruskin attempted to save the friendship by proposing the avoidance of certain contentious topics: 'You shall bar Parma [that is, Correggio] and I Japan' (*Works* 36. 492), a phrase which neatly catches the difference between the enthusiasms of the Theoretic critic and the Aesthetic Japoniste.

[20] See *Works* 36. 488–9 for Ruskin's letter to Rossetti of 1865 explaining that he keeps *Golden Water* and *Passover* at Winnington School, 'because I go there often, and enjoy them more than if they were hanging up here'. *Golden Water* anticipates Albert Moore's paintings of statuesquely beautiful women against floral backgrounds of the 1860s. See also *Works* 35. 638–41 for an unfinished discussion of the painting, intended for *Dilecta*.

[21] *The Collected Works of William Morris*, ed. May Morris (London, 1910–15), iii. 1.

later, on 11 August 1865, Swinburne wrote to Ruskin enclosing, at Ruskin's specific request, another manuscript copy of the poem.[22]

This is a profoundly Aesthetic poem, about the self-containedness, the autonomy of beauty ('But one thing knows the flower; the flower is fair'),[23] which is, in turn, inspired by a key Aesthetic Movement painting (of a beautiful woman contemplating her own beautiful image in a mirror). Yet it was so admired by Ruskin that he, like Whistler, asked Swinburne for a manuscript of the text. The Ruskin of this story is not easily reconciled with Ruskin the enemy of the Aesthetes.

Yet Ruskin the friend and inspiration of the Aesthetes will not quite do either. His attacks on Aestheticism cannot simply be wished away. And two of the most fundamental principles of his theory of art, its moralism and its naturalism, are incompatible with the amoralism and the commitment to artifice which stand at the heart of the Aesthetic position.

So are there ways of mediating between these conflicting accounts of Ruskin and the Aesthetes? I would like to suggest two further stories which attempt, in different ways, to make sense of the contradiction. One of these (my third story) would be of a Ruskin who changes his position over time, shifting from hostility to sympathy and back again. The Ruskin of the 1840s, with his commitment to Evangelical Christianity, was clearly hostile to Aestheticism. But in the 1850s, and more particularly after the 'unconversion' in Turin in the summer of 1858, Ruskin becomes more open to its claims.[24]

In the January of 1858, Ruskin, in his Kensington lecture on 'The Deteriorative Power of Conventional Art', had attacked the notion of 'art . . . practised for its own sake' (*Works* 16. 268). Back from Italy in the Autumn, speaking at the Cambridge School of Art for Workmen on October 29, Ruskin could argue like this:

. . . good Art has only been produced by nations who rejoiced in it; fed themselves with it, as if it were bread; basked in it, as if it were sunshine; shouted at

---

[22] *The Swinburne Letters*, ed. C. Y. Lang, 6 vols. (New Haven and London), 1959–62, i. 118–19 and 130. The painting, now in the Tate Gallery, is no longer in its original frame. But a photograph of the painting, showing the entire poem printed on gold paper and stuck to the frame, with an inscription to Swinburne from Whistler, was sold at Sotheby's on 11 July 1996 (Sale LN 6412; Cat. no. 236).

[23] A. C. Swinburne, *Poems*, 6 vols. (London, 1904), i. 130.

[24] For the term 'unconversion' see *Works* 29. 89. For Ruskin's summary, at the time, of its implications for his theory of art, see his letter to C. E. Norton of 24 Oct. 1858: 'positively to be a first rate painter—you *mustn't* be pious;—but rather a little wicked—and entirely a man of the world. I had been inclining to this opinion for some years; but I clinched it at Turin' (*Correspondence of John Ruskin and Charles Eliot Norton*, 46).

the sight of it; danced with the delight of it; quarrelled for it; fought for it; starved for it . . . (*Works* 16. 184)

Ruskin explains this view by referring to his work during the summer, copying the Veronese paintings in Turin, and more particularly the costumes in *The Presentation of the Queen of Sheba to Solomon*. The feebleness of British culture is demonstrated, Ruskin suggests, by its inability to take real pleasure in such beauty:

Take, for instance, the simplest example, which we can all understand, in the art of dress . . . Of course, all ladies like their dresses to sit well, and be becoming; but of real enjoyment of the beauty of the silk, for the silk's own sake, I find none . . . The pleasure of being well dressed . . . is quite a different thing from delight in the beauty and play of the silken folds and colours themselves, for their own gorgeousness or grace. (*Works* 16. 184–5)

'The beauty of the silk, for the silk's own sake'—this Ruskin, who here, without inhibition, speaks the very language of art for art's sake, becomes increasingly prominent in the next ten years.

These are years in which the old appeal to the divine ('the full comprehension and contemplation of the Beautiful as a gift of God', in the words of *Modern Painters*, ii (*Works* 4. 47)) is no longer readily available to him. In its place, he is obliged to seek alternative foundations for his theories, whether of art or of society. Discussing economics, for example, in 1862 in the *Fraser's Magazine* articles which would become *Munera Pulveris*, Ruskin turns to Greek myth as his source of symbolic value. In the process he celebrates the Homeric enchantress Circe as 'pure Animal life' or the 'power . . . of frank and full vital pleasure' (*Works* 17. 213). This unexpectedly sensual enthusiasm led him in 1863 to commission a drawing of Circe from Burne-Jones.[25] By 1869 Burne-Jones had developed this into the painting *The Wine of Circe* (sold, in the end, not to Ruskin but to Whistler's patron Frederick Leyland). This was a key Aesthetic image, celebrated in D. G. Rossetti's sonnet of 1870 for its power 'to proclaim . . . all rapture in Love's name',[26] and described by John Christian in 1984 as 'a "harmony in yellow", comparable to colour schemes found in contemporary works by Moore and Whistler'.[27]

---

[25] See Ruskin's letter to Ellen Heaton, 18 Nov. 1863, printed in *Sublime & Instructive: Letters from John Ruskin to Louisa Marchioness of Waterford, Anna Blunden and Ellen Heaton*, ed. Virginia Surtees (London, 1972), 251: 'I'm devoted to Circe . . . and he's making me a drawing of her poisoning the meat and going all round the table like a cat—it will be lovely'.

[26] *The Works of Dante Gabriel Rossetti*, ed. W. M. Rossetti (London, 1911), 211.

[27] *The Pre-Raphaelites*, The Tate Gallery, 1984. Catalogue by Alan Bowness *et al.*, 305.

The sympathy with Aestheticism reaches its peak during the friendship with Swinburne in 1865–6, when Ruskin (drawing, one assumes, on the concept, first expressed in *The Stones of Venice*, of Naturalist artists who 'perceive and pursue the good and evil together', *Works* 10. 221) so bravely defends the shocking texts in *Poems and Ballads* (First Series). Resisting attempts to suppress Swinburne's poems, he writes on 14 September 1866 that 'He is infinitely above me in all knowledge and power, and I should no more think of advising or criticising him than of venturing to do it to Turner if he were alive again' (*Works* 36. xlix). Writing to Swinburne himself, on 9 September, Ruskin had said: 'For the matter of it—I consent to much—I regret much—I blame, or reject nothing. I should as soon think of finding fault with you as with a thundercloud or a nightshade blossom.'[28] In 1867 he would even refer to Rose La Touche as 'Atalanta', the heroine of Swinburne's shockingly anti-Theistic verse play *Atalanta in Calydon*.[29] As Ruskin had put it in his lecture 'The Study of Architecture in Our Schools', at the Royal Institute of British Architects on 15 May 1865: 'Gentlemen,—I am no Puritan, and have never praised or advocated Puritanical art' (*Works* 19. 29).

But quite soon after his defence of *Poems and Ballads* in 1866 Ruskin begins to withdraw from this position of sympathy with Aestheticism. His friendships with Swinburne and Rossetti lapse. He starts to worry about the Aesthetic cult of the Greek, feeling an increasing need to distinguish his own understanding of Greek culture from the view articulated by Aesthetes like J. A. Symonds and Walter Pater. He begins to find his views attacked, sometimes by proxy, when disciples are roughly handled by Aesthetic Movement critics. The Reverend R. St John Tyrwhitt, for example (who would serve as Ruskin's secretary during the Slade Professorship), published a very Ruskinian *Handbook of Pictorial Art* in 1868. Emily Pattison dismissed it, in the *Saturday Review* of 22 August, for its tediously didactic theory of art, '. . . work which is not done for its own sake, in which the chief place is claimed for the historical or the moral . . . loses its aesthetic character, and cannot possess

---

[28] *Swinburne Letters*, i. 182.
[29] See Van Akin Burd, *John Ruskin and Rose La Touche* (Oxford, 1979), 111. See also Ruskin's letter of 28 Jan. [1866] to C. E. Norton, in which he calls the play 'the grandest thing ever yet done by a youth—though he is a Demoniac youth' (*Correspondence of John Ruskin & Charles Eliot Norton* 96–7). Ruskin seems especially to have enjoyed discussing Swinburne with Dora Livesey, a pupil at Winnington School and the supposed original of 'Dora' in *Ethics of the Dust*. See his letter to her of 25 Oct. 1867 (Burd, *John Ruskin and Rose La Touche*, 111) and his letter to Margaret Bell of 24 July 1868 (*The Winnington Letters of John Ruskin*, ed. Van Akin Burd (London, 1969), 651).

those poetic elements which fire the fancy and rouse the emotions'.[30] In the same year Swinburne attacked Ruskin's views on paintings more directly, in his *Notes on Some Pictures of 1868*.[31] Ruskin's sympathy for Aestheticism, always somewhat tentative and intermittent, began to decline very rapidly.

His lecture 'The Mystery of Life and Its Arts', delivered in 1868, suggests a returning enthusiasm for religion. Simultaneously the Aesthetic Movement was becoming more obviously shocking. In 1871 Robert Buchanan attacked Rossetti as the leader of 'the Fleshly School of Poetry'. The resulting furore over 'fleshliness' almost certainly helped to prompt Ruskin's attack on the nude in art, and on the study of anatomy in the training of artists, in his *Eagle's Nest* Oxford lectures in the Spring of 1872. The artistic carnality supposedly prompted by the anatomy school, as well as the scientific vivisection practised in the medical laboratory, prompted Ruskin's growing discomfort in his Oxford chair. Swinburne's celebration of sexual passion in the Prelude to *Tristram of Lyonesse* had been published in 1871. Pater's *The Renaissance* and the first volume of J. A. Symonds's *Studies of the Greek Poets* (a book which argued that 'we too often attempt to import the alien elements of metaphysical dogmatism and moral prejudice into the sphere of beauty')[32] both appeared in 1873. In the Autumn of that year Ruskin made the first of his attacks on Whistler, and seems thereafter to be irretrievably committed to a position of hostility to Aestheticism.

Ruskin, then, can be both a friend and an enemy of the Aesthetes without contradiction—it is simply a matter of where in his career you look. This is a more attractive story than the previous two, but still, I fear, not a wholly satisfactory one. Ruskin's statements of opinion do not fall into chronological groups as clearly as one might wish. The final volume of *Modern Painters*, for example, appears midway between the

---

[30] *Saturday Review*, 26 (22 Aug. 1868), 262.

[31] See Swinburne's letter to W. M. Rossetti of 4 Jan. 1875 about his plans to reprint his own portion of this jointly written pamphlet in *Essays & Studies* (1875): 'I am not at all minded to cancel the other passages of a combative kind; that on Frère I stick to as correct in the teeth of all the Ruskins in the world' (*Swinburne Letters*, ii. 363). In the *Academy Notes* of 1857, Ruskin could find 'no words tender enough nor reverent enough' for the paintings of French peasant life by Edouard Frère: they combined 'the depth of Wordsworth, the grace of Reynolds, and the holiness of Angelico' (*Works* 14. 142–3). Swinburne, in 1868, commented, 'He has been likened to Wordsworth; it must be a Wordsworth shorn of his beams . . . [who] would pass off on us . . . mere trickeries of coarse and easy sentiment' (*The Bonchurch Edition of the Complete Works of Algernon Charles Swinburne*, ed. E. Gosse and T. J. Wise, 20 vols. (London, 1925–7), xv. 207–8).

[32] J. A. Symonds, *Studies of the Greek Poets* (London, 1873), 416.

Turin unconversion and the friendship with Swinburne. One might therefore expect it to contain evidence of a sympathy with the Aesthetic view of art. In fact it is based, even in 'The Wings of the Lion' (the chapter which most directly incorporates the Turin experience), on the same, fundamentally Theoretic approach as the previous volumes. J. B. Bullen usefully draws attention to a passage in 'The Wings of the Lion' which praises the sensuality of Venetian art.[33] But this praise needs to be read in the context of the moralism of the end of the chapter, where Ruskin dwells on the way in which 'the great Venetians . . . in wanton compliance . . . fostered the folly, and enriched the luxury of their age' (*Works* 7. 299). Eight chapters later, in 'The Hesperid Aeglé', Venice will come to stand for 'the death which attends the vain pursuit of beauty' (*Works* 7. 437).

By the 1870s Ruskin's texts are rarely sufficiently single-minded to permit neat pattern-making of any kind. I would therefore like to attempt one final story, which may perhaps bring us a little closer to the truth. The key feature of this narrative is that it no longer focuses solely on Ruskin and the Aesthetes. The reason for this is that a simply binary division between a Swinburnian or Whistlerian Aestheticism, on the one hand, and the Theoretic or moral view of art, on the other, will not suffice.

Ruskin's argument with the Aesthetes had the bitterness and intensity often associated with internecine quarrels, and an internecine quarrel is precisely what it was. Both Ruskin and the Aesthetes were, in fact, more significantly opposed to a common enemy than they were to each other. That common enemy was Puritanism, with its iconoclastic suspicion of visual imagery and its ascetic hostility to sensory pleasure.

Puritanism, of course, is no longer the power in the land that it was 150 years ago. When Matthew Arnold called the Nonconformist British middle-class 'Philistines'[34] he intended to give a dog a bad name and hang it, and by and large he succeeded. The religious hostility to art, once so widespread, has almost vanished from contemporary consciousness. Today we assume that a hostility to art can be the result only of ignorance—an assumption enacted on the level of public policy in the view that it is proper to subsidize the arts from general taxation.

33 See J. B. Bullen, *The Myth of the Renaissance in Nineteenth-Century Writing* (Oxford, 1994), 260. Bullen is referring to *Works* 7. 296–7.

34 Arnold began to use the term in his Oxford lecture on 'Heinrich Heine' (13 June 1863; repr. in the *Cornhill* in August 1863 and in *Essays in Criticism*, First Series, 1865). He links the term most directly to the middle class and the 'Protestant Dissenter' in Chapter 3 of *Culture and Anarchy* (1869), originally an article in *Cornhill*, 17 (Feb. 1868).

It was not so in the Britain of previous centuries. Rejection of the arts was a coherent intellectual position, rooted in an ancient tradition (Plato, after all, had banned poets from his ideal society in the *Republic*), and demonstrated in tens of thousands of unadorned Protestant churches and chapels, and in hundreds of thousands of piously austere homes. In the 1840s and 1850s the British press found it hard to distinguish Aestheticism from Tractarianism and Roman Catholicism—a significant confusion, indicating the extent to which making a case for the importance of art necessarily involved a quarrel with a long-standing religious tradition. Ruskin and the Aesthetes were both involved in that quarrel, on the same side but with different tactics.

Ruskin, in this analysis, is continuously involved, from the early 1840s to the end of his career, in a complex negotiation between the Philistines (in Arnold's serious sense of that word) on the one hand and the Aesthetes on the other. The Aesthetes are happy to separate art from religion. The Philistines, or Puritans, are happy to separate religion and the conduct of life from art. Ruskin occupies an intermediate position between them, sympathetic with both, and endeavouring to maintain a constant contact. He is, in other words, neither an Aesthete nor an anti-Aesthete, but rather a moderate Aesthete, on a scale which includes, at one extreme, the Puritan rejection of art. Properly to understand the theoretical landscape of art criticism in the mid-nineteenth century we need not two but three terms: Puritanical, Theoretic, and Aesthetic.

One consequence of this intermediate stance is that Ruskin is frequently engaged in an attempt, not to reject, but rather to modify or moderate Aesthetic arguments. His quarrel with the Aesthetes over the Greek is one instance of this; his contest with Pater over Botticelli is another. Ruskin responds to Aesthetic discoveries by trying to bring them into the realm of the moral and spiritual. But it would be surprising if he did not, in the process, sometimes also make statements which seem to be exclusively the property of one or the other camp. Wishing to maintain contact with both the religious and the Aesthetic factions, the Theoretic critic speaks both of their languages, as well as an intermediate one of his own.

I quoted earlier from Ruskin's Inaugural Address to the Cambridge Art School, with its strikingly art-for-art's-sake argument about the sensory pleasure of dress fabrics. The same lecture goes on to assert that 'there is no chance of our getting good Art unless we resist our delight in it' and that 'Art has always destroyed the power and life of those who pursued it for pleasure only'. Ruskin's argument is built up as a patchwork of conflicting views, working towards the complex conclusion that 'you must not follow Art without pleasure, nor must you follow it for the sake of pleasure' (*Works* 16. 187–8, 197).

This patchwork technique is the reason why we can find a remarkable prototype of 1870s Aestheticism in a work so profoundly dedicated to the idea of morally and socially responsible art as *The Stones of Venice*. Another striking example is provided by 'The Hesperid Aeglé' in *Modern Painters* V. On the one hand, Ruskin here deplores the way in which Venice represents 'the death which attends the vain pursuit of beauty' (*Works* 7. 437). On the other, he offers a hostile definition of Puritanism:

Religious asceticism, being the refusal of pleasure and knowledge for the sake (as supposed) of religion . . . All . . . asceticisms have their bright and their dark sides . . . None [is] a healthy or central state of man. (*Works* 7. 424)

Ruskin is endeavouring to mediate between extreme positions, and is speaking a mixed, or composite, dialect as he does so.

He was not, in fact, the only writer who could be seen as operating in an intermediate zone of this kind. Gautier, in the 1830s, had defined the Aesthetic position as one which kept art distinct from both religion and utility. If Ruskin's partial, or impure, Aestheticism arose from an endeavour to negotiate between art and the claims of religion, the Epicurean ethics and social libertarianism of the purer Aesthetes could sometimes involve a corresponding overlap with Utilitarianism. A stress on art as 'pleasure, not truth' carries with it a flavour of Bentham's hedonic calculus, and of the more philosophical meanings (at least) of utility; Swinburne's political liberalism and quarrel with Christianity would carry him frequently into the purposeful camp of John Stuart Mill.

But Swinburne's Aesthetic and non-Aesthetic writings tend to be clearly marked as such: *Poems and Ballads* (First Series) is, almost wholly, art for art's sake, while *Songs before Sunrise* is commitedly political and irreligious. The mingling, or patchwork, effect remains distinctively Ruskinian. I would therefore like to end my fourth story with one of the most striking of all Ruskin's patchworks, which also conveniently brings us back to the *Whistler v. Ruskin* trial of 1878.

At some time after the April of 1877 (when Fairfax-Murray joined him in Venice)[35] Ruskin sent copies by Fairfax-Murray of the Lippi Madonna and Carpaccio's *Reception of the Ambassadors* back to the

---

35 See Jeanne Clegg, *Ruskin and Venice* (London, 1981), 157.

newly founded St George's Museum in Sheffield. They were, according to the curator, Henry Swan, 'the first pictures sent by the Master to the Museum' (*Works* 24. 451). Swan produced an undated pamphlet of commentary on them, mostly taken from previously published works by Ruskin, but with a few paragraphs of new material. In these new paragraphs (presumably written in 1877 or early 1878) Ruskin turns from a discussion of Titian and Angelico to a brief description of Carpaccio's *Dream of St Ursula* and Botticelli's *Spring*. The 'perfect power' of the schools of Venice and Florence is

better recognised by two exquisite pictures of more simple men—Carpaccio's 'Dream of St. Ursula,' a harmony of crimson and white, with subdued gold and green; and Botticelli's 'Spring,' a harmony of green and white, with subdued gold and crimson. (*Works* 24. 453)

This, you will remember, is the critic who in October 1873 had attacked Whistler for 'a daub professing to be "a harmony in pink and white" (or some such nonsense;) absolute rubbish', and who in the June of 1877 would attack him again for 'wilful imposture'. To steal Whistler's distinctive concept of paintings as 'harmonies' of colour (rather than moral, religious, mimetic, or social statements), at this time and so blatantly, is either the most deplorable instance of inconsistency and self-contradiction or an audacious demonstration of the way in which the Theoretic critic can, without embarrassment, use the discourses of both religion and Aestheticism to construct a view of art intermediate between them.

There is no escaping the fact that Ruskin, in the 1870s, expressed views fiercely hostile to Aestheticism. But in the same years he could also speak and act in ways which seem unexpectedly Aesthetic. He borrowed his enemies' language. And one might even find an Aesthetic assumption at work in the very pattern of Ruskin's career in this decade. In January 1871, in the first letter of *Fors Clavigera*, he announced an intention to separate his social and his artistic utterances:

I have been ordered to endeavour to make our English youth care somewhat for the arts; and must put my uttermost strength into that business. To which end I must clear myself from all sense of responsibility for the material distress around me, by explaining to you, once for all, in the shortest English I can, what I know of its causes . . . (*Works* 27. 13)

In previous decades, art and society had been increasingly mingled in Ruskin's writings. Now he proposes, instead, to keep them sharply distinct, channelling his social concern into *Fors Clavigera* and his thoughts on art into his Oxford lectures. Those thoughts on art remain Theoretic. But their segregation is distinctly reminiscent of the Aesthetic separation of art from moral and social responsibilities. The Ruskinian position, improbable though it may seem, is a sustained combination of two apparently contradictory stances and, as such, has its own peculiar coherence.

7

Myth and Gender in
Ruskin's Science

SHARON ARONOFSKY WELTMAN

In *Love's Meinie* (1873–81), *Proserpina* (1875–86), and *Deucalion* (1875–83), John Ruskin creates an alternative science. Critics have rightly noted that Ruskin's natural history is old-fashioned, mythic, and opposed to some of the greatest scientific innovators of his time, such as Charles Darwin and John Tyndall.[1] However, his mythological approach to knowledge has one surprisingly radical side-effect: he feminizes science.

Within Victorian culture, science stands in gendered opposition to the Nature it studies; this has been well documented.[2] As a by-product of Ruskin's effort to devise a new kind of science on principles different from his contemporaries, he undermines the gender hierarchy that partially constitutes Victorian science. He feminizes science in a variety of ways. Most simply, in Ruskin's 'grammars' of botany and ornithology, as he called *Proserpina* and *Love's Meinie* (*Works* 25. xxx), as well as in his books on geology and mineralogy, *Deucalion* and *Ethics of the Dust* (1866), Ruskin includes women as participants in scientific inquiry,

---

[1] Among critics who have commented on Ruskin's late science are Jeffrey L. Spear, *Dreams of an English Eden: Ruskin and His Tradition in Social Criticism* (New York, 1984); John Rosenberg, *The Darkening Glass: A Portrait of Ruskin's Genius* (New York, 1963); Robert Hewison, *John Ruskin: The Argument of the Eye* (London, 1976); Raymond Fitch, *The Poison Sky: Myth and Apocalypse in Ruskin* (Athens, Oh., 1982); Dinah Birch, *Ruskin's Myths* (Oxford, 1988); Paul Sawyer, *Ruskin's Poetic Argument: The Design of the Major Works* (Ithaca, NY, 1985); Frederick Kirchhoff, 'A Science against Sciences: Ruskin's Floral Mythology', in U. C. Knoeplfmacher and G. B. Tennyson (eds.), *Nature and the Victorian Imagination* (Berkeley and Los Angeles, 1977). All these critics have influenced my own position, but none explores the constitutive role gender plays in Ruskin's science.

[2] See Anne K. Mellor, '*Frankenstein*: A Feminist Critique of Science', in George Levine (ed.), *One Culture: Essays in Science and Literature* (Madison, 1987), 287–312; Brian Easlea, *Science and Sexual Oppression: Patriarchy's Confrontation with Women and Nature* (London, 1981); Cynthia Eagle Russett, *Sexual Science: The Victorian Construction of Womanhood* (Cambridge, Mass., 1989).

appealing to authorities they would know and using arguments de-signed—however condescendingly—to appeal to them. He also attacks violent and intrusive aspects of traditional science that have been gen-der-coded as masculine; he offers instead a gentle and frankly more pas-sive science based on quiet observation, a science which corresponds to stereotypically feminine characteristics. More surprisingly he revises Darwinian evolution, which depends upon deadly competition for re-sources and for females, into a mythic principle of metamorphosis that Ruskin identifies as feminine. Ruskin also rewrites Linnaean taxonomy, based on a hierarchy of male over female parts of flowers, into a system of moral classification that privileges the female.

The most subtle and most pervasive feminization of science comes from Ruskin's placing all animals and other natural forms under the syn-cretic and formative power of the Greek goddess Athena as part of a sys-tem of natural hieroglyphs, in which every living and non-living object represents something else. An aspect of learning to decipher this natural language is to study what in *The Queen of the Air* Ruskin calls 'living hi-eroglyphs' or 'Words of God' (the snakes, birds, crystals, and flowers Ruskin analyses in his scientific texts); empirically observing how the liv-ing signifiers move or grow or die leads to an understanding of what they mean. Because he feminizes language in *The Queen of the Air* by mak-ing it the province of Athena, and because science is a mode of reading Athena's natural hieroglyphics, science is feminized, too.

Technologies that ravage the landscape have long been figured as male: the common image of 'raping the earth' expresses this tradition. Even pure science—exclusive of technological application—has generally pictured its object of study as feminine. Certainly Darwin follows this convention in *The Origin of Species*, where he personifies Nature as fe-male, and other instances abound. This construction of science and sci-entists as male and the subject they study as female implies not only bipolar opposition but also a power dynamic. Critics particularly point to Francis Bacon, father of empiricism, who spoke of science as bind-ing Nature and all her children to service and making her a slave.[3] Ludmilla Jordanova cites an iconographic example: the late nineteenth-century statue in the Paris medical faculty of a robed woman with ex-posed breasts removing her veil, called *Nature Unveiling Herself before*

[3] Mellor offers quotations with comparable imagery from Isaac Barrow, Robert Boyle, and Henry Oldenberg. For 19th-cent. examples, see Evelyn Fox Keller, *Secrets of Life, Secrets of Death* (New York, 1992), 56–72.

Science, implies an erotics of gender hierarchy in scientific culture.[4] Even when scientific inquiry involves no cruelty to organic creatures and no plunder of the earth, the controlling metaphor of the Rational conquering the Mysterious, of the quest to penetrate the unknown and unseen, contributes to the stereotype of male scientist mastering female nature.

Substantial research suggests that nineteenth-century science regarded women as not only more closely tied to nature than men, but also so inferior to men as to be almost a different species, less evolved, not fully human.[5] Londa Schiebinger points out that most European visual depictions of apes were of females, and that debates about whether apes could be educated paralleled those about women and Negroes, suggesting the liminal position all three groups held in Victorian scientific imagination.[6] Darwin would not be so sloppy as to hint that women belong to a different species; Darwin and Spencer usually present women's supposedly lower development in terms of their being childlike rather than animalistic. Woman is 'intermediate between the child and the man'.[7] In other words, because women generally do not grow as big or as hairy as men, they have appeared to these thinkers to remain less fully developed: the male appearance is considered the appropriate adult human state, while the smaller, less hirsute female appearance seems immature. The need for women's arrested development was explained in reproductive terms: the energy required to come to full maturity was necessarily spent producing and nurturing young.[8] But, like Freud, other Victorians managed to suggest that 'ontogeny recapitulates phylogeny', so that a less developed human is a less evolved and less human one, after all.[9] In each of these examples, women are understood by Victorian scientists to be

4 Ludmilla Jordanova, *Sexual Visions: Images of Gender in Science and Medicine between the Eighteenth and Twentieth Centuries* (Madison, 1989), 87.

5 See Gill Kirkup and Laurie Smith Keller, *Inventing Women: Science, Technology, and Gender* (Cambridge, 1992), 73; Donna Haraway, *Primate Visions: Gender, Race and Nature in the World of Modern Science* (New York, 1989), 292; Nancy Paxton, *George Eliot and Herbert Spencer: Feminism, Evolutionism, and the Reconstruction of Gender* (Princeton, 1991), 171–3; Anne Fausto-Sterling, *Myths of Gender: Biological Theories about Women and Men* (New York, 1985), 175–87; Russett, *Sexual Science, passim*; Nancy Tuana, *The Less Noble Sex: Scientific, Religious, and Philosophical Conceptions of Women's Nature* (Bloomington, Ind., 1993), *passim*.

6 Londa Schiebinger, *Nature's Body: Gender in the Making of Modern Science* (Boston, 1993), 186.

7 Charles Darwin, *The Descent of Man, and Selection in Relation to Sex* (1871; repr. New York, 1901), 717.

8 Ibid. 295–6.

9 See Tuana, *Less Noble Sex*, 34–50, for a clear overview of this issue.

closer than men to nature; indeed that notion goes back at least as far as Aristotle.

Ruskin's writing undermines the general hierarchy of masculine science over feminine nature. Ruskin redefines science as an exercise in wonder at nature rather than control over nature. He rejected those aspects of Victorian science and technology that were tied to aggression, to imperialism, to control, to mastery over nature, to greed that would result in bad stewardship of the earth, or to harsh use of colonial women and children.[10] Whereas the early nineteenth-century scientist Humphrey Davy applauded chemistry for inventing gunpowder,[11] Ruskin cites the power to blow up people as an example of precisely how science has failed (*Works* 34. 314). Ruskin loathed dissection to learn anatomy and hated vivisection for any scientific purpose. He named the university's decision to allow vivisection in Oxford laboratories as his reason for resigning the Slade professorship. He disdained 'materialist science' that kills birds or insects in order to study them, and reviled technology that pollutes as it harnesses nature's power. A spiritual or mythic science, science grounded in love of beauty rather than in its denial, would conserve rather than exploit.[12]

The cultural associations of aggression, control, and mastery as traditionally masculine are obvious; that Ruskin advocates a science founded on principles traditionally considered feminine may not be so clear. He promotes scientific study that appreciates and protects rather than kills. Such a nurturing role figured as feminine should not surprise us in cultural context, but Ruskin does not so far feminize science as to imagine its giving life. The nineteenth century construes that as monstrous usurpation, as in *Frankenstein*.[13] Nevertheless, in retreating from the common vision of science as aggressor, Ruskin feminizes it. By imagining a reverential science that values life and champions meticulous but passive observation of nature, rather than dominates or destroys it, Ruskin subverts the masculine/feminine hierarchy that partly constitutes Victorian scientific culture.

In *The Stones of Venice* (1851–3), written long before Ruskin's angriest diatribes against contemporary scientists in the 1870s and 1880s,

---

[10] Sawyer, *Ruskin's Poetic Argument*, 271.

[11] Mellor, 'Frankenstein', 292.

[12] Sawyer, *Ruskin's Poetic Argument*, 272.

[13] For two salient readings of *Frankenstein* as feminist critique of 19th-cent. science, see Mellor, 'Frankenstein', and Robin Roberts, *A New Species: Gender and Science in Science Fiction* (Urbana, Ill., 1993).

Ruskin describes two kinds of knowledge-seekers, the scientist and the artist. Robert Hewison identifies the artistic, perceiving man as Ruskin the naturalist:[14]

The thoughtful man is gone far away to seek; but the perceiving man must sit still, and open his heart to receive. The thoughtful man is knitting and sharpening himself into a two-edged sword, wherewith to pierce. The perceiving man is stretching himself into a four-cornered sheet, wherewith to catch. (*Works* 11. 52)

Ruskin presents both men positively, but he represents their opposition through sexual imagery. Given the gender polarity conventionally assigned to the pairs of terms that Ruskin includes (active/passive, seeking/sitting, sword/sheet, pierce/catch) and given Ruskin's choice of other words associated with the feminine that he gives to the perceiving man (open, heart, receive), the artist or perceiving naturalist becomes feminized within this dyad. This feminine type is Ruskin's model for scientists who perceive without piercing; who need no phallic swords or dissection tools or engines of war; and who open their hearts to receive the knowledge nature provides.

Ruskin also feminizes science by removing scientific education from an exclusively masculine province; by constructing a female audience within his scientific prose; by teaching science to girls (such as those at the progressive Winnington school, where he sometimes worked in the 1860s); and by often lecturing to women on scientific topics. He repeatedly comments that his books on botany and ornithology are for young people, explicitly including girls (*Works* 25. 35, 413, 456, 483, 504). He writes a mineralogy textbook for 'little housewives' (*The Ethics of the Dust*), despite the fact that mineralogy was not typically seen as a proper subject of study for the female sex. An additional way in which Ruskin endeavours to include women in scientific study is to quote profusely from botanical authorities that women readers would know and find non-threatening. The source of this kind that he most frequently alludes to (albeit condescendingly) is Lindley's *Ladies' Botany*, and he refers to 'Aunt Judy' (Mrs Gatty) whose 1859 *Tales* were well known, on more than one occasion. By giving authorities like these almost equal footing with Linnaeus, Ruskin undermines the privilege that the 'master' texts (aimed at and written by men) normally have, especially since in this case the standard authorities are by far the more respected, with good reason. He also implicitly gives an aura of feminine authority to scientific inquiry by subordinating empirical knowledge to mythical, so

---

[14] Hewison, *The Argument of the Eye*, 176.

that he invokes Proserpina, Demeter, Athena, Iris, and the Egyptian Neith as authorizing his scientific texts.[15]

Despite the patronizing tone Ruskin often uses when directly addressing his female readers and listeners in his scientific treatises, the mere fact that he includes them at all is significant. An example is a lecture in *Deucalion* on gems called 'The Iris of the Earth', where he urges women to be tabernacles and to adorn themselves wisely with jewels. As Paul Sawyer points out, Ruskin uses his 'characteristic tone of saccharine condescension' when speaking to young women.[16] Yet by constructing the readers of *Deucalion* as women, Ruskin alters the notion that geology—or any science—is the exclusive province of men. The effort is compromised by his patronizing attitude and by the sudden address of this particular lecture, on jewelry, to women, when the lectures in *Deucalion* on glacial movement are addressed to a universal (and thus silently understood as male) reader. However, even in *The Eagle's Nest*, his Oxford lectures of 1872 reconciling science and art, where the audience is specifically identified as male, Ruskin conjures the image of women as successfully engaging in scientific investigations. He asks his readers to imagine two young women resolute in pursuit of astronomy, and he applauds the one who braves catching a cold in the observatory to view the night sky (*Works* 22. 141–3). Despite his grating sweetness in referring to the starry-eyed girls, he puts them in the masculine preserve of the observatory, where serious astronomical observation takes place.

Ruskin envisions scientific activity as suitable for women; nevertheless, he retains the traditional sense that the material studied is feminine, complicating his diffusion of the rigid gender hierarchy he writes against. For example, he names his book on botany *Proserpina* and then claims that every young woman is Proserpina (*Works* 25. 435), indicating every girl's right to study science and simultaneously every girl's identity with the topic itself: young women are both subject and object of botanical inquiry.[17] He thus intensifies the convention that positions women closer than men to nature. He repeatedly identifies women as women with birds, flowers, gems. These are entirely traditional identifications; for example, calling a young woman a 'bird' goes back to the fourteenth century. Naming a girl a 'jewel' or a 'flower' is just as trite. But Ruskin

[15] See Dinah Birch, '*The Ethics of the Dust*: Ruskin's Authorities', *Prose Studies*, 12 (1989), 308–24.

[16] Sawyer, *Ruskin's Poetic Argument*, 27 n.

[17] Schiebinger points out that botany was considered the most appropriate science for ladies in the nineteenth century, citing several famous examples of women botanists (*Nature's Body*, 36).

makes unusual use of the convention, because these traditionally feminine objects are exactly those he examines in his natural histories and encourages women to examine, too. The clearest example of how he redoubles women's connection to the material studied is his description of the swallow from *Love's Meinie*, an ornithological incarnation of the ideal housewife in 'Of Queens' Gardens'.

When describing the swallow's virtues, Ruskin echoes that essay from *Sesame and Lilies* (1865), Ruskin's best-seller and a volume often presented to young women as a gift (*Works* 18. 5). First, here is the passage from 'Of Queens' Gardens':

This is the true nature of home—it is the place of Peace; the shelter, not only from all injury, but from all terror, doubt, and division. In so far as . . . the hostile society of the outer world . . . is allowed . . . to cross the threshold, it ceases to be home . . . But so far as it is a sacred place, a vestal temple, a temple of the hearth, . . . so far it vindicates the name, and fulfils the praise, of Home.

And wherever a true wife comes, this home is always round her. The stars only may be over her head; the glowworm in the night-cold grass may be the only fire at her foot; but home is yet wherever she is. (*Works* 18 122–3)

Kate Millett's famous attack on Ruskin in *Sexual Politics* has prompted decades of debate between critics who, agreeing with Millett, consider Ruskin's mythic vision to limit women's role and those who consider the essay to widen women's sphere of action by redefining domestic power.[18] Complicating either conclusion about 'Of Queens' Gardens' are the parallels between the wife and the swallow in *Love's Meinie*. Here the bird seems always to be female:

Understand the beauty of the bird which lives with you in your own houses, and which purifies for you, from its insect pestilence, the air that you breathe. Thus

---

[18] See Kate Millett, *Sexual Politics* (London, 1977), 88–108, and 'The Debate over Woman: Ruskin Versus Mill', *Victorian Studies*, 14 (1970), 63–82; David Sonstroem, 'Millett Versus Ruskin: A Defense of Ruskin's "Of Queen's Gardens" ', *Victorian Studies*, 20 (1977), 283–97; Sandra Gilbert and Susan Gubar, *The Madwoman in the Attic: The Woman Writer and the Nineteenth-century Literary Imagination* (New Haven, 1979); Nina Auerbach, *Woman and the Demon: The Life of a Victorian Myth* (Cambridge, Mass., 1982); Elizabeth Helsinger, Robin Lauterbach Sheets, and William Veeder (eds.), *The Woman Question: 1837–83*, 3 vols. (New York and London, 1983), i: *Defining Voices*; Dinah Birch, 'Ruskin's "Womanly Mind" ', *Essays in Criticism*, 38/4 (1988), 308–24; Deborah Epstein Nord, 'Mill and Ruskin on the Woman Question Revisited', in James Engell and David Perkins (eds.), *Teaching Literature: What is Needed Now* (Cambridge, Mass., 1988), 73–83; Sharon Aronofsky Weltman, ' "Be no more Housewives, but Queens": Queen Victoria in John Ruskin's Domestic Mythology', in Margaret Homans and Adrienne Munich (eds.), *Re-making Queen Victoria* (Cambridge and London, 1997).

the sweet domestic thing has done, for men, at least these four thousand years. She has been their companion, not of the home merely, but of the hearth, and the threshold; companion only endeared by departure and showing better her loving-kindness by her faithful return. . . . In her feeble presence, the cowardice, or the wrath, of sacrilege has changed into the fidelities of sanctuary. (*Works* 25. 71–7)

Like the 'true wife', the 'sweet domestic' swallow guards the home, the hearth, the threshold. Both keep their homes for men, and have done so for as long as there have been women and birds. The swallow purifies the home from pestilence, cowardice, wrath, and sacrilege; likewise, the woman protects from injury, terror, doubt, and division. The woman is at home in the wilderness, the wild creature is at home in a house. Like any 'true wife', the bird is a faithful companion, loving and kind. In making the swallow so startlingly like the famous woman from 'Of Queens' Gardens', Ruskin does more than emphasize attractively do-mestic qualities in the feral bird: he mythologizes both real women and real birds, investing each with far more power than a practical Victorian audience might willingly admit. He also exalts the notion of identity between observer and observed, between the female naturalist and the objects of nature she studies. Women's special connection to birds or flowers does not disable their understanding. A sense of disconnection and objective distance from the material studied is more debilitating to genuine knowledge than a sympathetic bond.

Besides feminizing science by rejecting aggressive methods and by en-couraging women to participate in scientific study through the variety of rhetorical tactics we have just discussed, Ruskin also feminizes science by resisting recognition of Darwinian evolution that occurs meaning-lessly through cut-throat competition and by seeking instead an al-ternative paradigm that allows for transformations to occur without competition and with transcendent significance through the feminine medium of mythic metamorphosis. In other words, Ruskin revises Darwin by substituting metamorphosis for evolution.

Natural selection depends on excess population and on rabid compe-tition to produce conditions in which only the 'fittest' survive; Ruskin ex-iles such a scenario to a nightmare landscape exemplified in the barren, choking brambles he describes at Brantwood (*Works* 25. 293). For him there can be no excess population when, famously, 'there is no wealth but life' (*Works* 17. 105). He disapproves of competition in any form, even among students (*Works* 22. 243). He offers instead a rich world of chaotic flux, traditionally characterized as feminine. The identification of competition as masculine is clear from 'Of Queens' Gardens', where women guide men away from the fatal competition of political economy. Because women 'enter no contest', they remain morally untainted by the 'inevitable error' that corrupts men, who must enter the rough world of the free market-place (*Works* 18. 122).

Critics often talk about Ruskin's disagreement with Darwin's ideas: he repeatedly makes fun of Darwin's theory of evolution, much to his friends' and editors' embarrassment (*Works* 25. xlvi). In the overtly scientific books, *Love's Meinie* and *Proserpina*, Ruskin's speculations on the descent of various plants contain numerous low jokes and irritated outbursts about the theory of evolution that support the critical commonplace that Ruskin opposed Darwin (*Works* 25. 263, 268, 291, 301). But despite Ruskin's often deserved reputation as an anti-Darwinist, his position is not so simple, and he even agrees with Darwin occasionally. For example, in *The Queen of the Air*, Ruskin claims that his own theories 'are in nowise antagonistic to the theories which Mr. Darwin's unwearied and unerring investigations are every day rendering more probable' (*Works* 19. 358 n.). Even in *Proserpina* Ruskin uses Darwin to uphold his point when it is convenient; for example, he twice respectfully refers to Darwin's work with carnivorous orchids as an authoritative source for his own analysis (*Works* 25. 224, 25. 546). In fact, Darwin epitomizes what Ruskin demands from scientists: a meticulous observer who loves the profusion of nature without exploiting it, who records resemblances in richly metaphorical language.[19] But after claiming no antagonism to Darwin's 'unerring investigations', Ruskin continues: 'The aesthetic relations of species are independent of their origin' (*Works* 19. 358 n.). He shifts the significance of species from their origin through natural selection to their mythic or aesthetic or moral meaning.

Why does Ruskin display such ambivalence toward Darwin's ideas? For two reasons: aesthetics and spirituality. Darwin's discussion of the peacock provokes two of Ruskin's most blatant attacks in both *Love's Meinie* and *Proserpina* (*Works* 25. 36, 25. 262–3). To Ruskin, explaining those fabulous feathers as the result of generations of sexual selection misses the point by distracting the observer's attention away from what is really important about the peacock, its beauty.[20] Far different from the

---

[19] See Gillian Beer, *Darwin's Plots: Evolutionary Narrative in Darwin, George Eliot and Nineteenth-Century Fiction* (London, 1983), 62.

[20] That the sexual aspect of both these arguments should be the very one that Ruskin dislikes should not surprise us, knowing his apparent discomfort with adult sexuality. Yet Ruskin sublimates the rejection of sexuality in birds and plants, disguising his response as an aesthetic rather than prudish repugnance.

creationist arguments brought against Darwin by Wilberforce and others, Ruskin's objections to natural selection stem from his sense of aesthetics as moral: natural selection seems ugly and meaningless, while for Ruskin the world's beauty manifests intensely felt spiritual truths. Darwinian correlations among species depend on mere descent, on accidents of time, and on deathly competition, not on mythic significance.

Ruskin cannot deny evolution through natural selection on empirical grounds. Like Darwin he knows that organic forms shift continually. But he is hostile to a science that degrades the meaning of these variations into a mere quest for beginnings. He alters the explanation of continual change in natural forms from linear evolution to free-flowing metamorphosis. Gillian Beer has pointed out that Darwin draws on the notion of metamorphosis to establish the idea of evolution through natural selection,[21] so in a sense Ruskin reverses Darwin's revision. But when Ruskin provides a mythic alternative to evolution, he unwittingly feminizes it, for mysterious shape-shifting has long had feminine associations in Western culture.

The wifely swallow from *Love's Meinie* serves as an example of Ruskinian flux as opposed to Darwinian evolution. Ruskin describes the swallow metamorphosing from one creature to another:

You can only rightly describe the bird by the resemblances, and images of what it seems to have changed from,—then adding the fantastic and beautiful contrast of the unimaginable change. It is an owl that has been trained by the Graces. It is a bat that loves the morning light. It is the aerial reflection of a dolphin. It is the tender domestication of a trout. (*Works* 25. 57)

The metamorphic quality of Ruskin's description self-consciously invokes evolutionary change, only to debunk it a moment later: 'the transformations believed in by the anatomist are as yet proved true in no single instance, and in no substance, spiritual or material'. Ruskin opts instead for a mythological understanding of animal significance: 'the transformations believed in by the mythologist are at least spiritually true; you cannot too carefully trace or too accurately consider them' (*Works* 25. 57). The parallel structure of the prose here gives the two kinds of transformation equal weight, even though Ruskin knows perfectly well that, though not proven, Darwin's theory of evolution is very likely (*Works* 19. 358 n.). His point is not curmudgeonly disapproval of new-fangled science, but to enjoin his reader to love and appreciate the natural beauty around him or her: 'I cannot too often, or too earnestly,

---

[21]   Beer, *Darwin's Plots*, 104–45.

urge you not to waste your time in guessing what animals may once have been, while you remain in nearly total ignorance of what they are' (*Works* 25. 57). Seeing the swallow as potentially owl, bat, dolphin, and trout helps us understand not only the spiritual truths about the swallow, but also that everything can be similarly seen as incipiently something else. Since both nature and the principle of change are typically figured as feminine, to picture nature in constant chaotic flux (as opposed to linear evolutionary progress) is to intensify the feminine quality of what is already seen as feminine in Western civilization.[22] The swallow's seeming metamorphoses are part of its being the bird version of the housewife-queen of the earlier essay. There Ruskin praises women for their capacity for change, as we shall see.

This notion of the fluidity of form as feminine shows up appropriately enough in Ruskin's discussion of water plants in *Proserpina*. The leaves that remind Ruskin of Persephone's field of flowers he calls 'Arethusan' for the Sicilian fountain near the site of her abduction. Ruskin opposes these specimens to plants with 'Apolline' leaves:

> The Apolline leaf represents only the central type of land leaves ... of a fixed form; while the beautiful Arethusan leaves, alike flowing of their limb, change their forms infinitely,—some shaped like round pools, and some like winding currants, and many like arrows, and many like hearts, and otherwise varied and variable, as leaves ought to be. (*Works* 25. 241)

By calling the land leaves, typified by the laurel, 'Apolline', Ruskin slights Daphne, the nymph transformed into the laurel when she cried out to the gods to save her from Apollo's pursuit. But substituting Apollo's name allows the gendered opposition Ruskin suggests between water leaves as feminine and land leaves as masculine. The Arethusan fountain itself is a transformed nymph, who also fled from an unwanted pursuer; the water leaf is triply feminine by association with Arethusa and Persephone and by its opposition to the Apolline.

The chief characteristic of the Arethusan leaves is their capacity for infinite change in form, which is a traditionally feminine feature, based on the female body's changing shape in pregnancy. Ruskin specifically identifies the capacity for change as feminine, labelling it unflatteringly 'caprice' later in *Proserpina* (*Works* 25. 485). 'Caprice' becomes sinister as a characteristic of serpentine vines, which snake their way up poles and wind around tree trunks, choking them. Ruskin identifies the

---

[22] See Julia Kristeva, 'Woman's Time', in Toril Moi (ed.), *The Kristeva Reader* (New York, 1986).

honeysuckle (despite its pretty flowers and rich scent) strictly as a parasite (*Works* 25. 527), declaring that 'a serpent is a honeysuckle, with a head put on' (*Works* 26. 306). Ruskin stresses the capricious femininity of these plants: 'The reason for twining is a very feminine one—that it likes to twine' (*Works* 25. 485). He had more gallantly turned caprice into a feminine virtue in 'Of Queens' Gardens', where he explains his quoting Verdi's *La donna è mobile* to be a compliment to women's adaptability in helping others: women 'must be wise . . . with the passionate gentleness of an infinitely variable, because infinitely applicable, modesty of service—the true changefulness of women' (*Works* 18. 123). Flowers are in rapid, continual flux: 'they grow as you draw them, and will not stay quite the same creatures for half-an-hour' (*Works* 25. 253). This sense that the universe shifts as Ruskin attempts to record it, even in half an hour, pervades the whole of *Proserpina*, reflected in the book's wild attempts at codification and cavalier admissions of the impossibility of the task.

For Darwin natural forms are also in constant flux, and the agent controlling change is nature, personified as female, selecting the fittest characteristics of a given species from a competing over-abundance for that particular niche in space and time. However, there are several important differences between the two men's characterization of nature as feminine. Darwin's conventional personification is an extremely effective rhetorical device, an analogy that allows him to explain natural selection in familiar terms of breeders' artificial selection of traits. He does not really mean that nature selects as an intelligent agent; in fact, he dismisses the notion of agency implied in his personifying nature, explaining that he only uses such metaphors for brevity and convenience.[23] In contrast, Ruskin's personifications symbolize what he sees as spiritual truths. Darwin suggests a linear movement of descent or progress; Ruskin a chaotic profusion of unpredictable change. Darwin's metaphor of fitness (actually borrowed from Huxley and Spencer) implies a teleology without moral significance (although it quickly became available for use in hierarchies of moral as well as physical 'superiority'), since fitness depends only on temporary environmental circumstances; Ruskin's only *telos* is the moral significance of each natural form. So even though the metaphorical agent of change in Darwin's *Origin of Species* is Nature traditionally personified as female, competitive natural selection is very different from the mythic principle of change Ruskin identifies as feminine in his scientific works.

---

23 Beer, *Darwin's Plots*, 23.

For Ruskin, the aim of the fruit is the flower, not the other way around (*Works* 25. 250). 'How far flowers invite or require, flies to interfere in their family affairs—which of them are carnivorous and what forms of pestilence or infection are most favourable to some vegetable and animal growths,' are questions, typical of Victorian botany, which seem obscenely wrong-headed to Ruskin. He complains, 'They will next hear that the rose was made for the canker and the body of man for the worm' (*Works* 25. 414). He objects not to recognizing the fact of insects, cankers, and worms, or to empirical evidence of their roles in plant reproduction and digestion, but to a science that subordinates beauty to biological process, and whose greatest metaphor for change relies on chance and violence. Ruskin prefers the feminine paradigm of freeflowing multiple metamorphoses among types that carry eternal significance to the masculine paradigm of one-way movement dependent upon fatal combat, disregard for life, and spiritless sexuality.

While Ruskin's studies of plants and animals react to Darwin and to the Victorian acceptance of evolution, in *Proserpina* Ruskin also responds to the eighteenth-century Linnaeus, abandoning Linnaean method and the great taxonomist's gender-based hierarchy in plant classification. As with his revision of Darwin, Ruskin's impetus in rewriting Linnaeus is squeamishness about a taxonomy that focuses on reproductive organs instead of floral beauty. Ruskin turns to myth and literature for help in reorganizing botany. By developing a nomenclature that reverses Linnaeus and generally privileges women's names, Ruskin again inadvertently feminizes science.

Most people who set out to create a new and better terminology expect its success to depend upon its fixity, its reliability, its authoritativeness. Not Ruskin: he pokes fun at Linnaeus by basing his orders and classes and species of flowers on Greek goddesses and Shakespearian heroines, replacing the father of botany with myth and fictional females. Linnaeus organizes his Orders and Classes on plant morphology; physical similarities demonstrate relatedness. Ruskin, on the other hand, defines his orders of plants with a play on words: plant orders are like religious orders or orders of knighthood, based on the plants' symbolic spiritual or chivalric qualities, like grace (*Works* 26. 348). As in *The Ethics of the Dust*, in *Proserpina* Ruskin elides scientific education and ethical prescription. He delineates a hierarchy of ideal women very similar to his discussion of literary role models for girls in 'Of Queens' Gardens'. He ranks 'levels of loving tempers in Shakespearean wives and maids', from the most nobly spiritual and greatest to the simplest and most earthly, with Isabel (a novice) at the top, Viola and Juliet at the bottom (*Works* 25. 416–17). The heroines give their names to families of flowers in the order Ruskin calls Cytherides (Cytherea is a name for Venus; all her flowers are associated with love). The floral families of Viola and Giulietta each share a name with one of Shakespeare's characters; these two families, which comprise violets and pansies, are placed in Cytherides to emphasize their connection to 'those who love simply, and to the death' (*Works* 25. 416). Ruskin makes his botany into an opportunity to preach about ideal characters and behaviour for women; he can more successfully control his botanical Viola and Juliet than his lost Rose La Touche or even his little cousin Lily. The parallel listing again links flowers to females in Ruskin's world, and shows Ruskin at his most conventionally Victorian in ranking sexless over carnal love.

The eighteenth-century Linnaeus not only used plants' reproductive characteristics as the primary method of classification, but also—in contrast to Ruskin—describes plants' sexual relations with great gusto, although always through metaphors that replicated his society's gender relations. For example, for Linnaeus plants are not just male or female, but husbands and wives, who wear wedding gowns; more suggestively 'flower petals spread as "bridal beds", . . . while the curtain of the *corolla*' lends 'privacy to the amorous newlyweds'; and the marriages are either 'public or clandestine'.[24] Likewise, Erasmus Darwin viewed the plant world through the lens of human sexuality, as in his steamy botanical poem *The Loves of the Plants* (1789), where flowers indulge in wanton passion, incest, and suicide.

In response, Ruskin embarks on his project of creating new terms because the old ones are 'apt to be founded on some unclean or debasing association, so that to interpret them is to defile the reader's mind'. He continues, 'I will give no instance; too many will at once occur to any learned reader, and the unlearned I need not vex with so much as one' (*Works* 25. 201). He even scruples against pointing out when he has changed the authoritative term, so as not to call attention to the old corrupting name, even making up new ones in cases where he considered the old ones acceptable, to prevent arousing curiosity and pointing out the offending terms (*Works* 25. 202). Botany's emphasis on sexuality disturbs Ruskin, and his new system silently 'corrects' it. Although his motivation stems from personal and cultural sexual repression, Ruskin sees

[24] Schiebinger, *Nature's Body*, 23, 25.

the change in names as one that will enable him to teach botany to girls. In a letter to Daniel Oliver (herbarian and librarian at Kew Gardens) Ruskin complained that existing botanical nomenclature 'is in many ways disgusting and cannot be translated to girls'.[25] Ruskin's fanciful rejection of Linnaeus's botanical sexuality allows him to educate boys and girls identically in their scientific studies.

Ruskin revises an even more significant structural aspect of Linnaean taxonomy. Linnaeus defines Orders of plants by characteristics of the flowers' pistils or female parts, and defines Classes (above Orders in Linnaeus's taxonomy) on the characteristics of flowers' stamens, or male parts, resulting in a botanical reflection of eighteenth-century European gender hierarchy.[26] Because Ruskin avoids classifying kinds of plants along sexual lines, he resists inscribing Linnaeus's hierarchy in his botanical system. Ruskin takes advantage of linguistic gender in assigning Latin names to flowers in order to create a syrupy compliment to women: masculine endings indicate a flower's strength and endurance; feminine endings may also label strong flowers, but they must in addition be good and/or pretty to achieve a feminine name. Flower names that are already established names for women as well 'will always signify flowers of great beauty, and noble historic association' (*Works* 25. 345). In his effort to avoid reproductive discussion, Ruskin reverses Linnaean hierarchy by ranking the female higher than the male.

Proserpina is amazingly fragmented, with chapters that start sometimes twenty years before they finish, often recording their own evolution—including dates—as much as any subject matter. Just as the natural world that Ruskin tries to define and seemingly to fix is always in flux, so his 'grammar of botany' is a process rather than a product (*Works* 25. 216).[27] The instability of Ruskin's system coupled with the fragmentation of the text undercuts not just his own classifications, but all scientific classifications; as he says in *Deucalion*, 'no existing scientific classification can possibly be permanent' (*Works* 26. 418).[28] To expose flaws in existing scientific systems, Ruskin performs what Kirchhoff calls

[25] See Dinah Birch, 'Ruskin and the Science of Proserpina', in Robert Hewison (ed.), *New Approaches to Ruskin* (London, 1981), 152.

[26] Schiebinger, *Nature's Body*, 17.

[27] For example, Ruskin first describes 12 orders based on Greek mythological names, then supplements them with 16 more, arriving at 28 orders (*Works* 25. 348–58). In *Hortus Inclusus*, the number is 25 (*Works* 37. 288). Ruskin's inconsistency parodies the inconsistency he humorously objects to in the scientific authorities whose work he revises.

[28] In French feminist terms, Ruskin reveals the inadequacy of Lacan's symbolic order, represented by the language Ruskin inherits from Linnaeus. *Proserpina* demonstrates several characteristics of what French feminist theorists have called '*l'écriture feminine*'.

'systematic desystematization'.[29] This scientific deconstruction produces a text that remains always unfinished; the nomenclature never
gels. Ironically, like Darwin's tangled bank, Ruskin's depiction of
botany produces more ideas and images than can possibly survive in a
single text. The result is a dizzying picture of nature that is as untamable
and unstable and prolific as Ruskin himself. But in that superabundant
chaos lies the opportunity to revise science as feminine.

We have seen that Ruskin destabilizes the gender hierarchy typically implicit in Victorian science by rejecting aspects traditionally considered
masculine, such as violent exploitation of Nature imagined as female;
by creating a botany and ornithology designed to be attractive to women
(however unsuccessfully); by including women as participants in scientific investigations; by appealing to feminine authorities; by refusing
to accept the notion of linear evolution through merciless competition;
and by revising the gender hierarchy of Linnaeun taxonomy. He offers
instead a science based on non-invasive observation, conservation, and
loving guardianship; and he replaces the competition-driven violent
progress of evolution through natural selection with chaotic flux in the
manifestations of natural forms through imagined metamorphosis. But
there is another, much more subtle way that Ruskin subverts the
Victorian sense of science as masculine, and that is by reading the objects of Naturalist study mythically, as living hieroglyphs within the
Greek goddess Athena's 'natural language'.

  The Athena that Ruskin creates in *The Queen of the Air* governs language in several ways: she is goddess of the air, personifying and controlling the medium through which sound waves and thus spoken
discourse travel; she wields 'formative' or syncretic power, bringing together like and unlike elements to build crystals, to give life, to make
metaphors, to bind signifier to signified; and she controls a system of
'natural hieroglyphs'. In Ruskin's thinking, each corporeal animal is a
hieroglyph: real living, breathing, flying, crawling creatures are signs,
and the 'grammars of zoology' that followed *The Queen of the Air* during the next fifteen years interpret Athena's hieroglyphics. Every item in
Ruskin's hieroglyphic code, in which serpents and birds are 'living
Words', is 'wholly under the rule of Athena' (*Works* 19. 345). His most
vivid example is the snake, which Ruskin describes as 'that running
brook of horror on the ground'; the serpent evokes 'horror . . . of the
myth, not of the creature' (*Works* 19. 362). It is 'a divine hieroglyph of

---

[29] Frederick Kirchhoff, 'A Science against Sciences', 257.

the demoniac power of the earth. . . . As the bird is the clothed power of the air, so this is the clothed power of the dust; as the bird is the symbol of the spirit of life, so this of the grasp and sting of death' (*Works* 19. 362–3).

Ruskin thus feminizes signification itself, not only by giving Athena governance over the 'living hieroglyph', but also and more importantly by having Athena's formative power forge the linguistic link between each hieroglyphic signifier and its inevitable signified.[30] Because for Ruskin all living things and natural objects are signs in Athena's grand system of hieroglyphics, and because scientific investigation is in part an effort to decipher their meaning, Ruskin's sciences on any topic are already positioned under Athena's control. But even more to the point, two of his science books treat animals specifically identified as Athena's hieroglyphs in *The Queen of the Air*: *Love's Meinie* on birds and *Deucalion*'s 'The Living Wave' on snakes. Furthermore, the crystals in *The Ethics of the Dust* (and therefore the jewels from 'The Iris in the Earth' in *Deucalion*) are the province of Neith, whom Ruskin identifies as the Egyptian Athena.

Flowers ruled by Proserpina also fit into Athena's hieroglyphic code. One way Ruskin manages this is to turn flowers into birds and snakes. For example, each plant has two parts: 'one part seeks the light; the other hates it. One part feeds on the air, the other in the dust' (*Works* 25. 218). Just as bird and snake represent the eternally opposed elements of air and earth, in plants these elements also coexist without coalescing. Ruskin carries the comparison further, and makes the root into a serpent: 'a root contorts itself into more serpent-like writhing than branches can; and when it has once coiled partly around a rock, or stone, it grasps it tight, necessarily, merely by swelling' (*Works* 25. 221).[31] As a corollary, Ruskin compares blossoms to birds by explaining an etymology for 'petalos' in Greek meaning 'to fly' 'so that you may think of a bird as spreading its petals to the wind' (*Works* 25. 231). He recognizes the fundamentally metamorphic method of his hieroglyphic thinking by humorously quoting Charles Bonnet, the eighteenth-century discoverer of parthenogenesis, to say 'sometimes it was difficult to distinguish a cat

---

[30] For a fuller explanation of the ways in which Ruskin feminizes language in *The Queen of the Air*, see Sharon Aronofsky Weltman, 'Mythic Language and Gender Subversion: The Case of Ruskin's Athena', *Nineteenth-Century Literature* (Dec. 1997).

[31] Ruskin's insistence on the double nature of the plant, divided above and below the dirt line, is itself unstable, as he leaps from the dust to the air, pointing out the resemblance between the earthly root and the clasp of the bird's claw (*Works* 25. 219).

from a rosebush' (*Works* 25. 220). Ruskin is joking, but he also means it; Athena's living hieroglyphs shape-shift not only across species, but also from animal to vegetable to mineral and back again.

Ruskin details the serpent as a symbol of degeneration or devolution at length in *The Queen of the Air*. Evil change manifests itself through the snake, which brings 'dissolution in its fangs, and dislocation in its coils' (*Works* 19. 362–3). Athena wields this destructive force as a corollary to her formative power. It is the same power we have already seen in 'Of Queens' Gardens', where women are praised for the capacity to change. It is the same power we saw in the water leaves whose variability so delights Ruskin. It is the same power that Ruskin recoils from when he calls it 'caprice' in women or in strangling vines. 'Serpent nature' and 'serpent charm' corrupt flowers in the order of Draconidae (*Works* 19. 372). For example, the foxglove and snapdragon 'decorate themselves by spots, and . . . swollen places in their leaves, as if they had been touched by poison. . . . The spirit of the Draconidae . . . enters like an evil spirit into the buttercup, and turns it into a larkspur' (*Works* 19. 376–7). The serpent quality metamorphoses one originally good species into an evil one, so that in Ruskin's botany, snapdragons and gladioli are subverted irises.

Even flowers not in the order of Draconidae seem to suffer from degrading serpent influence. The 'Brunella', for instance:

But if any of the petals lose their definite character as such, and become swollen, solidified, stiffened, or strained into any other form or function than that of petals, the flower is to be looked upon as affected by some kind of constant evil influence; and . . . it will be felt to bear the aspect of possession by, or pollution by, a more or less degraded Spirit. (*Works* 25. 466)

In case the reader does not recognize this polluter or possessor as the serpentine influence found in the Draconidae, Ruskin explicitly points to the relevant paragraphs in *The Queen of the Air*. The masculinity of the evil power is suggested by snake imagery and by images of tumescence: 'swollen, solidified, stiffened,' the petals sound remarkably phallic. Nevertheless, the serpentine power of degeneration remains Athena's, and part of its mythic horror for Ruskin is the sense of aberration such feminine potency implies.[32]

Outside the order of Draconidae, the Viola Cornuta's stalk is 'thickest in the middle, like a viper' and its calyx has a 'fanged or forked effect;

---

[32] Similarly degraded flowers inhabit the orders Ruskin calls Contorta and Satyrum: another gender-loaded term, which Ruskin uses to designate ugly plants (*Works* 25. 467).

feebly ophidian or diabolical'. Ruskin sums up this flower by complaining, 'On the whole, a plant entirely mismanaging itself,—reprehensible and awkward, with taints of worse than awkwardness; and clearly, no true "species", but only a link' (*Works* 25. 40–2). The corruption of this flower is not just in its being half violet, half pansy, but in its inability to decide if it is a runner or not. Ruskin expects his hieroglyphs to incarnate eternal types, so that pansies and violets, as similar as they are, remain distinct, and runners stay runners and not individual stems. He envisions a universe where living signifiers transmute themselves metaphorically rather than physically, where even while dissolving and reforming, the ideal forms and what they represent are still identifiable. Yet he knows, even in his feebly joking use of the Darwinian terms 'species' and 'link', that there are no fixed species and there are myriad links. Ruskin considers everything hybrid and mutated and half-evolved abominable, but he evokes the aberrations in fascination, and he fascinates his readers with powerful descriptions of their existence, because finally mutations are hieroglyphs, too.

As with the codification of flower names and their mythic significances in *Proserpina*, the correlation of gemstones with moral qualities in *Deucalion* builds a readable language of 'natural hieroglyphs', like that described in *The Queen of the Air*. In *Deucalion*'s 'The Iris in the Earth', Ruskin matches real gem colours to the colours in heraldry, which traditionally carry moral significance. By dressing themselves in the right jewels (which are not so much the gold, crystal, and onyx of the subtitle as moral characteristics, such as charity), and in sharing them with others, women bring back a kind of Eden; the tabernacle they should decorate turns out to be both their own bodies, equally with those of their 'poor sisters' (*Works* 26. 196).[33] As Sawyer explains,

In the logic of the lecture, jewels are the primary signifier that renders three other systems interchangeable—women, the nation (Tabernacles), the natural order. In all these 'grammars,' and in so much of Ruskin's thought, the unacknowledged wish appears to be to control the world through signs, which are made ontologically primary to the things they signify.[34]

Again women become both the subject and object of study. Like the crystals personified as little girls and the little girls themselves as readers of crystal-signs both within and without *The Ethics of the Dust*, like the

---

33 Comparable poor sisters are incarnated as feeble florets in 'Of Queens' Gardens' (*Works* 18. 142).
34 Paul Sawyer, *Ruskin's Poetic Argument*, 275 n.

women-as-flowers and readers of flower-signs in *Proserpina*, like the wives and swallows in *Sesame and Lilies* and *Love's Meinie*, in *Deucalion* the reader, constructed here specifically as female, cannot stand outside the system to read from a meta-position, but is already implicated in it as another sign. Sawyer's suggestion that the psychological motivation for creating these signs is a wish to control (or at least to organize) the outer world through them is certainly true for Ruskin, as it is to some extent for all of us. It is the fiction that language offers us; we structure disorder and pretend to control it by naming what we experience and manipulating the names.

Ruskin's rhapsody on the swallow and his glorification of the wife in such similar terms sometimes backfire and belittle women rather than elevate them. But his syntheses emphasize that Ruskin not only sees everything hieroglyphically, but also that for him these likened terms are again interchangeable. Here a swallow is a woman; we have seen that a woman is a tabernacle; clearly a tabernacle is a church; a church is a crystal; a crystal is a girl; a girl is a flower; a flower is a snake; a snake is a bird (*Works* 26. 195–6; 26. 196; 18. 320–4; 18. 271, 221; 25. 388; 25. 221, 283; 26. 308–9). The circle works in any other direction, and the distinction between girl and woman is not significant here: for example, a woman is also a flower, a bird is a flower, a flower is a crystal (*Works* 18. 142; 25. 242; 25. 250), and so on in a dizzyingly metamorphic vision of the world. Since all these objects, including women, are interchangeable signs, not only can everything be seen as something else metaphorically, but everything, including girls and women and swallows, is a hieroglyph in Athena's language. To pursue botany, mineralogy, geology, ornithology, or astronomy rightly, in Ruskin's view, brings the scientist to a better understanding of each hieroglyph studied and to a better chance of learning to read its meaning.

Ruskin's view of nature as revealing spiritual truth sounds at times like Natural Theology, which reads nature as God's other scripture. This movement was vanquished by Victorian science. Ruskin, like Tennyson and so many others, had already lost his childhood belief to the clink of geologists' 'dreadful Hammers' (*Works* 36. 115) even before *The Origin of Species* (1859) was published and rocked the world's religious confidence. Nevertheless, in rejecting so much that he felt was wrong about his century's science and technology, Ruskin did not simply return to the position of Natural Theology. Despite his interpreting the living hieroglyphs as 'Words of God' and despite the often reactionary tone

Ruskin takes regarding Darwin and others, his late scientific studies do not evince an orthodox Christianity; his luminous hieroglyphs have too much independent life and are simply too pagan to be satisfying evidence for the argument from design. Instead of religion, Ruskin uses myth to interpret transcendent truths that he feels materialist science necessarily overlooks.

In employing myth to remake scientific study into a way to read the natural world, to understand and love it better, to serve it and preserve it, Ruskin inadvertently feminizes science. Indeed, Ruskin's nineteenth-century vision of science presages twentieth-century eco-feminism, which also bases its philosophy on valorizing ancient claims of innate connections between women and the earth. Ruskin's lifelong effort to reconcile science and art culminates in his late 'grammars' of ornithology, botany, and mineralogy. That he should try to capture science as his ally is not surprising in a time when science had just become the 'new mythology'.[35] In effect, Ruskin tries to redefine science so that he can pursue it in good conscience. This is what makes it finally feminine, since in his view women are men's moral guides. In *The Laws of Fésole* Ruskin famously declared 'all great Art is Praise' (*Works* 15. 351). He picks up the aphorism again and applies it to history in *The Bible of Amiens*: 'all great Art is Praise. So is all faithful History and High Philosophy' (*Works* 33. 29). But what of all great science, of what Victorians still called Natural History and Natural Philosophy? The science Ruskin proposes in these books is a science of praise. This great task of praise that comprises the work of artists, historians, philosophers, and now scientists, happens also to be that of women. In 'Of Queens' Gardens' Ruskin charges women that their 'great function is Praise' (*Works* 18. 122). A science that nurtures and preserves the natural world, that sees beauty without destroying it, that builds upon a sense of identity with rather than antagonism to nature, that studies nature to understand it better rather than to enslave it, that praises rather than dissects, this is— in Victorian terms and in the terms Ruskin himself uses—a feminine science.

35 Levine, *One Culture*, 8.

8

Ruskin's Multiple Writing: Fors Clavigera

Dinah Birch

For many of Ruskin's readers, and also for those who know him largely by reputation, *Fors Clavigera* is a baffling text. Serially published from 1871 to 1884, and nominally addressed to 'the workmen and labourers of Great Britain', it is the most substantial publication of Ruskin's Oxford years—600,000 words of radical and innovative prose. In form, purpose, method of production, and range of reference it is notoriously hard to categorize. Of all Ruskin's major works, *Fors Clavigera* has attracted the slightest body of interpretative response. Its early critics were inclined to see it as mental disintegration on an impressive scale. Cardinal Manning memorably summed up the work as 'like listening to the beating of one's heart in a nightmare' (*Works* 36. lxxxvi), a remark which has been endlessly repeated since.[1] Frederic Harrison, in his generally sympathetic study of 1902, placed *Fors* on 'the very border line that marks off rational discourse from the morbid wanderings of the mind'.[2] Leslie Stephen summed up the general view in a truly magisterial put-down just after Ruskin's death: 'One can hardly doubt that the discursiveness and eccentricity were indicative of a morbid irritability of brain which was to cloud his intellect.'[3] R. H. Wilenski was among the twentieth-century critics who continued to identify it as a symptom of mental illness, referring to 'the manic tone in *Fors Clavigera*' in his hostile account of 1933.[4] Later commentators have been less ready to dismiss *Fors* as

---

[1] Judith Stoddart rightly notes that it is often presented as 'the final word on the subject.' See Judith Stoddart, 'The Rhetoric of Reform: John Ruskin's *Fors Clavigera* and the Politics of the 1870s', D.Phil. thesis (Oxford, 1990), 2.

[2] Frederic Harrison, *John Ruskin* (London, 1902), 181.

[3] Leslie Stephen, 'John Ruskin', *National Review*, 35 (Apr. 1900), 240–55; repr. in J. L. Bradley (ed.), *Ruskin: The Critical Heritage* (London, 1984), 421.

[4] R. H. Wilenski, *John Ruskin: An Introduction to Further Study of his Life and Work* (London: 1933), 121.

morbidity in print, and the tone of recent studies—most significantly, those of John Rosenberg, Brian Maidment, Judith Stoddart, and Linda Austin—has been less dismissive.[5] In his authoritative account of Ruskin's early life, Tim Hilton confirmed this change in critical mood by calling *Fors Clavigera* 'Ruskin's masterpiece'.[6]

One reason for both the difficulty and the achievement of *Fors Clavigera* is its multiplicity, a vertiginous diversity of method and intention. *Fors* develops a literary method that allows Ruskin to be at once public and private, self-effacing and self-involved. It is a method that now looks less eccentric than it did, for the inheritors of the fragmented interface between text and reader in these letters have turned out to be more numerous than Harrison and Stephen could have predicted. In a modern or even postmodern world, what used to look mad, morbid, or simply peculiar now seems much more fertile as a literary model. The very name of the work—*Fors Clavigera*—might be seen as representative of its richness. The titles of Ruskin's books are often cryptic, but none is more puzzling than this one. What does it mean? He was later to claim that his 'own conception of it was first got from Horace'.[7] Clearly the Horatian model of the satirical writer who withdraws into anger and solitude to comment on the follies of contemporary life is important to the dynamics of *Fors Clavigera*. Horace talked about 'stern Necessity' carrying nails, hooks, and molten lead, and this gave Ruskin his form of words—nail-bearing Fate, or Fors Clavigera. But the meaning of the name echoes far beyond Horace. In the second letter of the series, dated February 1871, Ruskin unravels part of what he intended in the title. He describes the words Fors as being 'the best part of three good English words—Force, Fortitude, and Fortune'. 'I wish you to know the meaning of those three words accurately', Ruskin very characteristically remarks (*Works* 27. 27–8). Energy (force), endurance (fortitude), and chance (fortune)—all necessary for work of the kind that Ruskin is

5 See John Rosenberg, 'Ruskin's Benediction: A Reading of *Fors Clavigera*', in Robert Hewison (ed.), *New Approaches to Ruskin* (London, 1981), 125–42; also his *The Darkening Glass: A Portrait of Ruskin's Genius* (New York, 1961); Brian Maidment, 'Readers Fair and Foul: John Ruskin and the Periodical Press', in J. Shattock and M. Wolff (eds.), *The Victorian Periodical Press: Samplings and Soundings* (Leicester, 1982), 29–58; 'Interpreting Ruskin, 1870–1914' in *The Ruskin Polygon: Essays on the Imagination of John Ruskin* (Manchester, 1982), 158–171; Judith Stoddart, 'The Formation of the Working Classes: John Ruskin's *Fors Clavigera* as a Manual of Cultural Literacy', *Bucknell Review*, 34, no. 2 (1990), 43–58; Linda M. Austin, *The Practical Ruskin: Economics and Audience in the Late Work* (Baltimore, 1991).

6 Tim Hilton, *John Ruskin: The Early Years* (New Haven, 1985), p.x.

7 *Works* 28. 106; see Horace, *Odes*, I, 35.

undertaking in these letters. These are the three images of Fors that Ruskin repeatedly refers to in later letters as the first Fors, the second Fors, the third Fors. The following word—Clavigera—is, as Ruskin interprets it, also triple in meaning. 'Clava means a club. Clavis, a key. Clavus, a nail, or rudder' (*Works* 27. 28). Thus Clavigera may mean club-bearer, key-bearer, or nail-bearer. Ruskin goes on to explain that the triple meaning contained in Clavigera corresponds to the triple meaning in Fors:

Fors, the Club-bearer, means the strength of Hercules, or of Deed.
Fors, the Key-bearer, means the strength of Ulysses, or of Patience.
Fors, the Nail-bearer, means the strength of Lycurgus, or of Law. (*Works* 27. 28)

Here a dense network of meaning begins to expand into myth. Hercules' strength is for action: 'for subduing monsters and cruel persons', Ruskin reminds us. Ulysses' patience is 'portress at a gate which she cannot open till you have waited long . . . her robe is of ashes, or dry earth.' The strength of Law, the power of Lycurgus, 'is Royal as well as legal'. Ruskin tells us that 'the notablest crown yet existing in Europe of any that have been worn by Christian kings, was—people say—made of a Nail' (*Works* 27. 29). In that nail Ruskin refers to the legendary Iron Crown of Lombardy, supposedly containing one of the nails of the crucifixion, thus reminding his readers that despite the Greek and Latin references embedded in his title the primary character of his work is Christian. Though Ruskin doesn't mention it here, another hidden reference is to the Christian St Peter, the rock of the church, with the keys of Heaven and Hell, life and death, given into his hand. Robert Hewison has suggested a further, and darker, biblical reference concealed within the title, 'with the Jael of the Old Testament, who murdered Sisera by driving a tent nail through his head'.[8] Like much else in his work throughout the 1870s, the web of meaning contained within *Fors Clavigera* is in part the product of his continuing preoccupation with Rose La Touche, and the images of loss and destruction associated with his ill-fated love for her.

Ruskin's analysis of multiple meaning within the language of his title characterizes his method in these letters. Excavating layers of meaning from the history of words, the stories attached to them, and their existence in other traditions and other languages, is a literary process readily associated with early twentieth-century modernism. Ezra Pound, T. S. Eliot, and James Joyce developed the method to a high level of

[8] Robert Hewison, *John Ruskin: The Argument of the Eye* (London, 1976), 181.

sophistication. In many of its essentials, however, it is a process that Ruskin initiates in *Fors Clavigera*. The primary reference is often to Englishness—'good English words', as Ruskin approvingly notes. But this national identity is placed within an expansive context. Here too, Ruskin's method anticipates the dynamics of high modernism. Throughout *Fors*, Ruskin juxtaposes the splintered images of temporal history with those of timeless myth. Hercules, Ulysses, and the Iron Crown are interwoven in his account of the ramifying meanings to be traced in his title.

This elaborate construction of meaning contained in the title of *Fors Clavigera* has much to do with the placing of authority, for like his modernist successors Ruskin constructs a voice which claims the right to direct. 'I wish you to know', 'I will tell you what you may usefully know', 'the notablest crown yet existing in Europe'. These are phrases of a kind which Ruskin repeatedly employs in *Fors Clavigera*. The implication is clearly that he, Ruskin, does know, that he is in control of the text and of the reader's response. He knows *all* of the crowns that have existed in Europe, and we are directed to trust his judgement as to which of them has been the most notable. That unusual superlative—'notablest'— represents a recognizable stylistic trait, drawing attention as it does to the absolute verdict that is being delivered. Here is the solid and paradoxically reassuring centre of this unpredictable work. Incorporated into the changing texture of Ruskin's language is the sustained implication that we are hearing a voice that can be depended on to guide us rightly, a voice that can discriminate good from evil, right from wrong, useful from useless.

That process of division and judgement, in which the reader is constantly and often aggressively implicated, is the energy which drives the text forward. Yet the ground on which this declamatory authority rests is continuously fractured, into complex and amplified patterns of Greek and Roman language and mythology, Homer and Dante, Christian tradition and history, personal memory, contemporary events, and much else besides. What Ruskin does here, and elsewhere in *Fors*, is to offer an almost autobiographical account of what is seen as a fissured but nevertheless precise and quite impersonal body of meaning—or of truth. Here again he prefigures a modernist dynamic. His writing is uncompromisingly personal, while it denies the influence of personality, just as it insists on its contemporaneity while defining itself against centuries of European tradition. This literary version of St Peter's rock is like the ageless stones that Ruskin had recorded so meticulously throughout his years as a geological draughtsman—solid and enduring, but deeply scored, split, and signed with meaning by the processes of time.

Such writing often approaches the form of a sermon. The apparently capricious subject matter of *Fors* might seem quite alien to the disciplined purposes of a preacher. Yet the pattern of the sermon, the first and in some ways the most persistent of Ruskin's literary models, runs through *Fors Clavigera*. The preacher takes a text, and, grounding his words in the vicarious authority derived from the church, expounds its layered meaning to the waiting congregation. Put in the simplest terms, this is what Ruskin does in *Fors*. But Ruskin's texts are not exclusively drawn from the Bible, or supported by the teachings of any one church, but from an enormously proliferating range of those cultural and literary traditions which he sees as authoritative, and among which no one tradition is ever finally given ascendancy. As readers of *Fors*, we are constantly asked to extend our sense of what carries authority, to augment the reach of the texts we refer to, in the Latin sense of the word *auctor*—to increase, or produce. Hence, in part, the reader's bewilderment. The tone of the writing invites us to look for a secure and fixed basis for Ruskin's pedagogic discourse. What we find, however, are sermons with a constantly moving and self-transforming centre.

One of the objections that has often been raised to *Fors* is that in their emphasis on spiritual and personal authority in all these manifold expressions the letters represent a voice that talks down to their readers. Ruskin, now in his fifties, Professor at Oxford and Master of the Guild of St George, is prone to treat his readers as children. Oddly associated with this condescension is an associated inclination to figure himself as a child—digressive, dogmatic, and irascible. But if Ruskin's writing in *Fors* is both childish and patronizing, the patronage is of a kind that assumes the active responsibilities of the educator, and the childishness is qualified by the assured ability to range over an expanse of cultural knowledge that few of his readers could emulate. Ruskin's didactic and personal voice is individual rather than institutional, the work of a wandering preacher rather than an established church. It suggests self-education rather than the education of the regulated classroom, or the competitive examination syllabuses that Ruskin despised. It is not an accident that for generations an enthusiasm for *Fors Clavigera* was seen as the mark of the self-educated man, or woman, for many of whom Ruskin's odd fusion of personal intensity and eclectic range of reference came as an intellectual liberation. The intelligent and obstreperous boys of Rudyard Kipling's *Stalky and Co.* (1899), thumbing sticky copies of

Fors in their second-division boarding-school, are representative of that element of awkward insurrection that seems to have characterized *Fors*-readers in Ruskin's lifetime and beyond.

One further point in Ruskin's exegesis of the title of his work sheds light on the way in which *Fors Clavigera* treats its readers as children. 'Clavigera' carries an association with 'gerere', meaning to carry, or to do. 'It is the root of our word "gesture" (the way you carry yourself); and, in a curious bye-way, of "jest".' Those two ideas, of gesture and jest, are closely connected in what Ruskin is attempting in *Fors Clavigera*. *Fors* can be read as significant gesture, and it is permeated throughout with the sense of play, or jest. 'True, the play of it (and much of it is a kind of bitter play) has always, as I told you before, as stern final purpose as Morgiana's dance; but the gesture of the moment must be as the humour takes me' (*Works* 29. 197), Ruskin reminded his readers in Letter 81. Ruskin frequently plays for us, in the sense of offering us a bravura performance. Still more often, he plays with us, jests with us, as he had played with the children of Winnington Hall, the girls' school with which he had been linked in the 1860s. It is worth noting that *The Ethics of the Dust* (1866), the book for and about children and education that arose from what he had learned from Winnington Hall, is often overlooked as a significant rehearsal for the more far-reaching ambitions of the 1870s. This sense of being played with is another reason for readerly exasperation with *Fors*, for any sense we might have of our own dignity as grown-up readers is rarely among Ruskin's concerns.

The play that *Fors* offers us is of a dark kind, closer to the grotesquerie that he had defined in *The Stones of Venice* than to the philosophical sport of Lewis Carroll. The spirit of mockery that is so strong in *Fors* is allied to the play that Ruskin spoke of in the final volume of *The Stones of Venice*, the frame of mind which 'plays with terror, and summons images which, if it were in another temper, would be awful, but of which, either in weariness or in irony, it refrains for the time to acknowledge the true terribleness' (*Works* 11. 166). In this sense, Harrison and Stephen are right. A sidelong morbidity colours what Ruskin has to say in *Fors*, where the creativity of the child's joke constantly threatens to tip over into destructive folly. In his second *Fors* letter, Ruskin famously remarks that 'during the last eight hundred years, the upper classes of Europe have been one large Picnic Party' (*Works* 27. 39). Such play is not, as Ruskin perceives it, of the kind that results in merriment. The high art of these irresponsible picnickers, as demonstrated by 'melodies illustrative of the consumption of La Traviata, and the damnation of Don Juan'

(*Works* 27. 40), is comparable with their mischievous domesticity or industry, signified by the poverty-stricken children allowed to starve in Wapping, or immense guns manufactured in Woolwich. This picnic has amounted to a deadly game. Here Ruskin's writing flickers between the timeless and the topical. He offers for our consideration two different kinds of text.

As I was revising this sheet,—on the evening of the 20th of last month,—two slips of paper were brought to me. One contained, in consecutive paragraphs, an extract from the speech of one of the best and kindest of our public men,[9] to the 'Liberal Association' at Portsmouth; and an account of the performances of the 35-ton gun called the 'Woolwich infant,' which is fed with 700-pound shot, and 130 pounds of gunpowder at one mouthful; not at all like the Wapping infants, starving on a half-chance meal a day. 'The gun was fired with the most satisfactory result,' nobody being hurt, and nothing damaged but the platform, while the shot passed through the screens in front at the rate of 1303 feet per second: and it seems, also, that the Woolwich infant has not seen the light too soon. For Mr. Cowper-Temple, in the preceding paragraph, informs the Liberals of Portsmouth, that in consequence of our amiable neutrality 'we must contemplate the contingency of a combined fleet coming from the ports of Prussia, Russia, and America, and making an attack on England.' (*Works* 27. 42–3)

Ruskin goes on to ponder his second text. It announces, he tells us, 'approaching help in a peaceful direction' (*Works* 27. 43). His play becomes a matter of biting irony:

It was the prospectus of the Boardmen's and General Advertising Co-operative Society, which invites, from the 'generosity of the public, a necessary small preliminary sum,' and 'in addition to the above, a small sum of money by way of capital,' to set the members of the society up in the profitable business of walking about London between two boards. Here *is* at last found for us, then, it appears, a line of life! At the West End, lounging about the streets, with a well-made back to one's coat, and front to one's shirt, is usually thought of as not much in the way of business; but doubtless, to lounge at the East End about the streets, with one Lie pinned to the front of you, and another to the back of you, will pay, in time, only with proper expenditure of capital. (*Works* 27. 43–4)

Ruskin's provocative and anti-technological militarism emerges in what he has to say of the lethal Woolwich infant. His hostility to Liberals and to liberalism, coloured by the privately complicated circumstances of his friendship with William Cowper-Temple, also directs his commentary. So too does his deep antipathy towards the advertising trade, projected

---

9 William Cowper-Temple (1811–88), the Liberal politician who with his wife Georgiana had become one of Ruskin's closest friends, was one of the first trustees of the Guild of St George.

here as a literally dehumanizing business, transforming its participants into walking declarations of those two-faced lies that constantly preoccupy Ruskin in *Fors*. Many ironic gestures, and many jests, are bitterly combined in this letter. 'Think over it', Ruskin characteristically urges. 'On the first of March, I hope to ask you to read a little history with me; perhaps also, because the world's time, seen truly, is but one long and fitful April, in which every day is All Fool's Day, we may continue our studies in that month' (*Works* 27. 44).

Among the difficulties and pleasures which readers of *Fors* will recognize is that this multiple text is also a seamless text. The succeeding letters build on each other, weaving references backwards and forwards to create an ever-expanding network of composite meaning. In claiming that the boardman's trade would pay, in time, Ruskin is ironically invoking the premises of capitalism, which threaten ruin as the inevitable long-term return for bad investment. This is partly a preacher's technique—the wages of sin is death. But it also has to do with Ruskin's sustained contemplation of time, and the legacies of history, throughout *Fors*. As promised, the third letter, dated 1 March 1871, begins by thinking about history and what might be learned from it. Like many of the earlier *Fors* letters, this one is written with the Franco-Prussian war very much in mind—that European drama which more than any other created the sense of national anxiety and turbulence that is such an important backdrop to the confrontational challenges of *Fors*. Here as elsewhere, Ruskin assumes a topical framework that his readers will recognize. His letters proclaim themselves to be a response to the inexorability of chance, grimly represented by the laws of fortune presently laying Paris to waste. 'The thing was appointed to them by the Third Fors' (*Works* 27. 46). But to understand those changeless laws must be, Ruskin suggests, more than a matter of reading reports of daily events. The image of the great picnic is in this letter transmuted to that of the great play. Ruskin explains: 'What happens now is but the momentary scene of a great play, of which you can understand nothing without some knowledge of the former action. And of that, so great a play is it, you can at best understand little; yet of history, as of science, a little, well known, will serve you much, and a little, ill known, will do you fatally the contrary of service' (*Works* 27. 45). Here again the controlling method is that of division—good knowledge must be distinguished from bad, useful service is necessarily separated from its destructive contrary. We are instructed to be more than an audience at this great play, more even than actors. We are to be critics.

Choosing to interpret the Franco-Prussian war and its implications for England in the light of the biography of the twelfth-century Richard the Lionheart, Ruskin is wholly in control of his performance. He reveals the story of 'Richard of England' in piecemeal fashion, constantly gesturing towards a body of significance within the tale that can only be partly and intermittently revealed, emblematic of much beyond itself. The tone, partly derived from Carlyle, is sometimes sentimental, sometimes mocking, always knowing. Richard emerges from Ruskin's account with mythical rather than historical significance: 'But the next point you have to note in Richard is indeed a very noble quality, and true English; he always does as much of his work as he can with his own hands. He was not in any wise a king who would sit by a windmill to watch his son and his men at work, though brave kings have done so. As much as might be, of whatever had to be done, he would steadfastly do from his own shoulder; his main tool being an old Greek one, and the working God Vulcan's—the clearing axe' (*Works* 27. 57). A king who would sit by a windmill? What king? What windmill? Who, without E. T. Cook's friendly footnote, would recognize this as an oblique reference to Edward III, and his supposed occupation of a stone windmill overlooking the site of battle at Crécy in 1346, so that he could watch his son the Black Prince at his martial work? From Richard as a true Englishman with a clearing-axe, and here of course Ruskin is transforming him into a most unlikely representative of his preoccupation with manual labour on the land, a sideways step slips us into Greek and Roman reference—the Greek axe, and the mythical axe of Vulcan. Note, too, how it is not just any Greek axe that Ruskin refers to, but an old Greek axe—the word 'old' functioning here as it often does in *Fors* as a crucially weighted and approving term. Richard, for all the irresponsibility and violence which Ruskin recognizes and castigates in his account of his life, emerges as a rough English hero—a prototypical squire, as opposed to an advertising businessman.

The sense of idiosyncratic personal utterance in such writing is so strong that it can conceal the extent of the debt to contemporary parallels, or older sources. These too are more multiple than might at first seem to be the case. Ruskin had not single-handedly invented the tactics that he develops with such assurance in *Fors Clavigera*. He had learned a great deal from a number of polemical texts dating from much earlier in the century. William Cobbett's engaged polemic in his long-running weekly journal *The Political Register* (1802–35: originally called, as Judith Stoddart reminds us, 'Letters to the Labourers and Journeymen

of the Kingdom'[10]) is important here; so too is Robert Southey's vigorously conservative and medievalist *Colloquies on the Progress and
Prospects of Society* (1829). But for Ruskin, as for Carlyle before him,
Coleridge was chief among those from whom he absorbed the terms of
personalized political debate, often cast in the form of intricate intellectual autobiography. Coleridge's political journalism in *The Friend*
(1809–10), the digressive polemics of *Biographia Literaria* (1819), and
the magisterially retrospective *On the Constitution of Church and State*
(1830) are all authoritative sources for the tradition that Ruskin inherited and transformed. Ruskin's experience of Coleridge, however, is
partly mediated through the potent voice of the contemporary figure
who formed his voice in *Fors Clavigera* more than any other—that of
Thomas Carlyle. Carlyle is the primary model for the hero-making that
runs through *Fors*. It should also be recognized that he is also a principal
source for the literary strategies of the work, and for much of its political
identity. After a sharp quarrel with Carlyle in 1867, Ruskin had renewed
his formerly close contact with his old 'master'. *The French Revolution*
was one of the last works he read aloud to his mother, in December 1869,
intensifying the connection in his mind between Carlyle's work and the
lost virtues of the past. 'It reminds her of old times'.[11] As the 1870s went
on, Ruskin was increasingly conscious of his alliance with Carlyle
against the forces of liberalism. In his 1872 republication of *Munera
Pulveris*, the papers on political economy that had first appeared in
Fraser's Magazine in 1862 and 1863, Ruskin made a very public affirma-
tion of his allegiance in dedicating the volume to 'the friend and guide
who has urged me to all chief labour, Thomas Carlyle' (*Works* 17. 145).
The provocative, bitterly bantering tone of Ruskin's writing, with its repeated comparisons between the honourable past and fallen present,
owes much to Carlyle's authority. So too does Ruskin's persistent self-
characterization as unheard prophet. Ruskin wrote to Carlyle in October 1873: 'I have not the least pleasure in my work any more, except
because you and Froude and one or two other friends still care for it. One
might as well talk to the March dust as to the English of today—young
or old; nor can they help it, poor things—any more than the dust can;—
the general dustman will deposit them I suppose, some day where something will grow on them—if some beneficent wateringpan, or Aquarius

---

10   Stoddart, 'Rhetoric of Reform', 49.
11   Ruskin to Carlyle, 3 Dec. 1869, *The Correspondence of Thomas Carlyle and John
Ruskin*, ed. George Allen Cate (Stanford, Calif., 1982), 150.

ex machina, lay them in the "mud-deluge" at rest.'[12] The personal significance that the idea of dust had for Ruskin looks forward to the meaning it was later to have for T. S. Eliot. Often appearing in association with ideas of fragmentation and mortality—'fear in a handful of dust'[13]—images of dust recur in works published in the 1860s: *Munera Pulveris* ('the gifts of the dust'), *The Ethics of the Dust*. But the mannered style of this letter to Carlyle, at once despondent, comic, and belligerent, is also an act of flattering homage to its recipient. In the reference to the 'mud-deluge' Ruskin is citing Carlyle's *Latter-Day Pamphlets* (1850), the work in which Carlyle had first developed the style of combative satire that Ruskin was to adopt in *Fors Clavigera*.[14] The *Latter-Day Pamphlets*, serially published attacks on the liberal follies of the age, had been a turning point in Carlyle's career as political satirist, and is the most immediately influential of *Fors Clavigera*'s models. Carlyle recognized Ruskin as the inheritor of his anti-democratic arguments, and took a gloomy relish in reinforcing the image of the lonely and suffering prophet. In November 1873, he wrote to Charles Eliot Norton: 'Ruskin is treading the winepress alone; and sometimes feels his labours very heavy. God be with him, poor fellow. I hear at the present time no other Voice like him.'[15] Carlyle is being a little disingenuous here, for a voice very like Ruskin's was still very audible at the time—his own.

A less likely analogue for the tone of social irony that lies behind Ruskin's mockery of the boardsmen can be identified in Matthew Arnold's satire. This might seem surprising, for while Carlyle was recognizably an ally, Arnold was not. Antipathy between Arnold and Ruskin was long-standing. In 'The Literary Influence of Academies', published in the *Cornhill Magazine* in August 1864, Arnold had made his disdain for what he termed Ruskin's 'note of provinciality'[16] public. His urbane and polished balance is worlds apart from Ruskin's passionate radicalism. Nevertheless, Ruskin knew Arnold's work, and respected it. In 'The Riders of Tarentum', a lecture planned as a supplement to *Aratra*

[12] Ibid. 173.
[13] T. S. Eliot, *The Waste Land* (1922), l. 30, *The Complete Poems and Plays of T. S. Eliot* (London, 1969), 61.
[14] See Thomas Carlyle, *Works*, ed. H. D. Traill, Centenary Edition, 30 vols. (London, 1896–9), xx. 65.
[15] *Correspondence of Carlyle and Ruskin*, 173. See Nicholas Shrimpton, ' "Rust and Dust": Ruskin's Pivotal Work', in Robert Hewison (ed.), *New Approaches to Ruskin* (London, 1981), 51–67, for a cogent account of Carlyle's influence on Ruskin's political writings in the late 1850s and 1860s.
[16] *The Complete Prose Works of Matthew Arnold*, ed. R. H. Super, 11 vols. (Ann Arbor, 1960–77), iii. 252.

Pentelici (1872),[17] he praised the 'acutest philosophical analysis' (*Works* 20. 393) of Arnold's view of the English aristocracy in *Culture and Anarchy* (1869). Ruskin's own perception of the 'roughness' of the type of English squire represented by Richard the Lionheart here acknowledges the precedent of Arnold's remarks on the class to which he had given 'the generic name of barbarians' (*Works* 20. 393). Both critics habitually ground their polemic in a dialectic of opposition, constructing their arguments out of antithetical conditions. In Arnold's case, culture is defined against anarchy and the poise of Hellenism is offset by the intensity of Hebraism, while the disputatious narrowness of nonconformism is set against the serene breadth of an enlightened national church. Ruskin is more inclined to contrast a noble past with the trivial present, or the virtues of faith and obedience with the vices of progressive liberalism. His method is different in that he characterizes the moral and political divisions in stark terms, and he always makes it abundantly clear where the right choice lies. Arnold composes a more nuanced and ironic dialectic, fearing as he did the 'loss of totality' that would follow any assertively one-sided ideological commitment.[18] However, both critics responded to a sense of national crisis in the late 1860s and early 1870s by framing a satire of play. In *Friendship's Garland*, a publication closely associated with *Culture and Anarchy*, Arnold embarked on a sharp and uncharacteristically comic series of letters attacking the condition of England's complacent and short-sighted culture. First published in the *Pall Mall Gazette* (1866–70), the letters appeared as a single volume in 1871, the year in which *Fors Clavigera* began to appear. The sometimes farcically ironic humour of *Friendship's Garland* is more exuberant and more cheerful than anything to be found in *Fors*, and is closer in tone to the earlier pyrotechnics of Carlyle's *Sartor Resartus* (1831). Yet a serious and sometimes dark purpose underwrites Arnold's play, and the disillusionment with which the reader is addressed often prefigures Ruskin's bitterness in *Fors Clavigera*. 'You, my dear friend, live in a country where at present the idea of claptrap governs every department of human activity,'[19] Arnold wrote in the first letter of *Friendship's Garland*. Such a sentence would not be out of place in *Fors*. For all the political and intellectual differences that lie between the two works, there are points of comparability that remind us that Ruskin was not wholly without companions and rivals in the 1870s.

[17] *Aratra Pentelici* was originally a course of lectures on sculpture, delivered in Oxford in 1870.
[18] Arnold, *Works*, v. 254.   [19] Ibid.

This is not, however, how he saw himself. 'I am so alone now in my thoughts and ways that if I am not mad, I should soon become so, from mere solitude' (*Works* 28. 206), Ruskin told his readers in his Christmas letter of 1874. As an appeal for sympathy, this is not without its effect. Ruskin's self-image as lonely eccentric is powerfully formed, and it is hard not to take him at his word. To do that too simply is dangerous, for he was less isolated from his culture than he chooses to have us believe. Nevertheless, it remains true that Ruskin is a singular writer, and that the peculiarities of his position in the 1870s enabled him to open out the culture of his age in unique ways. *Fors* is a brilliantly innovative text, though innovation is the very thing that Ruskin deplores in these conservative and elegiac letters. The closest parallels come after his death. The fluent and fragmented nature of this writing, with its sense of biting play, is moving towards the construction of a literary language adequate to the disorienting multiplicity of modern experience.

Ruskin's twentieth-century reputation has suffered from his identification as one of the chief eccentrics and reactionaries of his age. This is particularly true of the output of his later years, after he acquired the bearded and august air of the quintessential Victorian sage. That was how writers of the modernist generation often wanted to categorize him—even Ezra Pound, whose economic theories of art are profoundly influenced by Ruskin.[20] He seemed to be identified with the rigid thinking of their parents' generation, cut off from the aesthetic issues of the twentieth century—irrevocably part of what Lytton Strachey contemptuously termed 'the Glass Case Age'.[21] Yet Ruskin now seems, to a remarkable extent, one of the writers who made the evolution of modernism possible. Joyce, Pound, Eliot, Woolf, and their inheritors could not have written as they did if Ruskin had not written as he did. In *Fors Clavigera*, he developed a vehicle that could combine what he had learned from the tradition of European culture with the expression of the alienated and disaffected individual voice, adrift amid the disintegration of that culture. In this remarkable late work, Ruskin rejected and assimilated the changing Victorian world with a vehemence and assurance that enabled his successors to maintain their own ambivalent continuities with the past.

---

[20] 'Came not by usura Angelico; came not Ambrogio Praedis, Came no church of cut stone signed: *Adamo me fecit*'; Ezra Pound, *The Cantos*, No.45, 11. 33–4, rev. edn. (London, 1975), 230.

[21] Letter from Lytton Strachey to Maynard Keynes, 1906; see Michael Holroyd, *Lytton Strachey: A Biography* (Harmondsworth, 1971), 312.

Index